INTERNATIONAL POLITICAL I
AND THE GLOBAL SOUTH

International Political Economy and the Global South provides students from both the Global South and the Global North a textbook that speaks to distinct concepts, categories and issues of International Political Economy (IPE) from a Southern and Northern perspective, while identifying how they differ.

The primary goal is to provide an alternative or complementary reading of IPE derived from the experiences of the periphery. The textbook asks: how has the Global South responded to the demands of a global economy? What is the meaning of sovereignty to those who have experienced colonialism and imperialism? How can the Global South claim the "international" when the Global North sets its norms, institutions and practices? It opens with a standard introduction, offering an intellectual history of key IPE concepts, including state, firm, capital, power, labor, globalization and finance. Each subsequent chapter follows a similar structure: exploration of the problem; discussion of what may be missing from dominant understandings of the problem and/or how orthodox IPE may tell us something different about the problem compared to what is experienced in the Global South; and identification of alternative frameworks and perspectives.

Aiming to de-Westernize and decentralize the production of knowledge, the textbook introduces students to the discipline and phenomenon of IPE with a genuinely global perspective.

Zaynab El Bernoussi is Associate Professor of Political Science at the Africa Institute, Global Studies University, UAE. She is the author of *Dignity in the Egyptian Revolution, Demands and Protests* (2021).

Adriana María Garriga-López is Associate Professor of Anthropology at Florida Atlantic University in Boca Raton, Florida, USA. She was born and raised in San Juan, Puerto Rico.

Giuliano Martiniello is Associate Professor of Political Science and Political Economy at Sciences Po Rabat, Université Internationale de Rabat, Morocco. He is the co-editor of *Uganda: The Dynamics of Neoliberal Transformation* (2018).

Bashir Saade is Interdisciplinary Lecturer in Politics and Religion at the University of Stirling, UK. He is the author of *Hizbullah and the Politics of Remembrance* (2016).

INTERNATIONAL POLITICAL ECONOMY AND THE GLOBAL SOUTH

Perspectives from Africa, Asia, Latin America, and the Middle East

Zaynab El Bernoussi, Adriana María Garriga-López, Giuliano Martiniello and Bashir Saade

Routledge
Taylor & Francis Group
LONDON AND NEW YORK

Designed cover image: Tijuana by Adriana María Garriga-López

First published 2025
by Routledge
4 Park Square, Milton Park, Abingdon, Oxon OX14 4RN

and by Routledge
605 Third Avenue, New York, NY 10158

Routledge is an imprint of the Taylor & Francis Group, an informa business

British Library Cataloguing-in-Publication Data
A catalogue record for this book is available from the British Library

ISBN: 978-1-032-20581-6 (hbk)
ISBN: 978-1-032-20574-8 (pbk)
ISBN: 978-1-003-26425-5 (ebk)

DOI: 10.4324/9781003264255

Typeset in Times New Roman
by Apex CoVantage, LLC

CONTENTS

TABLES AND FIGURES

Tables

Figures

ACKNOWLEDGMENTS

This project could not have been born without the support of Emily Ross, who trusted, nurtured and diligently encouraged the idea of an IPE and the Global South textbook back in 2016. The project idea arose from a frustration with the textbook choices available in terms of how much they integrate the Global South as part of "big" and "central" IPE conversations. Since then, Emily has left Routledge but made sure, in her unwavering support, to pass our project onto the caring hands of our editors Jennifer Vennall, Hannah Rich and Lydia de Cruz. To all four of them we express our gratitude.

We thank our anonymous reviewers who have been generous with feedback and support, and we can proudly name one of them, Jorg Wiegratz, for his constructive comments that shaped our book.

We are indebted to the Arab Council for Social Sciences (ACSS), based in Beirut, Lebanon. Seteney Shami, Omar Dahi, Sami Hermez, Jana Chammaa, Jamil Bazzi and other wonderful people of the ACSS helped us tremendously in pushing this project forward. The ACSS funded our wonderful writing retreat in the beautiful, proud and resilient Lebanese mountains in resistance, reflecting the magnanimous and proud Levantine spirit. We were lodged in Aaqoura at Guita Bed and Bloom, a most charming guesthouse. At Guita, Philippe Germanos, the founder and proprietor along with his team composed of Hanin, Sleiman, Habib, Laure and others who welcomed us, filled our bellies with gloriously delicious food and cared for our needs as we strove to write together during five beautiful and unforgettable days. Thank you all. Lastly, we stand in solidarity with the people of Palestine and all those who resist occupation and colonial practices in Lebanon, Puerto Rico and across the Global South.

The authors, Guita, Aaqoura, Lebanon, 2023.

1

INTRODUCTION – IPE AND THE GLOBAL SOUTH

Toward a Locally Informed Inquiry

> I have often remarked that you cannot change Jamaica if you do not change the world. I have never meant by this anything so naive as to suggest that little Jamaica could change the world. Nor do I mean that Jamaica can avoid its responsibility to itself. We must use our resources intelligently and manage them effectively. No one owes us charity nor should we wish to take it were it available. On the other hand, the system works against countries like ours. Hence it is that international economic system which we must work to change.
>
> Michael Manley, *Jamaica: Struggle in the Periphery*, 1982, p. 65

Introduction

Late President of Jamaica, Michael Manley, decried Jamaica's poverty since the 1960s and tied it to an aggressive mining industry (bauxite from which aluminum is extracted) and harsh financial restrictions (particularly from the Internal Monetary Fund, IMF), which took away resources from the local economy and channeled them abroad. These relationships of extraction, production and redistribution between far-flung territories of the world are part of what we will define in this book as the international political economy (IPE). And as Manley claimed repeatedly these relationships have constrained the Global South economies in a peripheral and disadvantageous position. The Global South here refers to middle-income and low-income countries mostly in Africa, Asia and Latin America that have been at the periphery of former imperial economies. However, high-income countries in Asia and Africa, such as the Gulf and South Africa, are still spaces of the Global South because they are still heavily dependent and even at the mercy of Global North economies in terms of financing and political influence.[1] More broadly, the Global South extends beyond the geography of former colonies to a multitude of marginalized political spaces and communities that struggle for a fairer share in the world economy.[2] Some of the main IPE issues of the Global South are dealing with sovereignty, extractivism, the cost of climate change, unemployment and precarity of jobs, unequal distribution of costs and benefits of globalization, and migration. What makes the South a distinct space of IPE is its condition of economic and political peripheralization. So, to go back to Manley's quote to change IPE in the Global South is to change the rules of the game of IPE mid game.

DOI: 10.4324/9781003264255-1

Now let us ask, what is IPE? IPE looks at both domestic political economies, meaning the relationship between markets and governments, and the role of strategic interaction among nation-states and non-state actors (Frieden & Martin, 2003). IPE is like observing a game in which states act as major players trying to advance their economic and political interests through various policies by competing and cooperating. Game theory, a mathematical paradigm that studies the cost and benefits of different strategies of action, has been central to the study of IPE, particularly as it relates to actions of international trade. But IPE is not just international trade and game theory is not the only way to explain IPE.

Indeed, the space of maneuvering that certain countries have in the international domain means that some countries can do less than others in terms of policymaking. Indeed, in some countries the domestic policies do not seem to be serving local interests (even if nationalist discourses say so creating a form of cognitive dissonance regarding the policy process) and are instead serving the interests of foreign partners (El Bernoussi, 2024). For example, the security policy in Morocco is presented as one that guards national security interests and helps human development when in reality it works as a security protection to the European Union preventing unwanted migrants and as a pillar of the US Global War on Terror.

Not only IPE is worth studying to learn and understand about all of these dynamics but also because it is encompassing and underpinning our daily lives. Open your closet. Look at all the clothes and shoes that you wear. Look at all what you are using and pay attention to the labels. They might be for the most part made in China. But even the labels don't tell you the full story because it is only the last stage of assemblage, therefore hiding the labor time and effort needed to manufacture them. The raw materials are probably coming from the four corners of the world as well as the labor involved in the process of production.

But despite being all around us, the discipline of IPE is itself fairly recent as a subject of study in academia. Susan Strange is viewed as one of the pioneers of the discipline of IPE (Palan, 2013) who identified the emergence of the field back in the early 1980s (1984) and viewed IPE as an offshoot of international relations (IR) theories that advanced a critique of capitalism. This approach challenged IR theories for its exclusion, silences and marginalization (Griffin, 200, 721) trying to incorporate different disciplinary perspectives. Many economists and other scholars have strongly engaged with important topics that are directly relevant to IPE such as the unequal distribution of the benefits and costs of globalization (Hirst & Thompson, 1992; Radice, 2000; Amin, 2014; Stiglitz, 2019), the impact of security–humanitarian aid nexus on local economies and politics (Duffield, 1994; Sachs, 2006), poverty traps (Banerjee & Duflo, 2011) and capital growth and gender and class relation (Piketty, 2013, 2020; Cagé, 2020; Streeck, 2016; Enloe, 2014) that we see as important to our approach to the discipline. Most publications on IPE anchor their analysis within the confines of international relations and international economics. Our book takes a different approach to bring in multidisciplinary perspectives to understanding the dynamics of IPE in our societies.

Our core argument is that IPE looks and works differently when we examine its historical context (i.e., historicize), when we pay attention to underlying political interests that frame the core assumptions of the discipline (i.e., repoliticize), and when we focus on a Global South critical perspective (meaning including actual local intellectual concerns and policy priorities). Understanding this context of IPE involves centering critical perspectives that have heretofore remained marginal and incorporating them through a reframing of the subject of history and politics away from the West to "the rest", or away from the Global North and into a World perspective that analyzes IPR and the Global South more seriously than merely adding it as a supplement. This equates to a process of contextualizing and broadening the perimeter and scope of IPE. In doing so, we identify a number of dynamics that work as common denominators and involve forms of value, human work, dispossession, mobility and violence. Throughout this text, we will be looking at the Global South through select locations in Africa, Asia, Latin America and the Middle East.

This premise of our book's argument should change not only our understanding of the Global South as an integral part of making IPE but also, and perhaps most importantly, the analytical lens through which we read the Global South. Another underlying theme is that the subordinate role of the Global South has been a key factor in the hegemony of capitalism. Indeed, it is the exploitation of the Global South that has enabled major "achievements" such as the formation of the Western civilizational ideal, modernity, the Industrial Revolution, the integrated world economy and the contemporary neoliberal development model. In this sense, the book is not a call for particularism but rather aspires to transcend the Eurocentrism within which IPE has historically been embedded and give legitimacy to alternative claims to universalism (Hobson, 2004, 2012, 2020, useful concept of defective agency) or alternative modernities (Gaonkar, 2001).

In short, we intend to de-Westernize and decenter the production of knowledge about IPE to recognize the historical formation of concepts that emerged in a specific time and place within the political and epistemological rationale that has been called "the West" and engraved within dominant discursive formations. It is important to note that we understand how difficult it may be to de-Westernize IPE because of the hegemony of Euro-centric discursive and academic tropes within IPE as a disciplinary formation. Therefore, we aim first to historicize knowledge in IPE while joining the growing trend of de-Westernizing and decolonizing knowledge in the social sciences to engage within a plurality of intellectual perspectives. Two main objectives thus underpin this textbook: (1) to introduce students to the discipline, concepts and phenomena of IPE through a genuinely global perspective that is grounded in examples from different geographies; and (2) explore ways of thinking about IPE from the Global South.

In this book, we emphasize multidisciplinarity allowing us different entry points to our IPE topics: informed ethnography, case studies, genealogy of concepts, critical methodologies and history. We invite our readers to consider a locally informed inquiry on the Global South because it allows us to deepen, decenter, de-Westernize, historicize and contextualize economic and political issues for people in the Global South. We are coming from various disciplinary backgrounds: anthropology, international relations, political ecology, political economy, political philosophy and political sociology. Most importantly, the Global South is our very home and not just our field of study.

In what follows, we will frame some key economic and political research problematics[3] to then discuss why IPE is currently in dire need of alternative Global South perspectives. We will finish with the organization of the book. This introductory chapter is guided by two main questions:

1) What are some key economic and political problems in our communities and how are they addressed by major schools of thought of IPE?
2) How has IPE in the Global South been studied and how can its analysis be expanded?

Economic and Political Problematics

There are three major economic and political problems:

- The problem of redistribution: how are human, political and natural resources appropriated and shared? What are the mechanisms and trade-offs involved in the process?
- The problem of valuation: how do we think about value? Are prices a reflection of values? What effect do they have on the economy and politics?
- The problem of accumulation/dispossession: what is the relationship between accumulation and dispossession? By which means some actors are appropriating while dispossessing others? And how does this shape inequalities?

Victorian historian Thomas Carlyle in the nineteenth century defined economics "the dismal science". In fact, the main economic problem, as framed in orthodox economics, is about making choices and incurring opportunity costs. For example, a student can choose to stay at school but might thereby forgo the possibility of earning an income. When we add considerations on international politics to economics, this issue of necessary trade-offs can become a competition over state survival in a realist tradition and/or a competition over control of resources in a nationalist tradition (Watson, 2014). This competition creates problems of allocation and redistribution of resources (such as privatization of public goods) leading to all sorts of political conflicts and violence.

Prices matter too. A market is a system in which producers and consumers come together, directly or indirectly and physically or virtually. Producers and consumers generate forces that we call supply and demand, respectively, and it is their interaction for their interests within the market that creates one-price mechanism (there are others!), which was famously described as the "invisible hand" by eighteenth-century Scottish political economy pioneer Adam Smith, and presupposed access to information. The crudest form of exchange is barter, but the evolution of money as a medium of exchange and unit of accounting accelerated the development of both processes. Yet, as it was argued later in a critique of the liberal political economy, the major transformations of a global and imperialist capitalist world system did not simply result from the action of market forces, but were also the result a political hierarchy, of exploiters and exploited, colonizers and colonized, dispossessors and dispossessed (Polanyi, 1956).

In this sense, a key contribution of Karl Marx, the famous nineteenth-century German philosopher who inspired communist movements around the world, was a critique of that capitalist system, being a mode of production and social order supported by mercantilist and liberal ideologies. The system, Marx argued, had its origins in the processes of divorcing producers from the objective means of their social realization (land), a process that he defined as "primitive accumulation": (the original sin constituting a social relation between those who own the means of production and those who are left with labor as a means of survival). Capitalism as a historical social system of production and accumulation, whose global character was evident from its inception, seems to flourish not only within the box of the nation-state but rather projected as a political project on a global scale through conquest, colonialism, imperialism, wars and destroyed ecologies that defined the experiences of modernity.

Before IPE, there was political economy (PE), a discipline concerned with a political critique of economic relations and interested in the economic interpretation of decision-making by governments, institutions and individuals. Some PE theoretical orientations include the following: liberal/classical political economists (utility/individualist), Marxist political economists (class conflict), Keynesian political economists (state as an economic actor) and feminist political economy (the political economy of care).

In its beginnings, IPE focused first on statist, mercantilist and liberal ideologies for the policymaking process as it related to controlling markets and trade. Later we will briefly survey some traditions of IPE (but for further analysis of schools of thought in IPE, see John Ravenhill's *Global Political Economy*, Oxford University Press, 2014; and Bill Dunn's *Global Political Economy: A Marxist critique,* Pluto, 2008).

Liberalism

First, liberalism is the economic doctrine advancing the idea of "free market", one in which the role of voluntary exchange and markets is emphasized as both efficient and morally desirable, as captured in the famous phrase by Adam Smith: "it is not from the benevolence of the butcher, the brewer or the baker, that we expect our dinner, but from their regard to their own self-interest" (*The Wealth of Nations,* vol. 1, chapter 2). To Smith, wealth was the commodities that can circulate freely. The assumption is that free trade and the free movement of capital will ensure that investment flows to where it is most profitable to invest and where there is a comparative advantage (hence, e.g., flowing into under-developed areas where maximal gains might be made). In other words, each country can exploit its own natural advantages, resources and endowments and gain from specialization. The economy is oiled by freely exchangeable currencies and open markets that create a global system of prices, which, like an invisible hand, ensures an efficient and equitable distribution of goods and services across the world economy.

Mercantilism

Second, the mercantilist tradition, inspired by the works of Friedrich List, assumes that the world economy is an arena of competition among states seeking to maximize relative strength and power (Levi-Faur, 1997). Simply put, the international system is like a jungle in which each state has to do what it can to survive. For this reason, the aim of every state, its raison d'être, must be to maximize its wealth and independence. States will seek to do so by ensuring their self-sufficiency in key strategic industries and commodities, and by using trade protectionism (tariffs and other limits on exports and imports), subsidies and selective investments in the domestic economy. Obviously, within this system some states have more power and capability than others. The most powerful states define the rules of the game and the limits of the system of exchange; and they do this through hegemony, alliances and balances of power.

Marxism

The Marxian tradition also sees the world economy as an arena of competition, but not among states rather among socioeconomic classes in society. Capitalism is the driving force in the world economy. Using Marx's language, this means that world economic relations are best conceived as a class struggle between "oppressor and the oppressed", in the sense of subjugating interest. The oppressors or capitalists are those who own the "means of production" (trade and industry). Robert Gilpin (1987) highlights four key elements of Marxist writings:

1) That social life is not static but rather dynamic and conflictual (i.e., the dialectical approach), which challenges a liberal conception of social reality that tends toward harmony and equilibrium.

2) A materialist approach to history that sees changes in production as the motor driving the movement of history.
3) The assumption that capitalist development is an experience of modernity.
4) The idea that a moral commitment to socialism is a better deal for people.

Every one of these four key ideas relates to the dynamic of class struggle. And there are critics to those ideas. For example, some question the dominant assumption of a Western origination of so-called civilization (Pomerantz, 2000; Hobson, 2004). Marx contends that capitalism as a system of private ownership and wage labor is the most productive system of production, but three laws challenge its survival:

1) The law of disproportionality: as opposed to Say's law, the supply/demand loop does not match. As famed Marxist economist Rosa Luxemburg explains, capitalism results in over-production essentially due to a lack of internal demand, which pushes capitalism to look for new markets and resources in the Global South, and thus externalizes the contradiction of capitalism to the periphery (Lee, 1971).
2) The law of accumulation: capitalism as an inherent trait of concentrating wealth in the hands of a minority widens inequalities.
3) The law of falling rates of profit: with the tendency toward technological innovation as means to gain an edge over competitors, capital reduces the quantity of the labor in the productive process. In Marxist terms, if the total amount of labor time in the productive process is reduced, profits fall.

Each one of these laws relates to various crises of the system (revolution, protests) that represent a threat to capitalism. For Marx, capitalism is unsustainable and self-destructive in its own nature. This is something we can observe in the many instances of crisis in our economies caused by the dominance of capitalist ideology.

From a Marxist perspective, capital is not just money as for the liberals: it is a social relation, a new social form with distinctive social property relations and unique laws of motion and modes of exploitation. The origins of capitalism must be searched through the transformation of social property and labor relations.

Summary

Overall, it becomes clear in contrasting these different ideological traditions of thinking about international economic relations that each tradition and debate focuses on different actors and driving forces in the world economy (Table 1.1).

TABLE 1.1 Summary points on the three IPE ideologies

Ideology	*Liberalism*	*Mercantilism*	*Marxism*
Main actor	Market	State	Laborers
Main problem	State	Competition between states	Capitalism
Main solution	Free markets	War	Revolution

IPE emerges from the recognition that inter-state politics and the international economy cannot be studied separately or understood in isolation from each other. Despite a lively debate about the causes of underdevelopment and inequality among nations by scholars in the Marxian and dependency theory traditions, which rarely permeated into the central concerns of mainstream IR, IPE remained a rather neglected subject until the 1970s. However, the inception of the Cold War impacted both the Global North and Global South and brought to the fore issues of decolonization and post-colonial state structures within IR. Before then, the power and predominance of the United States had been unquestioned in the Western alliance from the end of World War II, until the Vietnam debacle and the economic strain began to erode US hegemony in the late 1960s. Since then, IR also began to change as the events outlined above forced policymakers and scholars alike to pay more attention to economic affairs.

The Need for a Global South Perspective

What comes to your mind when you think about politics and the economy in the Global South? Chances are that you imagine people living in poverty surrounded by absent or precarious infrastructure and little or no means to change their conditions. This image is in contrast to a prosperous, highly urbanized and organized Global North where democracy and the rule of law thrive. This dichotomy between the Global South and Global North is an imagination that has legitimized a paternalistic tone from the latter toward the former particularly when it comes to prescribing development and aid programs to "help".

Our focus on IPE and the Global South joins a storied tradition of anti-imperialist critique within IPE that challenges these tools of development with Samir Amin (2014), Immanuel Wallerstein (1987), Giovanni Arrighi (1983) and Christopher Chase-Dunn (1998) among others, which presents the particularities of the Global South as a dependent subordinated political and economic space with enduring colonial legacies. Much of this literature has addressed an obsession of IPE of the Global South, which is particularly concerned with how to bridge the gap between "developing" and "developed".

A notable theory in IPE that has tried to explain the problem of development in the Global South is dependency theory. The developing countries' push for reform of the international economic system reflected dependency and structuralist theories of international economic relations which highlighted negative aspects of interdependence (Frank, 1969). Dependency theorists were concerned to identify aspects of the international economy and institutions which impeded the possibilities of development in the Global South: producing in Gunder Frank's words, the development of underdevelopment. Their central concern was to answer why so many countries within the world economy remained under-developed, despite the promises of modernization, development and global growth.

IPE scholars Melisa Deciancio and Cintia Quiliconi show that a major problem of IPE is that it is too confined to Western paradigms (2020b). For example, in examining politics and economics and the relationship between markets and states, little attention is given to how much such examination is impacted by the type of state discussed. Therefore, we see the need to introduce a question of relativity when observing state market relations, broadening the prism of how states and market forces operate. For example, issues of IPE in Africa tend to be studied as cases in development studies and in the political economy of foreign aid and are not situated at the core of IPE knowledge production. In the case of IPE with Chinese characteristics, the focus is on state-led development and more specifically on the role of the Chinese Communist Party in doing so. In Chinese IPE, there is also much attention to contain the political and economic dominance (i.e., hegemony) of the West. Lastly, in the case of IPE in Latin America, the concern with dependency has been key, but there is also a growing interest in regional political and economic integration. More generally, IPE in the Global South is concerned not only with issues of development as we saw previously but also with issues of access to credit, debt repayment, adding value to exports, and developing mutually beneficial economic relations with regional partners. Global IR expert Amitav Acharya is also a notable voice in promoting the need for going beyond Western paradigms and moving the positionality of Global South economies and polities from victimhood (needing/lacking development) to agency (2014).

When we look at IPE and the Global South, we find controversial debates such as how we define the Global South, and disagreements on solutions for issues of poverty and economic stagnation. For the last point, we often have a stand-off between defenders of socialist systems that collectivize resources (from the Marxist tradition we saw above) and those prescribing better institutions and governments. The work of Bangladeshi-British economist Mushtaq Khan on Global South economies is an example of the institutionalist trend in IPE or institutional political economy. Khan notes countries in the Global South launched development programs before consolidating institutions and rule-based contexts, not the other way around, like in economies of the Global North, which helps understand the weakness of these economies (Khan, 1999). This emphasis on the impact of institutions, such as the state, on socioeconomic practices does come with interventionist policies and new forms of state-led capitalism. Labor, as an important concept of IPE, has also continued to be neglected (more attention to the state) in studies on the Global South as mostly a factor of production of little variation, whereas labor captures major transnational changes in our societies. There is also the weight of the COVID-19 pandemic and unfinished popular turmoil around the world that is simmering.[4] Neoliberal reforms have had a significant cost on political development in various countries because they often bypassed popular voting and create a crisis of democracy, since the impact of the reforms is often contested in the streets (Cagé, 2020).

In reading IPE from the Global South, one should also pay attention to how the rules of the game can be changed. While observing international economies and polities from different locations of the Global South, there is a concern for broader and more comprehensive themes such as South–South cooperation, developmentalism and decolonization, which requires deepening the analytical framework. In addition, Deciancio and Quiliconi argue that mostly academic bodies are presented as places where the IPE thinking is originating, but this is also limiting because such bodies are not necessarily influential in shaping the local policymaking as IPE is not only academic discipline but also a socio-political practice shaped by institutional and non-institutional actors (2020a). In our chapters we hope to show practical ways for how to think about changing IPE and our global economic system to increase equity and wellbeing for all.

As we will be learning together about IPE, we recommend following the yearly agendas of and reporting on the annual Davos (Switzerland) meeting by the World Economic Forum, an organization that was started in 1971 by a German academic and that brings together major political leaders, celebrities of all sorts and young activists to talk about pressing issues affecting the world's prosperity and peace. Davos is much critiqued for being elitist and a celebration of neoliberalism. A counter-event to Davos that is important to follow is the World Social Forum based in Porto Alegre (Brazil) as it brings together civil society organizations and promotes alter-globalization, calling for solidarity, climate protection and preservation of indigenous cultures.

Organization of the Book

The textbook begins with an introduction to the volume, which you are reading, followed by a select number of key concepts for IPE. Each subsequent chapter generally aims to do the following, in different ways: (1) explore the problem of IPE and (2) link it to the specific context of the Global South. The eight thematic chapters are organized in two parts: first, key concepts of IPE and the Global South, these being value, food, labor and globalization; second, key themes of IPE and the Global South being financialization, securitization, migration and social movements.

Chapter 1 helps us define for the book IPE, the Global South and our core goals to give interdisciplinary perspectives and locally informed observations. Chapter 2 looks at changing notions of value in the Levant area in the gradual changes that took place during the colonial encounter, after the collapse of the Ottoman empire as well as through the gradual consolidation of the modern state in Lebanon. Chapter 3 deals with the role of food in IPE. It explores the relevance and limitations of the notion of an international food regime to unravel the ways in which agricultural commercialization shapes dynamics of wealth creation, capital accumulation and state formation. Chapter 4 looks at labor and unions and shows how systems of production and specific industrial strategies impact the labor force. The key discussion is about the relationship between workers and capitalist development and the negotiation of workers' interests in the face of capital expansion. The textile manufacturing sector is an example for discussion. Chapter 5 explores the relationship between sex work and forms of global capitalist development. Through the example of sex work (defined as sale of sexualized labor time), this chapter discusses the sex economy as a global formation of formal and informal labor. Chapter 6 broaches the topic of migration and borders in our globalized world by looking at the militarization of border zones. The chapter focuses on the US/Mexico border as a crucial example of the IPE of migration. Chapter 7 examines the IPE of finance by looking at the expansion of financialization and the multiplication of money. It argues that global finance adds a layer of inequality to the world economy because of finance's inherent dysfunctions. Chapter 8 untangles the intertwined relationship between security and economy. The chapter shows how the formation of a political regime of order, often at many costs, is vital for the functioning of the world economy. Chapter 9 explores the role of social movements particularly in the agricultural sector as they represent a response from below in IPE. Chapter 10 concludes our book by emphasizing the need to contextualize IPE for a better understanding of the phenomenon and the discipline. We also explore there some prospects for IPE's big discussions in the future. The chapters tackle the topics of IPE differently using a variety of disciplinary approaches to reflect the wealth of perspectives in social studies. Questions of discussions are embedded directly in the text so they can be used for further conversation in the classroom. Often, the chapters contain boxed cases to highlight particular examples for discussion.

Notes

1 These countries can be considered as semi-peripheral countries that work as a trade union between Global North and Global South, for example, Saudi Arabia and Brazil.
2 Ballestrin, L. (2020, July 3). *The global South as a political project*. E-International Relations. https://www.e-ir.info/2020/07/03/the-global-south-as-a-political-project/
3 We use the term "problematic" to refer to the complex processes that create those problems.

4 We start this book with the tenth-year anniversary of the Arab Uprisings in which the unemployed youth, among others, revolted. El Bernoussi, Z. (2021, February 4). *Opinion: The Arab Spring ten years on*. E-International Relations. https://www.e-ir.info/2021/02/04/opinion-the-arab-uprisings-ten-years-on/

Bibliography

Acharya, A. (2014). Global international relations (IR) and regional worlds: A new agenda for international studies. *International Studies Quarterly*, *58*(4), 647–659.

Amin, S. (2014). *Capitalism in the age of globalization: The management of contemporary society*. Zed Books.

Arrighi, G. (1983). *The geometry of imperialism: The limits of Hobson's paradigm*. Verso Books.

Banerjee, A. V., & Duflo, E. (2011). *Poor economics: A radical rethinking of the way to fight global poverty*. Public Affairs.

Cagé, J. (2020). *The price of democracy: How money shapes politics and what to do about it*. Harvard University Press.

Chase-Dunn, C. K. (1998). *Global formation: Structures of the world-economy*. Rowman & Littlefield.

Deciancio, M., & Quiliconi, C. (2020a). Widening the "global conversation": Highlighting the voices of IPE in the global South. *All Azimuth: A Journal of Foreign Policy and Peace*, *9*(2), 249–266.

Deciancio, M., & Quiliconi, C. (2020b). IPE beyond Western paradigms: China, Africa, and Latin America in comparative perspective. In E. Vivares (Ed.), *The Routledge handbook to global political economy* (pp. 457–471). Routledge.

Duffield, M. (1994). Complex emergencies and the crisis of developmentalism. *IDS Bulletin*, *25*(4), 37–45.

El Bernoussi, Z. (2024). The high stakes of differentials. *International Studies Review*, *26*(3), 1–3.

Enloe, C. (2014). *Bananas, beaches and bases: Making feminist sense of international politics*. University of California Press.

Frank, A. G. (1969). *Latin America: Underdevelopment or revolution*. Monthly Review Press.

Frieden, J., & Martin, L. (2003). International political economy: Global and domestic interactions. In I. Katznelson & H. Milner (Eds.), *Political science: The state of the discipline*. W.W. Norton & Company.

Gaonkar, D. P. (Ed.). (2001). *Alternative modernities*. Duke University Press.

Gilpin, R. (1987). *The political economy of international relations*. Princeton University Press.

Hirst, P., & Thompson, G. (1992). The problem of 'globalization": International economic relations, national economic management and the formation of trading blocs. *Economy and Society*, *21*(4), 357–396. https://doi.org/10.1080/03085149200000017

Hobson, J. M. (2004). *The easter origins of Western civilization*. Cambridge University Press.

Hobson, J. M. (2012). *The Eurocentric conception of world politics: Western international theory, 1760–2010*. Cambridge University Press.

Hobson, J. M. (2020). *Multicultural origins of the global economy': Beyond the Western-Centric frontier*. Cambridge University Press.

Khan, M. (1999). *The political economy of industrial policy in Pakistan 1947–1971* (Department of Economics Working Paper). SOAS University of London. http://eprints.soas.ac.uk/9867/

Lee, G. (1971). Rosa Luxemburg and the impact of imperialism. *The Economic Journal*, *81*(324), 847–862.

Levi-Faur, D. (1997). Friedrich list and the political economy of the nation-state. *Review of International Political Economy*, *4*(1), 154–178.

Manley, M. (1982). *Jamaica: Struggle in the periphery*. Third World Media.

Marx, K., & Engels, F. (1967). *Capital: A critique of political economy*. International Publishers.

Palan, R. (Ed.). (2013). *Global political economy: Contemporary theories*. Routledge.

Piketty, T. (2013). *Capital in the twenty first century*. Harvard University Press.

Piketty, T. (2020). *Capital and ideology*. Harvard University Press.

Polanyi, M. (1956). The magic of Marxism. *Bulletin of the Atomic Scientists*, *12*(6), 211–214. https://doi.org/10.1080/00963402.1956.11453726

Pomerantz, K. (2000). *The great divergence: China, Europe, and the making of the modern world economy*. Princeton University Press.

Radice, H. (2000). Globalization and national capitalisms: Theorizing convergence and differentiation. *Review of International Political Economy*, *7*(4), 719–742.

Sachs, J. D. (2006). *The end of poverty: Economic possibilities for our time*. Penguin.

Scott, J. C. (1990). *Domination and the arts of resistance: Hidden transcripts*. Yale University Press.
Stiglitz, J. (2019). *People, power, and profits: Progressive capitalism for an age of discontent*. Penguin.
Strange, S. (1986). *Casino capitalism*. Manchester University Press.
Strange, S. (1998). *States and markets*. Bloomsbury Publishing.
Streeck, W. (2016). *How will capitalism end? Essays on a failing system*. Verso Books.
Wallerstein, I. (1987). World-systems analysis. *Social Theory Today*, *3*, 310–313.
Watson, M. (2014). Theoretical traditions in global political economy. In J. Ravenhill (Ed.), *Global political economy* (Chapter 2, pp. 29–66). Oxford University Press.

2

HISTORICIZING IN IPE

What Is This Thing Called "Value"?

Introduction

Sometime in 1883, Mikhayel stood up in front of his mansion, overlooking a thorny hill, a mile away from where he lived. His house was a mix of Italian and Ottoman architecture, filled with the latest European furniture and typical of nineteenth-century Levantine wealth. Mikhayel had multiplied his wealth (inherited from his father) by trading in the items that most Levantine merchants of his time traded in: silk, tobacco and salt. Mikhayel's father was already quite wealthy and influential when he was born and was said to have been one of those who lent money to the Emir Bashir al-Shihab II, the nineteenth-century influential lord of Mount Lebanon. Mikhayel was also said to be among the few who possessed golden coins, a sign of wealth and status.

Overlooking the other side of the mansion were other green hills, filled with olive, apricot, almond, walnut and other types of trees. There, in the northern part of what was to be called Lebanon, farming land often consisted of hoping that trees planted in orchards would bear fruit the following year. On that day, Mikhayel looked at the barren hill that had not been used in a few generations. Out of all his domains, this one seemed the least attended. This piece of land was not much, relative to his overall possessions, and given that nothing grew there it was at best just a pretty landscape that gave way to the sea on its horizon.

On that day, Mikhayel was trying to decide whether he would give this land to Bassam, the idle brother of his wife, after the latter's insistence that her brother did not have anything for himself. Both Bassam and his sister were the grandchildren of a French consul appointed to Tripoli toward the end of the eighteenth-century who decided to settle there and marry a local woman. The French element (although not much of it was left by that time) brought a certain kind of status, but they needed to marry into more "established" families (*bayt* in Arabic which literally means house) for it to make a difference. And it did as Mikhayel conceded in giving the land to his brother-in-law.

While the hill stayed barren, its ownership passed down from one generation to the next. And during this time, the various transformations of the twentieth century inevitably unfolded, witnessing the collapse of the Ottoman Empire, the breakup of the Levant area into French-mandated and British-mandated states, drastic changes in living conditions and sources of wealth as

DOI: 10.4324/9781003264255-2

individuals or whole families migrated from rural to slowly forming urban areas, or traveled across continents to find alternative sources of livelihood. In the case of the colonial world, these transformations entailed the wholesale creation of cities such as Beirut that subsequently became the capital of the newly born state of Lebanon, triggering the gradual marginalization of more prominent Ottoman commercial hubs such as Tripoli, Damascus, or Aleppo. These transformations were paralleled by the unprecedented political, legal and social reforms for which the modern age had become a stigma including the rise and partial dismantling of colonial projects, the breakup of territories into clearly delineated nation-states, the import of social and political institutions such as parliament, secular courts, modern nationally conscripted armies, the establishment of monetary systems with a central bank in each state and, more specifically for our discussion here, the adoption of private property and the shift from family or social group as the legal category that can make claim to property.

The wealth of Mikhayel's generation, a generation that held decisional power in the family structure, was so great that his sons and daughters lived from it their whole lives and never worked. After some time of spending these resources, though, sustaining their lifestyle without new income implied selling one piece of land after another, until what was left were a few plots here and there. By the mid-1940s, the descendants of Mikhayel decided to have a second home in Beirut, like most families in that region. The capital of this newly born country was becoming the main pole of power, culture and economy. Living off the savings accrued from selling land but never developing a trade, the family reserves dwindled to the extent that at some point even the furniture started being sold. The generation after that, the great-grandsons, and daughters of Mikhayel were living above their means by squandering the wealth established by their ancestors and that was mainly comprised of land they considered disposable. Interested mainly in the arts, as well as political and intellectual endeavors, this generation could sustain itself and keep a certain social status, but they never accumulated anything like what Mikhayel and his generation once had. The vast swaths of family land were now gone for good.

In the 1990s, one of Mikhayel's great-grandsons decided he wanted to retire, and because he had a nostalgia for the family home he grew up in, he decided to go back to that region and buy a piece of land to build a house on. By that time, the once-barren hill was slowly becoming one of the trendiest residential areas of the region; the great-grandson of Bassam had started a real estate project, a gated community with 24/7 security, shops around the corner, large pavements, decorated with a variety of trees none native from the area, making the whole area look like a small separate town, in the middle of a region that had turned into a magnet for factories and industries established on what was once considered cheap land. As a result, this great-grandson of Mikhayel paid $40,000 in 1998 for a small piece of land on a hill that was originally given with a wave of his hand by his great-grandfather to the ancestor of this real estate complex promoter (see Figure 2.1 and Figure 2.2). At the time of the writing this chapter, meaning more than 20 years later, villas on this land were selling for about $2,500,000 each.

This story[1] exemplifies some of the themes that typically attract economic historians. Why did the value of the land change so radically? What are the factors that must be considered to explain such a change? How does value matter in explaining economic transactions? How and why do notions of land change over time? What does it mean to say that the economy is always socially and politically embedded? Between the two periods considered – the latter half of the nineteenth century and the end of the twentieth – the most significant major global, regional and local transformations occurred that have a direct bearing on the change in value and as we will

FIGURE 2.1 Photograph of some of the villas in the real estate project

Source: Bashir Saade, 5 June 2022

FIGURE 2.2 Photograph of the agro-food factory in a land behind the real estate project

Source: Bashir Saade, 5 June 2022

see, on what is meant by "land" and on how memory and notions of belonging shape understandings of value.

One way of understanding this change is to recognize that there is never a purely "economic" rationale without a footing in the "social", if not an explicitly "political" rationale. The "economic" notion of value that informed Mikhayel's actions held together because of an intricate social and political setting, that is, certain family relations and cultural traditions, and as we shall see later in the chapter, a history situated in an administrative and a legal context importantly shaped by an Ottoman and customary understanding of property and land, and a global set of forces, that includes European colonialism stretching to the four corners of the planet, and the latter's technological advancements that informed notions of wealth, and use of resources. Before we discuss this at length, let's look at how political economists and other scholars have understood the notion of value.

Theories of Value and Beyond

Although there may be many ways to understand this story, when we think about it we can see that value links how we use things; it's connected to how we deal with other people. Economists tend to abstract the "use" part of this equation into "capital" or a monetary or financial translation of the resource, objects or commodity in question (sometimes so it can be quantified and thus be studied more easily). Other social scientists such as anthropologists focus on the importance of human relations in achieving a certain quality of life on the shaping of value. But both economic and anthropological understandings of value, as we will see, depend on their understanding of a particular historical situation, where such understanding of reality gives rise to how we value things and how they become significant to us.

Anthropologist David Graeber (2002, pp. 1–2) posited that value tends to appear in three different academic contexts: sociology (value as the good in, or a certain quality of, human life), economics (value as object desired, exchange) and linguistics (meaning allocated to things, language and culture). From a cursory look, Mikhayel's story presents all three meanings. Mikhayel partly has an "economic" understanding of the land, he also has in mind a set of social and communitarian considerations, and finally, the very notion of land and of Lebanon itself in Mikhayel's time was significantly different from the one that emerges as political and legal reform of the modern age unfold such as the introduction of property rights, the idea that land can be bought and sold, and that owning land can translate as having access to capital.

As mentioned before, economists thought to find value in objects or commodities that partly emanate from how they are produced and exchanged between people in what has been called a market. Economists argue that markets have specific laws under which they operate. In that sense, the value of a commodity has a price tag to it and so cannot be understood, at least in a contemporary setting, without currencies and the complex financial system that withstand it. Early economists thought that value could be thought of as a substance that passes through goods, resources, etc. Here, the value could reflect the labor put into it, its quality, the time spent doing the good, the rarity of its component, and all kinds of other attributes, in a similar fashion as energy was thought to pass through different physical states, in physics. Economic historian Philip Mirowski (1991) argued that, in its quest to be labeled as a "science", economics as a discipline emerging in the nineteenth century mirrored theoretical developments in physics, and while the latter discipline abandoned the energy-as-substance model of the nineteenth century, in order to replace it with field theory, economics could never move away from their initial conceptualizations, that is, it always clung to a category of "value" that can be removed from its historical and social contexts.

Each conceptual attempt at defining value reflects the historical circumstances of its time. Substance theory and energy conservation principles worked well as the Western world was industrializing and developing these complex machines and manufacturing processes. Value was not just about a given agricultural output but circulated through the various stages that would deliver an industrial product (Pitts, 2020, p. 27). For early liberals such as Adam Smith, it was a matter of simple equation: labor plus time of production equals value. But if there is no production, there is no value. Later, Karl Marx criticized this approach by proposing that labor should count more than Smith would have it (Pitts, 2020, p. 28). In so doing, Marx elaborated one of the most seminal theories of political economy, bringing the aspect of the social back into the equation of value creation through its emphasis on the importance of human labor in the production process (Pitts, 2020, p. 70).

We can see how these understandings of "economy" or "society" reflect the concerns and political structures of their times. For example, theories of value of nineteenth-century Europe known as substantialists were motivated by large-scale mercantilist policies where national economies were sought to be organized for maximum wealth creation through specific trade and financial policies. By the time Marx came along, the human cost of industrialization in Western economies was starting to be felt. Therefore, to make sense of what mattered to people, thinking of value led Marx to focus more on the question of labor rather than on land or capital, as did other liberal political economists before him.

But the liberal–Marxist debate over a correct understanding of value, from an individual to a class-centered approach, both contained a few assumptions about how community life works that mirrored social and political developments occurring in nineteenth-century Europe and the Americas. Industrialization and the rise of the modern state in the West were paralleled with a gradual transformation in social relations of community bonds that turned upside down the very notion of family, larger social structures, and the relationship with state or political institutions and authority. But the transformations that mainly originated in the northern–western hemisphere spread in different ways and at various speeds and scales to the rest of the planet mainly through violent colonial encounters. What happens when the very categories of "land", "labor", and "capital" are redefined by drastic political, social, and economic transformations?

Anthropologist Marcel Mauss, writing in the early twentieth century, proposed that one could understand how we value things through the notion of the gift. Gifts and gift-giving are a universal feature of human cultures around the world, and yet their meanings and the customs and traditions connected to gifts and the exchange of gifts can vary enormously. Mauss began with the question "Why must gifts be repaid?" His answer was that at the level of culture the spirit of the donor lingered on in the object given and received, thereby constituting a kind of "organic" link between donor and recipient. Therefore, when one receives a gift from someone, one often feels the need, or even the pressure, to reciprocate with a gift of one's own. When these exchanges are multiplied over time, the communities involved each have their own complexities and are symbolically or even spiritually linked (especially if the gifts are of a religious nature). But for Mauss, this gift-exchange economy is very different from the contemporary "utilitarian" liberal one characterized by contemporary capitalist markets that are also premised on exchange. He contrasted two types of economic systems: one built on the mechanism of gift-exchange versus the one built on Exchange-Mercantile, which is a stigma of modern capitalist economies because it exchanges the worker's life force (labor) for someone else's profit.

How do different understandings of value change over time or co-exist in the same economy simultaneously? To understand this, we need to employ a historical perspective that can follow the dynamics of this change and track the continuity of meaning in certain categories or concepts like land. This historical perspective has several advantages. First, it permits us to decenter the analysis from an ethnocentric Western reading that is built into political economy as a discipline and IPE as an interdisciplinary area of study, as in many other areas of study. To be sure, other regions of the world have adopted Western dominant categories not just because of the impact of American and European colonial processes but also because of the continuing economic dominance and cultural hegemony exercised by Western academia and other hegemonic producers of knowledge on the rest of the world.

We will see how similar notions are deployed but they do not always mean the same thing as they reflect different sets of practices. Second, a historical perspective enables us to visualize the extent to which the allocation of value to things and people is manifest in the way they are exchanged, is what Mauss calls a "total social fact", meaning a multipurpose social action that blurs the boundaries between the political, economic, natural, and ecological, religious, etc. (Mauss, 1973, p. 147). To this end, International Political Economy must embrace the importance and centrality of "the social" and can only do so by looking in more details at historical change and continuity.

Attempting to Historicize

Let's first try to map out a few buzzwords that we find in the discipline, such as state, market, society, land, labor, or capital. One dominant debate in the political economy literature is over the proper role played (or that which ought to be played) by the state and the market in processes of economic production. Conventional wisdom holds that the market is a natural phenomenon where economic activity takes place, and the state is an outside agent that acts on or limits its action over the market. In a sense, the market is the field of economic activity, for the state, that of politics, and in the middle sit the people who are contained in "society".

The first critique to this approach came from the German economist Karl Marx, who argued that the state always ends up representing a certain social class of privileged actors that clamp down on the modes and means of production thereby controlling, to a certain extent, market activity. To this effect, Marxists argue that the liberal idea of a free market bringing about its own equilibrium and producing fairness, equality, freedom, etc., is indeed nothing more than a myth. The implication is that the relationship between the state, society and the market is much more intertwined than usually acknowledged (see Figure 2.3). As we will see below when we discuss transformations in the late Ottoman Levantine economy, the market implicates social relations if not "familial" or kin relationships. The state is made up of social forces, different groups of people co-ruling, and the state and the market shape each other in different ways depending on the context.

In the first half of the twentieth century, an Austro-Hungarian economist, Karl Polanyi would cause a watershed in the discipline by stating the opposite of what the liberals have been claiming, that in fact if we look at European history, especially that of the British economy, the gradual formation of the modern state brought about the formation, development and sustaining of "the market" through a myriad of institutions, legal innovations, social transformations and

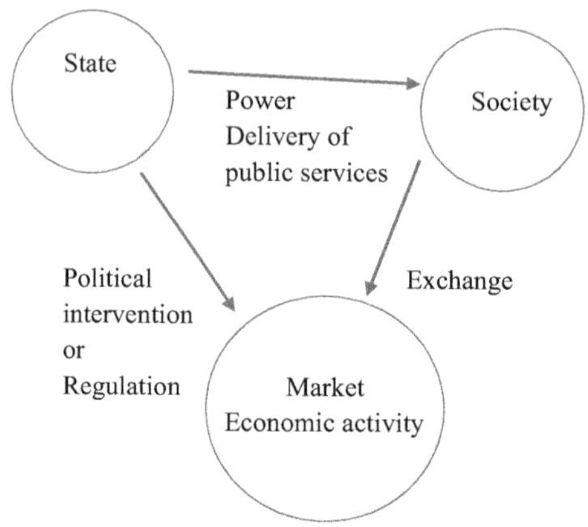

FIGURE 2.3 A Liberal or Classical view of Political Economy. States fulfill a "regulatory" role. They make sure the market is functioning properly, through protecting private property, enforcing contracts, etc.

the economic management of populations (Polanyi, 2002). Polanyi wrote in the 1940s, at a time when overarching states assumed ever-increasing roles in the management of the societies and economies with a heavy emphasis on interventionist and redistributive functions pushing for a certain level of social equality and access to resources. In a sense, Polanyi cut through the debate between those advocating more or less state, showing that the formation of the state has always been an integral part of the formation of the market. The political, institutional and legal assemblage that is the state/market departed from previous forms of human community life where economic production, management, exchange and consumption only played a minor role. Even though these debates were still peculiarly Western-centric in the sense that they responded to specific historical circumstances that developed in North America and Europe, Polanyi showed the importance of analyzing historical processes in understanding the political nature of economic transformations and that the meaning of things such as the market, land, labor, value, etc., reflects a particular historical and cultural process.

In colonial and post-colonial regions however, those questions of the good life or of community life were often channeled through different sets of (formal or informal) institutions not always affiliated or even obedient to the state, and this had a very significant impact not just on how "the economy" operates but also on the individual and social formation of value. Mikhayel's relationship with a fast-reforming Ottoman Empire trying to turn into some sort of nation-state project, or half a century later, his descendants' relationship with the Lebanese State that had just come out of a French mandate, and the radically transformed social and economic environment they operate in, would implicate significantly different understanding of value, land, etc (see Figure 2.4).

The Colonial Legacy and Private Property as a Political Project

Now that we've covered some of the implications of the transformations taking place in the run-up to the modern era, let's look at how this applied to nineteenth-century Ottoman provinces, the Levant area, and specifically the area that became known as Lebanon. Scrambling to

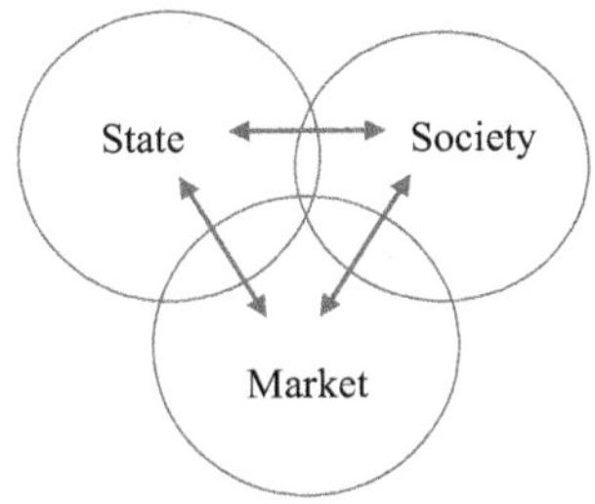

FIGURE 2.4 How the state and society shape each other and are dependent on each thereby also shaping and being shaped by economic activity

reform to keep up with European relentless "growth" quests, the Ottomans instituted a series of political changes and enacted land reforms in 1858, which introduced the notion of "land" as divorced from that of "labor". Hoping to improve the use of land for income and resource generation, this led to the firming up of the control of a few families over the land and dispossessed peasants enacting a short-lived, quasi-feudal system. Mikhayel represented a small example of such families, although he would have been more of a trader rather than a landowner (despite the sheer amount of land he came to have to his name).

In Philip Khoury's term, Mikhayel and his father were "merchant-moneylenders" who took advantage of the mid-nineteenth century relatively booming economic situation "to transform their landholding into outright landownership" (Khoury, 2003, p. 27) and acquire an important status with the tax collectors such as with the Emir Bashir Shihab who controlled Mount Lebanon. Similar events were taking place throughout the area including Egypt. The Ottoman reforms of the mid-1800s were dubbed *Tanzimat* (lit. regulating, ordering). Different colonial processes were at play here depending on the region. Egypt's early attempt at producing a "national economy" under the Khedivate rulers (who were technically representatives of the Ottomans) was spearheaded by Britain, whereas Mount Lebanon's new political regime called *Mutasarrifiyah* was sponsored by the French (Traboulsi, 2007, p. 41).

The Reforms sought to reassert Ottoman's hold over state-owned land called *miri* while being able to generate more revenue, by assigning agricultural land, to individuals who would have the right to usufruct over them (Provence, 2005, p. 33). In its quest to tax in a more exhaustive and systematic way by pinning down land to *registered* individuals, one of the main implications of the land reforms of 1858 was to produce a legal category for property that was divorced from what the land could produce or the "agricultural use" of the land. In so doing, it irremediably triggered a gradual change in notions of ownership and value assigned to land.

Premodern understandings of land could not be more different. Traditionally, property and ownership are bound by what can be done to the land, that is to say, how it can be used. In Islamic jurisprudence, a prophetic *hadith* (story or saying) governs the overall rationale of land ownership:

> every individual who leaves uncultivated for three years a piece of land of which he has possession shall lose his rights over the land; and if a third party appears who will cultivate it, this latter shall have a greater right to possess it than the former.
>
> *(Shehadeh, 1982, p. 83)*

This emphasizes the extent to which land use was more important than an abstract understanding of property. For example, Mikhayel's story exemplifies the recent legal change followed by the Ottoman reforms yet superimposed by an older "mentality" which is that if you cannot do much with the land then it is probably not worth much, and that could explain partly why Mikhayel was fine with giving such a vast amount of land away.

Egypt's colonial encounter with France and Britain, and other such large-scale initiatives all led to a standardization and codification process, in trying to keep up with the West, that created these abstract categories of "land" and "individual" or "person". Huri İslamoğlu (2000) analyzes in depth this Ottoman rush to consolidate state power and reorganize its territorial space through different categories of land all in the hope of extracting more resources and developing the kind of "economy" that Western countries have been boasting. For İslamoğlu, the Ottoman land code, among other things, separates the notion of property from that of taxation (İslamoğlu, 2000, p. 24). This is a very important point; it means that before the reforms, properties were valued in terms of how they could be taxed rather than as legally separate entities that could be bought or sold. This was only possible in the attempt of producing a notion of individual ownership. The point was to be able to think of land as having a "productive character" that would produce "an income to the owner" (İslamoğlu, 2000), and therefore to the state.

These reforms required a sharper and more precise mapping of territory and resources. They reflected a European conception of the land of that time that was subsequently exported everywhere in the world. As İslamoğlu argues:

> The belief that land was the chief source of value, that it was an economic asset, or a factor of production seems, in Europe and elsewhere, to have stimulated attempts at cadastral mapping as the scientific basis for the improvement of this most important asset and for the assessment of its taxes.
>
> *(İslamoğlu, 2004, p. 13).*

Ottomans started this process of delimiting land and ownership, but this was never fully completed by the time the empire broke down following the end of World War I in 1918. Not surprisingly, of the first initiatives the French would execute after establishing mandates over what becomes Lebanon and Syria is the launching of "cadastral mapping" a typical colonial practice design to ensure better control through organizing and delineating (Bhandar, 2018). This mapping was left unfinished by the time the French left Lebanon in 1943 and is still unfinished today and ironically is recently (at the time of writing this book) awaiting funding from France and the EU to be completed.

It is now clearer why looking at value and land as transformed through history matters to the International Political Economy scholar. While the Tanzimat prompted an unprecedented process of delimiting types of ownership, it precipitated a series of new social arrangements. Eager to follow the European model, the Ottomans were adamant that property should move from "the group" to the individual but again with less concern for the emergence of a European understanding of property rights but more efficient taxability and fungibility. For example, historically certain types of land were previously communally shared by a whole village or region. These were called *musha'* lands. They now had to be broken down into individually held parcels. After issuing the land reforms of 1858, the Ottoman state pressed its province's inhabitants to come forth and register their lands in their name. In most of the cases, those who registered land came from a more privileged social status. The peasants were reluctant to register so as not to incur taxes (Guéno, 2018, p. 135), but also made decisions, as we said earlier, according to specific social habits. Social practices and a certain notion of value here again prevail and show how a generic "liberal capitalist" logic could not apply. Another author argues that "[w]ith good reasoning based on past experiences, the appearance of any member of the government in a village was interpreted as (1) a census for military conscription, (2) an inventory for tax purposes, or (3) some sort of equally ominous change in the village structure. It is not surprising that many villagers were reluctant to declare their rights or holdings or to register their names on any sort of official registry" (Irby, 1971, p. 158).

And social habits were heavily conditioned by politics. As the state speeded up its attempts at producing a "modern economy", legal and administrative reforms paved the way for the emergence of different power relations. Reflecting on the case of Egypt, Timothy Mitchell summarizes more generally this rocky introduction of property rights in the Ottoman Levant area as such: "Power seems to operate through a chain of personal orders and inter-connected prerogatives rather than a generalized regime of government" (Mitchell, 2002, p. 58). As a result, "Private property emerged in the form of large agricultural estates" (Mitchell, 2002, p. 66) rather than a more atomized structure of ownership that would have empowered peasants as individual entrepreneurs, as the Tanzimat seemingly aimed for.

Old social hierarchies gave way to new ones: "The proprietor of the estates that spread across the Nile valley was a sovereign, an 'absolute master.' He was accountable to no one. He could imprison, expel, starve, exploit, and exercise many other forms of arbitrary, exceptional, and, if necessary, violent powers" (Mitchell, 2002, p. 70). In the case of Syria and Lebanon there was an expression that illustrated the kind of power large landowners exercised. It was said that "they had the power to untie the hanged man", meaning that they had the power to reverse a decision to hang someone through their networks and connections in high places. This is another illustration of how political, legal, social and economic historical transformations are all intertwined in changing in turn our understanding of value.

Families and the Economy

As was mentioned earlier, most land during the Ottoman era was nominally owned by the state. The main principle at work was to limit the accumulation of wealth and property. Moreover, inheritance laws in Islamic Shari'a have specific clauses to break inheritance among siblings and family members. One common strategy to keep inheritance community across generations was to register certain types of land and buildings as "*waqf*" (literally meaning "to stop", or freeze). Typically, *Waqf* land and property is known as made up of religious or other culturally important landmarks such as mosques, and churches and for communal use, no? But the historical records reveal a much more complicated story of intricate family strategies using *waqf* to transmit larger types of property be it land, constructions, resources, etc.

From the seventeenth to the early nineteenth century, the Maronite Church could acquire large swathes of land in Mount Lebanon through registering it as *Waqf*, building monasteries, which in turn required large agricultural plots. Richard Van Leeuwen (1994) shows how this strategy led to the rise of the church as an uncontested power in the region, but not without the help of powerful notable families such as the Al Khazen who built the monasteries and registered the Waqf. Bechara Doumani's work (1998, 2003) on the political economy of *Waqf* endowments and inheritance, what he calls property devolution strategies, in Tripoli (Lebanon) and Nablus (Palestine), preceding the nineteenth century is highly enlightening in this regard of the different strategy families employed to keep or expand property realms.

In the eighteenth- and nineteenth-century families such as Al Khazen mostly specialized in silk trading (rather than tax farming) with Europe which led to unprecedented fortunes but also to their downfall. By the mid-nineteenth century, the silk economy was just not competitive anymore as the east Asian trade opened to European colonial powers. But the Maronite church had by then prevailed as the dominant political actor in the region that would lead to the creation of a separate state called Lebanon. It was at the center of the Ottoman and European agreement to establish the *Mutasarrifiyah* administration in 1861 that involved political representation from the different religious communities and that lasted until the collapse of the Ottoman empire in 1916.

Families then were like institutions, the Al Khazen family in this case should be thought of as a larger clan than the modern nuclear family. They were not as organized as the Maronite church, for example, but they can be as resourceful and backed by similar foreign powers such as France or the Vatican. Social transformations introduced by the 1858 land reforms and the larger Tanzimat would force families and such institutions to rework their continuity, sources of subsistence, and control over property, through other types of trades, and political maneuvering. Mikhayel's family, for example, was involved in the silk manufacturing but also had the monopoly over salt trading in the region. Toward the end of the nineteenth century and after the virtual collapse of the silk industry in Mount Lebanon, many migrated to Latin American countries, some returning after some time and some settling there for good.

The Ottoman region during the nineteenth century was a peculiar place to be. Colonial encroachment, the struggle to reform, and a varied multi-communitarian society produced opportunities for merchant families to reinvent themselves, especially those coming from religious minorities. According to economic historian Timur Kurani (2004), Christian minorities (such as Mikhayel's family) in the Ottoman region benefitted from a two-level playing field where they could appeal to different legal jurisdictions (Islamic, and new secular Western), while being backed by Western chancelleries, and unlike their Muslim counterpart, developed significant economic and political leverage. In Box 2.1, we can see how this drastically changed the economic landscape of the Levant region.

BOX 2.1 THE SURSUQ FAMILY, THE ZIONISTS, LEVANTINE CAPITALISM, AND CHANGING CONCEPTIONS OF LAND

As soon as the 1858 Land Reforms were enacted, and before the Ottoman could finalize their implementation, influential families that had already established themselves as main trading powers, tax and silk farmers, and moneylenders in the Levant such as the Sursuqs moved fast to acquire large swathes of land from (what becomes) Turkey, Lebanon, Palestine and Egypt. In Palestine, the Sursuqs bribed Ottoman *walis* in Syria to put title deeds to the land in their name (Alff, 2018, p. 157). The way the Sursuq family could accumulate so much land was through a sophisticated scheme to circumvent Ottoman (aka Islamic) allergy to the accumulation of property by developing an extended listing of extended family's name on land registries, including families they married into such as the Tuenis, Butrus, or Debbas, all families that are part of the Greek-Orthodox community. Thus, as argued by Kristen Alff (2018) rather than espouse the corporate European model, the Sursuq family-run Levantine company found navigating Islamic law, ottoman reformed qanun, and extended family strategies more efficient at extracting value from land. The Ottoman Sultan Abdelhamid II himself grew alarmed by the expanding empire of the Sursuqs and registered land in his name in Palestine. Until the collapse of the Ottoman empire, the actual ownership of the land was contested. The Sursuq had the right to usufruct over them and peasants grew indebted to them by borrowing money in order to work the land, but according to Ottoman law they didn't "own" the land in the European capitalist sense of the term. Meanwhile by the late 1800s and specifically in 1901, the Sursuq family sold a significant chunk of its titles to the Jewish Colonization Association (JCA). These sales continued to be contested into the establishment of the British mandate in Palestine, not least by the peasants themselves and a set of influential notables in the region (Fakher Eldin, 2019; Alff, 2023).

Thus, introducing private property as a legal category of practice in certain non-Western areas of the world, such Egypt and the Levant, triggered a series or different social and political takeovers as new-found types of powers could be exercised. Far from the intended outcome of recentering the economic activity on "the individual", it forced new group arrangements to develop, such as a reinvention of the family, and new state political and legal strategies in attempting to assert control. This precipitated a change in the way people value assets and economic resources.

Ethics as an Alternative

Today, people's preferences and values are shaped by a more general "consumer culture" that is shaped by a myriad of institutions, groups, factors, experiences, etc. The modern discipline of economics pushes us to focus the unit of analysis on the individual as a source of value creation because it wants to dissociate itself from the other sphere of human life that affects it, namely here the political and the social. "An individualist, market view of the good [life] has the effect of trivializing values, needs, and wants – rendering them merely as personal preferences or tastes" (Sayer, 2011, pp. 262–263).

What we have seen so far is that value, the central analytical notion that aims to predict a certain agreed-upon standard as to how things, resources, social practices and sensitivities matter in producing different types of economic exchange cannot be understood independently from the more general social and political contexts. Throughout this chapter in fact, we have seen that where modern human and social sciences sought to disentangle different spheres of human life and activity, the reality is that these were and remain inextricably entangled. The Greeks, Arabs, Chinese, Mexicans and other people of the earth have another working notion to understand, analyze and evaluate the human quality of life: ethics.

Modern times are at the very least a witness to the decline of ethics as a discipline of study (rather than as a subject that is being studied) and the rise of the human sciences. Ethics is none other than the study of value or how and why things matter to people, to quote the title of a book by political economist Andrew Sayer (2011). If the "economic" is indissociable from other fields, then value gains a more holistic ground. What Sayer calls "Moral economy" is the economic field as such that he argues has always been saturated with ethical and moral concerns, in the sense that people evaluate how they "should behave with respect to others so as to harmonize conduct and maintain actors' well-being" (Sayer, 2007, p. 262). The main issue with values understood in their larger moral and ethical sense is that they were associated with the blurrier and messier world of emotions and faith. Establishing sciences in the modern era required a certain level of objectivity and judgments or analysis based on emotions or religious belief was deemed "subjective". But in fact, even early classical liberal political economists such as Adam Smith viewed values "as reasonable – that is, as being responsive to objective situations in their specificity" (Sayer, 2007, p. 267).

In these approaches, the state as a set of institutions sought to achieve certain types of tasks because it assumed it could and would benefit from doing them. The state in this case is given a certain moral/ethical objective. From a minimal perspective the state provides overall regulatory frameworks on which the "market" can operate fluidly. These contain clear moral injunctions or "value regimes" (Appadurai, 1988). Yet, we should "avoid treating the market as a boundless amoral force that ultimately commodifies (and destroys) so-called 'moral economies' (characterized by norms and non-instrumental values)" (Palomera & Vetta, 2016, p. 420).

Let's try to apply this to our story mentioned earlier. When Mikhayel gives the land to Bassam, one cannot say that he's just acting "rationally" in a utilitarian fashion nor that he is acting "emotionally" in a rash manner moved by a bout of anger or resignation, etc., following a conversation with his wife. The social or communitarian dimension in this gift, to use the Maussian term, to a certain extent structures Mikhayel decision-making process. Mikhayel contributed a tiny act to a more general balance of how community and kinship ties are maintained, and in the backdrop of the various transformations taking place in a late nineteenth-century Ottoman province.

No wonder why the colleague and friend of Marx, Friedrich Engels in his *The Origins of the Family, Private Property, and the State* (first published in 1884), studied "the family" in its multiple variants across history and its relationship with modes of production and political regimes. In the nineteenth century the family became the main link between the perdurance of private property and the state. The nuclear family, and specifically the unpaid reproductive and domestic labor performed by women to uphold it, was the necessary precondition of social stability without which wealth, the production of surplus value, or capital accumulation could not be possible. Marxist critics quickly saw that private property was mainly preserved and multiplied through marriage, inheritance and nuclear family structures and therefore sought to delink the family from the ownership and preservation of private property holdings. Marx and Engels clearly recognized clearly the inevitable social embeddedness of capitalism.

More recently, the triad state/society/market was studied in explaining Asian economies' impressive economic development and growth throughout the twentieth century. One great example is the economic effectiveness (accompanied by growing social dislocation and anxieties) of the chaebol system in South Korea where business organizations are depended on a complex set a family-based ownership and networks (Chang, 2010).

Thus, to understand political economy, down to how people make certain choices conducive to what we call the market today, one must look at the negotiated relationship between state, society and market that constantly varies especially in areas where the state is either still "unfinished business", failure, or where those relations of authority and value creation are just differently set up and practiced depending on social and familial ties.

We saw in this chapter how notions of land underwent severe changes due to parallel changes in the role of the state and the influence of colonial powers, which are still being negotiated today, in certain parts of the world such as the Middle East, the Caribbean and the African continent.

Was the gift of land on that scraggly hill to be reciprocated? According to the great-grandson of Bassam, the real estate property developer, there was nothing to repay as Mikhayel pretended that Bassam's great-grandfather bought the land in the first place! Even here at the end of this story, Bassam's great-grandson invoked a moral principle to justify his use of the land. Both in the 1880s and a century later in the 1980s, the Lebanese economy was moral, and value could only be understood through that prism, which relied on an intricate balance of social and political circumstances.

Note

1 This story comes from a close source whose family will remain anonymous.

Bibliography

Alff, K. (2018). Levantine joint-stock companies, trans-mediterranean partnerships, and nineteenth-century capitalist development. *Comparative Studies in Society and History*, *60*(1), 150–177.

Alff, K. (2023). Changing capitalist structures and settler-colonial land purchases in Northern Palestine, 1897–1922. *International Journal of Middle East Studies*, *55*, 675–692.

Appadurai, A. (Ed.). (1988). *The social life of things: Commodities in cultural perspective*. Cambridge University Press.

Bhandar, B. (2018). *Law, land, and racial regimes of ownership*. Duke University Press.

Chang, K. (2010). *South Korea under compressed modernity familial political economy in transition*. Routledge.

Doumani, B. (1998). Endowing family: Waqf, property devolution, and gender in greater Syria, 1800 to 1860. *Comparative Studies in Society and History*, *40*(1), 3–41.

Doumani, B. (Ed.). (2003). *Family history in the Middle East: Household, property, and gender*. SUNY Press.

Doumani, B. (2017). *Family life in the Ottoman and the Mediterranean: A social history*. Cambridge University Press.

Fakher Eldin, M. (2019). Confronting a colonial rule of property: The Al-Sakhina case in mandate Palestine. *The Arab Studies Journal*, *27*(1), 12–33.

Fakher Eldin, M. (2023). The middle class and the land struggle in Palestine revisiting the colonial encounter in the Beisan Valley, 1908–1948. *Comparative Studies of South Asia, Africa and the Middle East*, *43*(3), 249–261.

Gerber, H. (1987). *The social origins of the modern Middle East*. Lynne Rienner Publishers.

Graeber, D. (2002). *Toward an anthropological theory of value: The false coin of our own dreams*. Palgrave Macmillan.

Guéno, V. (2018). Land tenure and the concept of "property": The history of legal practice in Syria and Lebanon in the last century of the Ottoman empire. *Chronos*, *37*, 111–142.

Irby, J. K. (1971). Aspects of Musha land tenure in Lebanon. *Yearbook of the Association of Pacific Coast Geographers*, *33*(1), 153–160.

İslamoğlu, H. (Ed.). (2004). *Constituting modernity: Private property in the East and West*. I.B. Tauris.

İslamoğlu, H. (2000). Property as a contested domain: A reevaluation of the Ottoman Land Code of 1858. In R. Owen (Ed.), *New perspectives on property and land in the Middle East* (pp. 3–61). Cambridge, MA: Harvard Center for Middle Eastern Studies.
İslamoğlu, H. (1994). *State and peasant in the Ottoman Empire: Agrarian power relations and regional economic development in Ottoman Anatolia during the sixteenth century*. E. J. Brill.
Khoury, P. S. (2003). *Urban notables and Arab nationalism: The politics of Damascus 1860–1920*. Cambridge University Press.
Kurani, T. (2004, June). The economic ascent of the Middle East's religious minorities: The role of Islamic legal pluralism. *Journal of Legal Studies*, *33*, 475–515.
Makdisi, U. (2000). *The culture of sectarianism: Community, history, and violence in nineteenth-century Ottoman Lebanon*. University of California Press.
Mauss, M. (2002). *The gift: The form and reason of exchange in archaic societies* (p. 100). London and New York: Routledge Classics.
Mirowski, P. (1991). *More heat than light: Economics as social physics, physics as nature's economics*. Cambridge University Press.
Mitchell, T. (2002). *Rules of experts: Egypt, techno-politics, modernity*. University of California Press.
Owen, R., & Bunton, M. P. (2000). *New perspectives on property and land in the Middle East*. Harvard MES.
Palomera, J., & Vetta, T. (2016). Moral economy: Rethinking a radical concept. *Anthropological Theory*, *16*(4), 413–432. https://doi.org/10.1177/1463499616678097
Pitts, F. H. (2020). *Value (What is political economy?)*. Polity.
Polanyi, K. (2002). *The great transformation: The political and economic origins of our time*. Beacon Press.
Provence, M. (2005). Ottoman and French mandate land registers for the region of Damascus. *Middle Association Studies Bulletin*, *39*(1), 32–43.
Sayer, A. (2000). Moral economy and political economy. *Studies in Political Economy*, *61*(1), 79–103.
Sayer, A. (2007). Moral economy as critique. *New Political Economy*, *12*(2), 261–270.
Sayer, A. (2011). *Why things matter to people: Social science, values and ethical life*. Cambridge University Press.
Shehadeh, R. (1982). The land law of Palestine: An analysis of the definition of state lands. *Journal of Palestine Studies*, *11*(2), 82–99.
Skeggs, B. (2014). Values beyond value? Is anything beyond the logic of capital? *The British Journal of Sociology*, *65*(1), 1–20.
Traboulsi, F. (2007). *A history of modern Lebanon*. Pluto Press.
Van Leeuwen, R. (1994). *Notables and clergy in Mount Lebanon: The Khazin Sheikhs and the Maronite Church (1736–1840)*. E. J. Brill.
William, R. (1983). *Culture and society, 1780–1950*. Columbia University Press.

3

THE POLITICAL ECONOMY OF INTERNATIONAL FOOD REGIMES

Introduction

In March 2022, a few months after the beginning of hostilities between Russia and NATO (through the proxy of Ukraine), which contributed to the skyrocketing of food prices, hundreds of hungry people assaulted food stands in the popular market of Sale in Morocco, signaling the beginning of an acute food crisis. The actual geo-political and geo-economic conflict is tremendously affecting wheat, maize, barley and sunflower oil imports from the Black Sea region, an area known as the granary of the world as it hosts 30% of most fertile black soil in the world. The war in Ukraine and the economic sanctions to Russia have therefore gravely influenced the spike in food prices, which rings as an alarm bell, particularly for governments and policymakers in the MENA region, the largest global food importer. This event, and many others in the Middle East and North Africa region, raise a series of questions: what is political about food? What has been the relationship between food and capitalism? How did the integration of non-European regions within the mechanics of the international food regime affected local food systems? What have been the implications on national production and consumption patterns? What are the alternative paradigms which can help us rethink the existing hegemonic order of transnational food corporations?

The 2007/2008 economic and financial crisis and the skyrocketing food prices which ensued have brought the question of food to the attention of development agencies, national governments and academics. World food prices in 2008 were 83% higher compared with 2005 (FAO, 2009). The price of wheat rose 130% and that of rice doubled in the first three months of 2008 spearheading a sequence of food riots both in the MENA region and in sub-Saharan Africa (Bush & Martiniello, 2017).

The spike in food prices signaled the end of cheap food (Moore, 2010), that is, decades in which a combination of Green Revolution technological innovations along with heavy state subsidies contributed to rising agricultural yields (especially in cereals such as maize and rice), which were made available at cheap costs to cater for the consumption needs of urban populations. The Green Revolution was a colonial-inspired program of agricultural modernization conceived in the United States and extended to countries such as Mexico and India, aimed at

DOI: 10.4324/9781003264255-3

maximizing food productivity based on the intensive application of fertilizers, pesticides, herbicides, hybrid seeds and water irrigation.

The development of large-scale agro-industrial monocropping based on wage labor, that is, the dedication of large portions of farmlands to the cultivation of a single monoculture produced with intensive use of soil, labor, energy and water, and the making of a global food market pointed to the increasingly corporate nature of the international food regime which enhanced a growing concentration of power and wealth in what Jan Douwe van der Ploeg termed "food empires" (2013). Food empire can be defined as an extended network that exerts oligopolistic control over the production, processing, distribution and consumption of food and that simultaneously appropriates a large proportion of the value produced from these activities. The International Food Regime is a regime of food production, circulation and consumption on a global scale pivoted around the market and the state. It highlights the role of agriculture as a significant cluster in the development of capitalist state formation and global political economy.

The productivist emphasis on producing large quantities of food has, however, undermined both the quality and diversity of available food and raised a set of issues about the relationship between food consumption and the emergence of a series of health pathologies. Among the manifestations of these contradictions in the food system, the interlinked questions of malnutrition and obesity feature prominently. It is against this background that this chapter aims to revisit the debates about the dynamics shaping contemporary production and consumption patterns and diets globally. The case of sugar is a good example of navigating the history and politics of food on a global scale and its relationship with the dominant economic system and explore the ways in which the development of capitalism shaped what people consume.

This chapter provides a long historical overview of the processes of globalization of food and a discussion of the dynamics that have governed the making of the international food regimes. It does so in order to understand how food production and distribution have become key vectors of capitalist accumulation, shaping cultivation and food consumption patterns on a global scale. It discusses the main transformations that have occurred in the system of governance and the production of food with a particular interest in the adoption of key food groups of the neoliberal diet in the Middle East and North Africa (MENA) region and African countries south of the Sahara. It asks as follows: what is an international food system? How has the international food regime changed across time? How has it shaped food production and consumption patterns of countries in Africa and the Middle East?

It argues that countries in the region have progressively been incorporated in the international food regime and significantly adopted elements of the neoliberal diets though with important differences across the region. Gulf countries, in particular, seem to be driving processes of meatification in the region and the promotion of large-scale land investments producing monocropping for their internal food security, that is, for the satisfaction of the growing consumption needs of their populations, especially in grains and meats. This meatification implies a change in the patterns of meat consumption in everyday diets of people, especially but not only in the Western world. Most recently, the notion aptly captures the changes in the demand and consumption of meat by affluent societies in the non-Western world. Good examples are China, the United Arab Emirates, Kuwait, Brazil, Chile and South Africa. In what follows we begin with a literature review exploring key debates and themes around the continuities and discontinuities in the international food regime and the implications for diets and a focus on the rise of the neoliberal diet. We offer a concluding section summarizing the main points of the chapter and some future research trajectories.

A Tale of Three Food Regimes

According to economic anthropologist Sidney Mintz (1986), sugar has been at the core of the development of the early phases of capitalism, tying slavery in Africa, the development of plantations in the Caribbean, and the consumption of sugar in Europe. Adopting a multidisciplinary lens to the study of the International Political Economy of food allows us to open the study of the making of the "international" to socio-cultural and ecological dynamics. Seeing the making of the international food regime from Africa and the Middle East enables us to link global patterns of food production and consumption with agrarian, demographic and ecological transformations elsewhere. As Mintz noted, in the beginning sugar was a luxury commodity consumed exclusively by aristocrats along with the development of other food habits such as the consumption of tea and or coffee, both goods linked to the long-distance trade circuits in tropical commodities of the British colonial empire. As sugarcane cultivation expanded thanks to the persisting super-exploitation of slave labor along with industrial strategies that cheapened the production process and therefore its final price, sugar slowly started to be consumed also by the working classes. Here, the argument of Mintz gets compelling: sugar was cheapened in order to be accessible to the working classes, whose daily work efforts dramatically exceeded their meager caloric intake. In other words, sugar, with its "cheap", but "empty" calories (Richards, 2013), served the purpose of boosting the biological reproduction of workers providing them with the extra-caloric intake necessary to survive and be ready to work on the following day. This was so because the degree of exploitation during the Industrial Revolution was huge especially if the daily hours of work were weighed against the daily caloric intake and overall living and health conditions. In *The Wealth of the Nations*, Adam Smith maintained that during the Industrial Revolution a carpenter in London used to have an expectation of life of seven years. The cheapening of the reproduction costs of industrial working classes in Europe, and therefore their increased exploitation, was largely premised upon the super-exploitation of African slaves in the plantations of the Caribbean and Madeira Islands (see Patel & Moore, 2017), a process which triggered the insurrections led by Toussaint Louverture in Saint-Domingue in 1793–1794, and other insurrections in Cuba 1812, in the Southern plantations of the United States and Jamaica in 1820 (James, 1989). Here we see more clearly the nexus between food and the origins of capitalism, as well as the emerging forms of resistance to its emergence.

This example aptly shows that it was the combined effort of both state and capital forces paving the way for sugar toward Europe at certain costs and in certain quantities, rather than consumers' demand or preferences. Moreover, it is important to note that throughout history, thousands of plant species have been domesticated and used in agriculture but most of them are now underutilized. Around 7,000 out of the 250,000 identified plant species have been used in agriculture throughout human history (FAO, 1997). However, the expansion of agro-industrial monocropping has resulted in only 12 plant species and five animal species giving 75% of the world's food, and just three plant species (rice, wheat and maize) constituting 60% of total worldwide caloric input (FAO, 1997). Crop diversity has been drastically decreasing with less genetic diversity being used within species, fewer species being cultivated and genetically homogeneous cultivars replacing cultivated varieties since the beginning of the twentieth century. Such homogenization of crops, extended to cropping systems and products, is a very recent phenomenon considering the long history of agriculture and is part of the process that, following the Industrial Revolution, and later on the application of chemistry, transformed agriculture in an intensive industrial activity (Chable et al., 2020).

Abrupt homogenization and standardization, enhanced by the advent of industrial agriculture, have dramatically decreased the diversity of food available and therefore limiting the so-called consumers' choices. An illustrative example of this process is offered by a brief history of tomato cultivation. According to Riccardo Bocci, at the beginning of the twentieth century there existed at least 5,000 varieties of tomatoes. With the expansion of the global food market, especially after the Uruguay round of the World Trade Organization in 1993, in which agricultural commodities were first integrated into the norms of international free trade, and the connected processes of supermarketization, the number of tomato varieties currently commercialized on a global scale have been reduced to less than ten, *de facto*, determining what kind of tomatoes people eat, rather than what their preferences are. Supermarketization consists in the expansion of the supermarket model from Global North to Global South and Eastern Europe, displacing local vendors and local diets.

The globalization of food, the use of food aid as a political weapon in the US foreign policy, the concentration of power in the hands of corporate agro-chemical companies, the expansion of large-scale monocropping, commodity standardization and the enforcement of intellectual property rights on seeds have contributed to an "un-natural" selection of the varieties produced and consumed today. Global agricultural value chains have in fact focused on less than ten tomato varieties for reasons that include productivity, gestation to maturity, costs of cultivation, and perceived consumers' preferences in terms of color, brightness and roundness and taste. The result is a disastrous damage to the existing biodiversity built across millennia through peasants' horizontal exchange of seeds and practices.

A series of interlinked systems has resulted in the evolution of food production patterns across time and space, shifting from hunting and gathering modes of production to settled agriculture, paving the way for industrial society and eventually global food exchange, highly affecting the societies' food culture (Grew, 2018). "Produce for subsistence" was peasants' main rule of reproduction as long as they possessed the means of subsistence (Brenner, 2005). However, food systems have witnessed remarkable changes with the rise of capitalism.

As described by Wallerstein (1983), since the fourteenth century, feudalism's dissolution and capital accumulation led the European expansion, pushing for increased food production mainly sugar and wheat. The colonial era defined a new division of labor and activated an extractive relationship between Europe and the rest of the world, which resulted in turning the colonies into supply zones of raw materials and food to fuel European capitalism (McMichael, 2009). Since then, the relation between world capitalism and agriculture has been remarkable. Beginning in the sixteenth century, capitalism achieved its long-run economic expansion by means of imposing bourgeois property relations on the rural areas, which drove an uneven process of dispossession and differentiation forcing the transition from peasant production to capitalist farming. Capitalism set in motion successive agricultural revolutions and a series of extraordinary expansions of the food surplus; "every great wave of capitalist development has been paved with 'cheap' food" (Moore, 2010, p. 1). From the early modern era witnessing the Dutch and English agricultural revolutions to the Green Revolution of the mid-twentieth century, "modernization" narratives have resulted in and legitimized land expropriations. By driving down the relative cost of food and pushing forward uneven processes of proletarianization, agricultural revolutions enormously contributed to the course of capitalist development which itself resulted in further transition of food and nutrition regimes (Moore, 2010). Proletarianization is a process by which classes of labor are formed from previously "independent" farmers, artisans, etc.

The food-regime perspective situates agriculture in the context of capitalist development, articulating the geographical, historical and political dynamics that shape the norms and rules of the international division of labor in agriculture and food into different regimes (Friedmann & McMichael, 1989).

Establishing "a world price for staple foods" was considered the differentiating, and world-historical feature of food regimes (McMichael, 2013, p. 24). The First International Food Regime (1870–1930s) was based on colonial tropical imports of basic grains and livestock from settler colonies such as Australia, the United States, Canada and India toward Europe, fueling the emerging industrialization process and consolidating the British hegemony in the world economy. These imports were supported by the adoption of mono-cultural agricultures in the colonies of settlement (McMicheal, 2009).

In the mid-nineteenth century, cultivation of colonial export crops proliferated in the Middle East and North Africa (MENA) region. Turkey, Egypt and Iran were centers of cotton cultivation, which expanded later on in Sudan. Tobacco was produced in Turkey and Syria; vine in the Levant; and silk in Mount Lebanon and Iran. Turkey and Iran were major cultivators of opium as well (Riachi & Martiniello, 2023). Along with its integration in the colonial export trade, the MENA region witnessed a concentration of land ownership by a class of absentee landlords, most notably in Egypt, Iraq and Syria, and therefore growing social stratification. In general, the Middle East was self-sufficient in staple foods. During that same period, Africa was a major provider of slave labor. According to Bairoch and Etemdad (1985), Africa exported 9% of the Third World food exports in 1860, 11% in 1900 and 10% in 1913.

During the first food regime, the main nutrition transition was adopting calorie as an effective metric for human energy requirements (Levenstein, 1980; Dixon, 2009). According to Cullather, the use of calorie resulted in "food being considered as an instrument of power responsive to political and scientific interventions" (2007, p. 34). In addition, another important factor was the identification of animal food as the master nutrient. So, the first food regime resulted in considering the calories and protein as measurable sources of human energy exchanged for a measurable sum of money (Dixon, 2009).

The Second International Food Regime (1945 to 1973) under the US hegemony witnessed the growth of the international state system as well as the transnational transformation of the agricultural sectors under the growing control of the increasingly global agribusiness corporations and their role in creating agro-food complexes (Friedmann & McMichael, 1989). Premised on the centrality of the role of the state, the second food regime was characterized by (i) sweeteners made from grain and soy substituting sugars and vegetable oils; (ii) a massive expansion of meat production and consumption; and (iii) the manufactured durable "foods complex". In addition, agri-input corporations and agro-food industries led to high degrees of mechanization and chemicalization resulting in a more complete industrialization of agricultural production both in animal feeds and for the manufacture of "durable foods" (Bernstein, 2015).

The promotion of Western food export and the use of food surpluses as "food aid" to countries in the Global South, resulted in increased dependence on food imports, making food a political weapon. With wheat and maize heavily subsidized by the United States, hence overproduced, the US government passed the law PL 480, which allowed to sell cheap food aid as part of the US foreign policy with the aim of luring toward Western assistance states in Africa and elsewhere which were under the sphere of communist influence (McMichael, 2000). During the second food regime, and by the 1970s, all countries in the Middle East, for example, were heavily dependent on grain imports, paramount is the case of Egypt. In addition, various developing countries that had previously specialized in food production – including in Africa – lost their positions as food suppliers to the benefit of industrialized countries and ended up being marginalized in the international food trade (Daviron et al., 1988). After these countries had been expelled from the market for "temperate" products, they became focused on the production of "exotic" products such as sugar and tropical beverages including cocoa, coffee and tea (Fold & Nylandsted Larsen, 2008). This was particularly marked in Africa. Exotic products, which had accounted for 10% of food exports in 1913, increased to 26% in 1938, 40% in 1962 and reached 52% in 1972 (Lamartine, 1959; Bairoch & Etemdad, 1985; FAO, 2003a).

Dixon (2009) argues that this second food regime witnessed another highly significant nutrition transition including the development of "protective foods". Following the creation of the term "vitamin", this regime further promoted the chemically based nutrition science (Cannon, 2005), hence providing food-processing corporations with a new platform for profit. In addition, by succeeding in adding cheap inputs, mainly sugar and fats/oils sourced from the developing world, the second food regime resulted in a rapid rise in diet-related diseases.

The Third Food Regime is distinguished "as a new moment in the history of world capitalism characterized by the politics of Neoliberalism" (McMichael, 2005, p. 273). Referred to as the "neoliberal food regime" or the "corporate food regime", the third food regime has been a key vector of the deepening of capitalist relations on a global scale. In 1995, the neoliberal development was epitomized by the creation of the World Trade Organization (WTO) with its regime of liberalization and privatization which promoted the integration of transnational agribusiness and food markets. Consequently, the WTO's Agreement on Agriculture (AoA) forced Southern states to open their agricultural sectors while the European Union and the United States retained huge subsidies, hence resulting in the lowest prices in history for their meat, grains and milk products (McMicheal, 2008). The corporate food regime resulted in the determination of a world price for agricultural commodities strikingly divorced from costs, hence rendering farmers vulnerable to dispossession. Farmers were either displaced into urban areas or displaced as laborers on agricultural lands dedicated to exporting food to global consumers (McMichael, 2008). As a result, corporate globalization proceeded through mechanisms of accumulation by dispossession (Harvey, 2003).

In the last two decades, countries in the MENA region started exploring alternatives to enhance food security, which resulted in investments in overseas land. Food security exists when all people, at all times, have physical, social and economic access to sufficient, safe and nutritious food that meets their dietary needs and food preferences for an active and healthy life (FAO, 2001). Large-scale land acquisitions in African countries have been a highly controversial strategy, especially in terms of the arrangements being not transparent and often favoring the investors with, for example, tax exemptions in the host countries, in addition to imposing high risks of labor abuses. These land acquisitions can in fact threaten food security in the host countries. For example, in 2007, Saudi Arabia leased land in Ethiopia for the production of rice, wheat and barley while the World Food Programme spent around US$116 million for the provision of 230,000 MT of food aid to 4.6 million Ethiopians threatened by hunger and malnutrition between 2007 and 2011 (South Asia Partnership, 2011; Jane, 2011). In addition, although Sudan is the recipient of the largest food aid operation in the world, the Sudanese state is planning to set aside one-fifth of the country's arable land for capital investments by Arab governments (Jane, 2011). Since February 2019, the Land Matrix database reported a total of 1,105 large-scale land acquisitions (19,396,447 hectares) in Asia although, already in 2009 Asia was reported to host the largest number of undernourished people (more than 500 million) (WHO, 2009).

According to the collective GRAIN, African states have been signing an increasing number of deals with foreign investors giving them control over their countries' most fertile agricultural lands, including rice lands (KARAT, 2011). Since February 2019, the Land Matrix database reported a total of 574 deals covering 4,390,379 hectares being concluded in Africa, while 103 new deals covering 9,130,698 hectares are meant to follow thereafter.

The neoliberal food regime is characterized by the production of "empty calorie" foods lacking good nutrition, in addition to "nutritionalization" (chemical engineering) of foods (such as GMOs) for the purpose of boosting their nutritional value (Dixon, 2009).

"Nutritionalization", "nutrification" and "nutrition terrorism" are terms used to describe the modern diets that are being promoted on the single criterion of their nutritional qualities and that are ruled by bio-markers such as "good" and "bad" cholesterol, blood sugar levels, daily energy requirements (measured in kilojoules of calories), BMI (body mass index), GI (Glycemic Index) and the HWR (hip–waist ratio), regardless of the food production system and the ecological footprint of the produced food (Dixon, 2002; Levenstein, 1993; Scrinis, 2007). Araghi (2003) explains the empty calories as an aspect of forced under-consumption for the working class. This class may now be described as food over-consumers, but their overweight bodies are the result of their inability to afford fewer, less energy-dense foods (Drewnowski & Specter, 2004). The rise of supermarkets in developing regions of the MENA and Africa during this food regime further encouraged the promotion of modern diets, imposing serious challenges and excluding small-scale farmers and agro-food producers (Reardon et al., 2003). The entry of women into the workforce encouraged the rise of supermarkets; decreasing women's availability to cook healthy food increased their tendencies to shop for convenience and processed foods hence saving cooking time (Reardon et al., 2003). A significant characteristic of food regimes that has persisted throughout the different food regimes but intensified in the third food regime is the "prevalence of food consumed far from where it is produced, hence a kind of generic food from nowhere" (McMichael, 2009, p. 147).

A Neoliberal Diet in the Global South

In the contemporary period, the debate about people's diets has been increasingly framed through the lenses of demand, in the economic sense. Many scholars argue in fact that the food consumption pattern is a function of their aggregate demands of different food items and of the individual choices of the consumers. How can we understand the diverse drivers of changing food consumer choices? Scholars have connected them to issues of income, gender, age, price, etc. And yet, especially in the light of the dramatic changes in the international food regime, and the growing dynamics of power regulating the global food market in the last four decades, this argument has been put under close scrutiny. Tastes and choices do matter, however, it seems increasingly evident that what people consume today is no more, if ever been, a question of individual behavior and choice, but rather one connected to dynamics of power and wealth creation embedded in the production, circulation and consumption of food at the global level. In this regard, economics professor Raj Patel (2009) argues that farmers, in the Global South and Global North, lack the freedom of choice in their farming practices. Decisions on what and how to grow, where to sell and what to eat are now made by the market, which is controlled by food companies. By manipulating production and consumption decisions with the support of governments through international trade agreements, food corporations end up generating enormous profits limiting farmers' and consumers' choices.

Scholars such as Otero et al. (2015) have pointed to the narrow scope of demand-driven analysis of everyday diets, showing how major corporate interests have shaped the character of people's diets at a global scale toward what they have termed "neoliberal diet". They argue that a neoliberal diet is composed of what is popularly known as junk food but also a broader range of highly processed and convenience food products. In a study on the United States, they discuss how diverse classes or socioeconomic strata have different dietary patterns, with upper-income groups having access to higher quality and or higher value-added foods such as meats, imported fresh fruits and vegetables, wines and other alcoholic beverages, while diets of low-income to middle-income classes are heavily focused on the energy-dense pseudo foods.

The class dimension of this correlation is epitomized in Andrea Freeman's (2007, p. 2245) notion of "food oppression", a "form of structural subordination that builds on and deepens pre-existing disparities along race and class lines". According to Freeman, governmental support of the fast-food industry through industry-friendly subsidies for animal feed, sugar and fats serve to reduce the cost of fast food and create a structural constraint on dietary choices. The food choices are in fact structurally conditioned by income inequality and by what huge monopolistic and oligopolistic food producers and distributors have on offer, which is in turn facilitated by a neoliberal state intervention. Transcending individualistic and consumption approaches, we end up understanding that the political and economic assemblages of state and capital, not the individual consumer, are best positioned to implement change when it comes to food "choices" and food production (Otero et al., 2018, p. 537).

This transition to the neoliberal diet is a global phenomenon, but there are clear indications that the rate of adoption of this diet is occurring far faster in developing countries (Monteiro et al., 2004). The globalization of food is without doubt key in radically transforming the nature of agri-food systems, the quantity, type, cost and desirability of food available for consumption (Hawkes, 2006, p. 2). The adoption of the neoliberal diet is also a symptom of the massive dependency of Arab countries on the international circuits of food trade for the satisfaction of the consumption needs of their populations. The region is in fact the most food-dependent in the world with a rate of food dependency around 60%. Countries like Lebanon, for example, depend for 90% of their consumption needs on international markets, while Egypt, for example, shows particularly high rates of food dependency especially for cereals (70%), different vegetable oils (50%) and sugar (50%). On the other hand, and in a similar vein, the section on Sub-Saharan Africa grapples with the key corporate forces that have shaped the expansion of agro-industrial production and the promotion of neoliberal diet. Similarly to the Middle East, there are substantial differences between Western, Eastern and Southern Africa in the adoption of neoliberal diets depending on a series of political, economic, ecological and socio-cultural factors. However, differently from the Middle East, African countries showed a significant reliance on locally produced food systems, despite a growing trend toward some degrees of import dependency. An example is given by the fact that African countries still produce and consume significant quantities of goat and sheep meat, rather than the mostly industrialized chicken.

The emergence of neoliberal diets is inherently linked to the neoliberal food regime (Otero et al., 2013; Pechlaner & Otero, 2008, 2010) and is characterized by trade liberalization and legal frameworks favoring large corporations, such as the agribusiness multinationals and food processors. As a result, the world food system has become increasingly vertically structured and it has been characterized by the concentration of wealth and power in the hands of a few multinational corporations, which control significant shares of key agricultural commodities.

The sector of seeds clearly shows this process of concentration of market shares with few transnational corporations such as Monsanto, DuPont, Limagrain and Syngenta controlling approximately 65% of the global seeds market.

The neoliberal diet is structured by class differences into basic and luxury foods: the high-quality foods (luxury foods) available for the rich who can afford fresh fruits and vegetables from world markets; and the industrial nutritionally compromised food accessed primarily by the poor to middle classes, contributing to deepening North/South divide. "Basic" and "luxury" foods reveal how economic globalization resulted in the differentiated convergence of class diets. Basic foods are primarily cereals and sugar as well as vegetable oils, whereas luxury foods are fresh fruits and vegetables as well as economically added-value foods such as wine and meat (Otero et al., 2018). With the "meatification" phenomena, meat has become a central component of the neoliberal diet, having a devastating impact on food security, consumers' wellbeing and ecological health, as it requires an enormous share of grains production that could otherwise be consumed directly by humans (Weis, 2013).

The neoliberal diet is characterized by being energy dense with high calorie content but low nutritional value. This applies to the highly processed convenience foods and those available from fast-food restaurants addressed by "pseudo foods" (Winson, 2013) and "fake foods" (Pollan, 2008). The three main additives of these foods are salt, sugar and fat (Moss, 2013). Processed-food companies have been highly successful in "hooking" people onto these foods due to these companies' effective efforts to privilege taste over nutrition (Moss, 2013, p. 37). In addition, the substitution of real ingredients and the increased durability and shelf life of processed foods result in the neoliberal-diet foods being significantly cheaper than the more nutritious alternatives. Costing less per megajoule of dietary energy in comparison with the more perishable counterparts of fresh produce, the neoliberal diet foods are very appealing to the low-income to middle-income classes (Drewnowski & Specter, 2004).

The consequences of the neoliberal diet are highly apparent. In 2009, the World Health Organization declared that around 65% of the global population live in countries where more people die from obesity and overweight than from underweight because of various health implications such as ischemic heart disease, coronary heart disease, strokes, type 2 diabetes and various cancers, among others (WHO, 2009). Poor populations, especially in the Global South, are plagued by the "paradoxical double-headed specter of famine and obesity" both resulting from the prevailing economic system and increasing inequalities (Patel, 2012).

The transition to the neoliberal diet, with all its negative consequences, has been a global phenomenon; however, scholars have been arguing that the rate of adoption of this diet is occurring far faster in developing countries (Monteiro et al., 2004) with globalization being key to this rise. With its one-size-fits-all approach, globalization has been transforming the nature of agri-food systems, and modifying the type, quantity, cost and desirability of foods available for consumers (Guthman, 2004; Hawkes, 2006). Scholars have identified major class differences in the adoption of the energy-dense foods of the neoliberal diet arguing that inequality exposes the economically vulnerable to the neoliberal diet and its considerable health risks (Drewnowski & Darmon, 2005; Darmon & Drewnowski, 2008; Drewnowski, 2009; Drewnowski & Specter, 2004; Freeman, 2007; Harrington et al., 2011; Lee, 2011; McLaren, 2007). Notorious has become in the last decade the case of sugar industries in the United States which in the 1960s used to pay scientists to downplay the link between sugar and heart diseases and promote saturated fats, a tactic which had already been used by the tobacco industry, pointing to the nexuses between politics, business, lobbying and science.

Other factors, including gender, age and ethnicity, shape the relationship with diet. Women, for example, often score low in nutritional accounts in the Global South despite being the main agriculturalists. Age in some countries in the Global South is synonymous with food entitlements, while in the Northern hemisphere poorly paid pensioners may find themselves struggling with coping with decent food access. Ethnicity, and its politicization, in many countries massively influence access to resources including land and food. Otero et al. (2018) further argue that the more a country is inequitable, trade dependent, trade liberalized and urbanized, with higher rates of female labor-force participation and greater economic globalization, the more its population becomes exposed to the neoliberal-diet risk. For example, South Africa scored the highest from emerging nations on the neoliberal-diet risk index generated by Otero et al. (2018) for 2007. This is explained by South Africa being one of the main developing countries adopters of neoliberalism, with the highest degree of inequality, resulting in increasing its import dependency on numerous top-food sources as well as vulnerability to international food price fluctuations (Otero et al., 2018).

Otero et al. (2018) also maintain that the upper classes have an economic choice regarding what to eat; hence, they do not suffer from unavoidable neoliberal diet risk. However, they may still be highly tempted toward the energy-dense food due to its common availability and forceful marketing strategies. On the other hand, people with low to middle incomes suffer from limited (if any) food "choices" (Guthman, 2011). Moreover, urban families in which most, if not all, of their adult members have to work, are highly affected by the neoliberal diet risk. Urbanization, increasing the extent of pushing women into the labor force and rendering the households unavailable for food preparation, also reflects the extent to which peasant economies have been expelled from the agri-food systems (Otero et al., 2018).

In this regard, Freeman (2007) further argues that black urban communities in the United States suffer the harshest effects of poor nutrition since these communities often lack sufficient access to adequate education and health care, which further compounds the damaging effects of a diet monopolized by fast food. Members of these communities experience various forms of oppression, including food oppression, as a result of class and race bias. Rather than being a product of individual acts of discrimination, food oppression is structural because it stems from the institutionalized policies and practices of governments and the fast-food industry. Food oppression impedes the survival and wellbeing of low-income communities, hence resulting in the creation of an underclass community who becomes increasingly more vulnerable and marginalized as a result of the economic and health crises. Government policies fostering food oppression include the provision of insufficient public assistance unable to cover the cost of fresh food in addition to collaboration with the fast-food giants to ensure that their products dominate the nation. Freeman (2007) argues that this state-sponsored racial inequality is concealed by the distinction between private and public sectors of action and is maintained by the myth of personal choice, even where a lack of resources and options limits the poor's ability to exercise choice.

The third food regime resulted in more than one billion people being undernourished around the world. Recently, undernourishment has been further exacerbated by the global economic downturns resulting from the COVID-19 pandemic. With an aggravating economic crisis, the poor and middle classes are further relying on tasty and cheap food in such stressful conditions, a combination of characteristics inherent in the neoliberal diet. This was in the last decade witnessed in Mexico, for example, where new lines of fast food were introduced as a result of the liberalization of agricultural commodities with the largest trading partner, the United States, and companies have been distributing free junk food as part of their relief efforts (Fernandez, 2020). In parallel, with Mexico being one of the most obese nations – with three-fourths of adults being overweight, and at least one in ten having diabetes – the country's significant diabetes and obesity rates have resulted in further exacerbating the impact of the coronavirus pandemic (Fernandez, 2020). The MENA region has also been the victim of this food regime rendering it the most food insecure region. Global development and financial institutions argue that the reason behind its food insecurity relies on its environmental dryness and scarce resources and rising population, which are leading to the increasing dependency on food imports (World Bank et al., 2009). On the other hand, a counterargument to this deterministic and reductionist vision states that regional agriculture has shifted toward an extractivist production of water-intensive crops to satisfy European and Arab Gulf oil-rich consumers in fruits and vegetables (Riachi & Martiniello, 2023). In addition, sub-Saharan Africa has experienced a significant increase in the number of ultra-poor since 1990 (Ahmed et al., 2007). Around 30% of the continent's total population (218 million people) residing in Africa struggle with hunger daily (Garrity et al., 2010).

BOX 3.1 ENGINEERED FOOD INSECURITY IN THE MENA

There are several competing arguments around the drivers of the food crisis in the MENA region. The most prominent among them views the region as trapped in the Malthusian tragedy of the mismatch between demographic growth and weak agricultural productivity. Other analysts in the environmental determinist paradigm see causes for regional food insecurity in the allegedly scarce farmland and water resources supply. Small-scale family farmers themselves are often blamed by governments, donors and philanthropists for their scant integration within agricultural value chains, low levels of commercialization, poorly productive seed varieties, and backward agricultural techniques (AGRA, 2009; World Bank, FAO and IFAD, 2009). These arguments cement discursive formations, which depoliticize debates over the characters and drivers of the agrarian crisis by framing the question as a technical, rather than political issue, and thus offering technical rather than political solutions.

In this box, we will see how food crises in the region are "engineered". They are, indeed, the result of a long process of regional political and economic integration in the international food regime, initiated during colonialism, continued in the post-independence period, and concluded in the neoliberal era, with its annexed transformations in land tenure and use, food systems and agricultural practices.

The incorporation of the MENA region in the first international food regime, pivoted on Great Britain's imperial power, began during colonialism in the nineteenth century when the cultivation of cash crops proliferated in the Arab world to feed the industrial expansion and changing consumption patterns in Europe.

At the beginning of the twentieth century, about 80% of agricultural lands were cultivated with cereals in the Levant (Issawi, 1988, p. 271). Half of the cereal production was grown for subsistence, while the remaining was sold in local and regional markets. In Egypt, the growth of cotton caused a deficiency in the production of cereals, and the country was forced to import large quantities of staple food, rather than exporting them as before. On the eve of World War I, cotton made up 93% of Egyptian exports (Richards, 1982, p. 9).

After a sustained period of growth in agricultural production in the region (1800–1914), the trade blockade brought about by the burst of WWI generated massive social devastations: half a million perished in Greater Syria. Mount Lebanon was particularly affected as it had re-oriented most of its farmland toward mulberry trees and raw silk export (Firro, 1990). While it was a lucrative strategy during peacetime, the lack of cereal production proved disastrous during the war as no grain reached the coast, and the area lost income from silk as export-oriented agriculture halted during the crisis.

The second food regime (1940–1970s) was characterized by the completion of the nation-state system following the decolonization process. Synthetic fibers replaced cotton, and corn syrup and other sweeteners became a substitute for colonial export crops and were produced now in the center, especially in the United States (McMichael, 2009). Also, grain was subsidized and moved back to core countries. The United States-led "Green Revolution", a project of agricultural modernization, became a "solution" to the problem of hunger based upon the use of labor-saving technologies such as hybrid seeds, chemical pesticides and synthetic fertilizers (See Patel, 2013). The Green Revolution ideal was a driving force in the MENA region through the central control of resources and inputs, the promotion of large-scale infrastructure, water projects and irrigation schemes. Post-colonial settlements favored state-led agrarian transformation and in particular the establishment of stable peasantries alongside state-run farms such as in Tunisia and Algeria. Land reform in Egypt in 1952 redistributed about one-seventh of the country's cultivable land from large landowners to smallholders and tenants and some landless people. In Syria, the state appropriated about one-fifth of the cultivated land in 1958 and 1963, and in Iraq one-half of cultivated land was appropriated and redistributed after 1958 (Bush, 2016).

Despite implementing various large infrastructure, land reforms and rural development programs, there remained high rates of inequality, landlessness, infant mortality and illiteracy. Allotment of individual land rights were pro-male and pro-cash crops, which enhanced a reallocation of labor to the disadvantage of women. Also, the redistributive scope of agrarian reforms in Egypt, Morocco and Tunisia excluded the wage-dependent landless workers from the transfer of property rights (Bush & Ayeb, 2012). Foreign aid and investment in agriculture prioritized exporting industrial crops and importing farm machinery and seed breeds, therefore marginalizing indigenous food crops and local varieties.

In the 1960s, countries such as Morocco were largely self-sufficient, producing more than 80% of the wheat for domestic consumption (Murphy, 2017). This changed over the years. With growing urban populations and the inability to raise agricultural productivity, governments in the region found it extremely convenient to have large quantities of cheap wheat available in the form of food aid first, and food imports later from the United States. As a result of various political choices, countries such as Egypt, Morocco and Tunisia became inundated with soft wheat, a process which affected production, consumption and import patterns.

To keep the price of bread, a staple, low, governments heavily subsidized wheat consumption. Bread prices started to represent the thermometer of Arab governments' political stability. Since the 1970s, several food protests have plagued the region. Yet, food riots are seldom about only the price or accessibility of staple foods. Food riots are political in character and are part of larger political and economic crises.

An Alternative

The strongest reaction to the hegemony of trade-based and market-based food security has emerged under the heading of food sovereignty. This term refers to the right of nations and people to control their food systems, markets, modes of production, food habits and environment (Holt-Giménez, 2009; Wittman et al., 2010, p. 2). In 1996, La Vía Campesina, the transnational umbrella gathering peasant organizations all across the world, defined food sovereignty as the right of each nation to maintain and develop its own capacity to produce its basic foods respecting cultural and productive diversity (La Vía Campesina, 1996).

Food Sovereignty implies the right of peoples, communities and countries to define their own agricultural, labor, fishing, food and land policies which are ecologically, socially, economically and culturally appropriate to their unique circumstances. It includes the true right to food and to produce food, which means that all people have the right to safe, nutritious and culturally appropriate food and food-producing resources and the ability to sustain themselves and their societies. Food sovereignty means the primacy of people's and community's rights to food and food production, over trade concerns (2007 Declaration of Nyeleni). The Ugandan government has engaged since 2014[1] in a national campaign to promote the consumption and production of beans (Figure 3.1), a local staple food crop easy to grow for small farmers and a cheap source of protein.

Food sovereignty has been characterized as an attempt to develop a strategy that will reconstruct economic and ecological diversity and supersede the homogeneity of the exchange value

FIGURE 3.1 Bowls of a variety of beans, August 2015, Jinja district, Busoga, Uganda, Giuliano Martiniello

regimes (McMichael, 2013). Food sovereignty sets itself apart from the ideas and practices of food security that are rooted in notions of international trade, free markets and price equilibrium. Political discontent has mounted with a modern food system that has been so dependent upon uniformity, capital intensity, GMOs and green revolution technology, and the food sovereignty paradigm provides opportunities to define alternative modes of thinking about food besides possibly helping to solve its major challenges (Bush & Martiniello, 2017).

The pivot of the food sovereignty narrative is the centrality it gives to the rural world and the role of smallholders' knowledge and practices in it running against developmentalist narratives that posited the disappearance of the peasantry and the inevitability of urban futures.

In the food sovereignty framework, food cannot be treated simply as any other commodity to be traded or speculated on for profit. Food must be seen primarily as serving the sustenance of the community and only secondarily as something to be traded. Under food sovereignty, local and regional provisions take precedence over supplying distant markets, and export-orientated agriculture is rejected. The "free trade" policies which prevent developing countries from protecting their own agriculture, for example, through subsidies, tariffs and public policies, are also inimical to food sovereignty. Food sovereignty emphasizes locality and the control over territory, land, grazing, water, seeds, livestock and fish populations of local food providers. Privatization of such resources, for example, through intellectual property rights regimes or commercial contracts, is explicitly rejected. It therefore stresses the importance of anchoring control of food systems within local communities and their ability to build upon existing indigenous and traditional knowledge and skills needed to develop localized food systems. It therefore contests corporate-oriented research and the produced technologies such as genetic engineering.

La Vía Campesina's vision of food sovereignty emphasized ecology, entailing the sustainable care and use of natural resources, especially land, water and seeds. In doing so it helped opening social enquiry to socio-ecological interactions and to the synergisms with biological components as a foundation for sustainable agro-ecological systems. The debate was advanced further with the popularization of the ideas of agro-ecology and ecological farming. In this regard, Vandana Shiva has argued that the paradigm of industrial agriculture has been rooted in war. The twin laws of exploitation and domination she argues "harm people's health and the environment" (Shiva, 2016, p. 2). Her response has been to advance the importance of strategies that expand agro-ecology or relationships that link and embrace the interactions between soils, seeds, the sun, water and farmers. Her analysis, elaborated now for more than 30 years, is to remind policymakers that "[taking] care of the Earth and feeding people go hand in hand" (Shiva, 2016, p. 12). Food sovereignty therefore requires shifts in the food production and distribution systems in order to protect natural resources and reduce greenhouse gas emissions, avoiding energy-intensive industrial methods that damage the environment and the health of those that inhabit it.

Conclusion

By linking the shifts in the international food system with the changing food consumption patterns, this chapter argued that the everyday diets of people in the Middle East and African countries south of the Sahara have been historically, though unevenly, shaped by processes of globalization of food. These regions have been incorporated in the international food regime, shifting their agricultural production and consumption patterns. The "neoliberal diet", which is globally emerging as a symptom of the dominance of corporate power in the international food system and the adoption of market-based strategies to food security, is slowly but progressively being adopted in the Middle East and African countries south of the Sahara. Extensive processes of meatification and wheatification of diets, dependency on foreign cereals, growing reliance on fast-food and supermarket chains for the consumption needs of growing urban populations especially in Africa, and growing consumption of sugar and vegetable fats are likely to have significant implications in terms of nutrition and health for people in the Global South, with its effect further filtered according to class and gender lines. Wheatification is a process of change in food consumption patterns based on an excessive consumption of soft wheat. The process was first spurred through US food aid which aimed to lure African countries into the capitalist orbit in the context of the Cold War. With time food aid shaped patterns of production, consumption and import. Food sovereignty provides for a more sustainable alternative to support diets, particularly in the Global South.

Note

1 https://naads.or.ug/beans/

Bibliography

AGRA. (2009). *AGRA Annual Report 2008/2009*. AGRANA.

Ahmed, A. U., Hill, R. V., Smith, L. C., Wiesmann, D. M., & Frankenberger, T. (2007). *Most deprived: Characteristics, causes and extreme poverty and hunger*. International Food Policy Research Institute.

Araghi, F. (2003). Food regimes and the production of value: Some methodological issues. *The Journal of Peasant Studies*, *30*(2), 41–70.

Bairoch, P., & Etemdad, B. (1985). *Structure par produits des exportations du TiersMonde, 1830–1937*. Droz.

Bernstein, H. (2015). Food regimes and food regime analysis: A selective survey. In *Land grabbing, conflict and agrarian-environmental transformations: Perspectives from East and Southeast Asia* (pp. 5–6). An International Academic Conference. https://www.iss.nl/sites/corporate/files/CMCP_1-_Bernstein.pdf

Brenner, R. (2005). From theory to history: "The European dynamic" of feudalism to capitalism? In J. A. Hall & R. Shroeder (Eds.), *An anatomy of power; the social theory of Michael Mann*. Cambridge University Press.

Brenner, R., Ahmed, A., Hill, I., Smith, D., Wisemann, D., & Frankernburger, T. (2007). *The world's most deprived: Characteristics and causes of extreme hunger and poverty (2020)* (Discussion Paper 43). International Food Policy Research Institute.

Bunch, R. (2010). Can promoters of development and activist for land reform unite? *Journal of Peasant Studies*, *37*(1), 209–212.

Bush, R. (2016). *Family farming in the near East and North Africa*. International Policy Centre for Inclusive Growth (IPC-IG).

Bush, R., & Ayeb, H. (2012). *Marginality and exclusion in Egypt*. Zed Books Ltd.

Bush, R., & Martiniello, G. (2017). Food riots and protest: Agrarian modernizations and structural crises. *World Development*, *91*, 193–207.

Cannon, G. (2005). The rise and fall of dietetics and of nutrition science, 4000 BCE–2000 CE. *Public Health Nutrition*, *8*(6A), 701–705.

Chable, V., Nuijten, E., Costanzo, A., Goldringer, I., Bocci, R., Oehen, B., Rey, F., Fasoula, D., Feher, J., Keskitalo, M., & Koller, B. (2020). Embedding cultivated diversity in society for agro-ecological transition. *Sustainability*, *12*(3), 784.

Cullather, N. (2007). American pie: The imperialism of the calorie. *History Today*, *57*(2), 34–40.

Darmon, N., & Drewnowski, A. (2008). Does social class predict diet quality? *The American Journal of Clinical Nutrition*, *87*(5), 1107–1117.

Daviron, B., Petit, M., Daviron, B., & Mondiale, B. (1988). *Sécurité alimentaire et commerce alimentaire dans les pays en développement*. Rapport d'étude pour la CNUCED.

Desmarais, A. A. (2007). *La Vía Campesina: Globalization and the power of peasants*. Fernwood Books, Pluto Press.

Dixon, J. (2002). *The changing chicken: Chooks, cooks and culinary culture*. UNSW Press.
Dixon, J. (2009). From the imperial to the empty calorie: How nutrition relations underpin food regime transitions. *Agriculture and Human Values*, *26*(4), 321.
Drewnowski, A. (2009). Obesity, diets, and social inequalities. *Nutrition Reviews*, *67*(Suppl_1), S36–S39.
Drewnowski, A., & Darmon, N. (2005). The economics of obesity: Dietary energy density and energy cost. *American Journal of Clinical Nutrition*, *82*(1), 265S–273S.
Drewnowski, A., & Specter, S. E. (2004). Poverty and obesity: The role of energy density and energy costs. *American Journal of Clinical Nutrition*, *79*, 6–16.
Faber, M., Laubscher, R., & Laurie, S. (2013). Availability of, access to and consumption of fruits and vegetables in a peri-urban area in KwaZulu-Natal, South Africa. *Maternal & Child Nutrition*, *9*(3), 409–424.
Faber, M., Schwabe, C., & Drimie, S. (2009). Dietary diversity in relation to other household food security indicators. *International Journal of Food Safety, Nutrition and Public Health*, *2*(1), 1–15.
Fairbairn, M. (2010). Framing resistance: International food regimes and the roots of food sovereignty. In H. Wittman, A. Desmarais, & N. Wiebe (Eds.), *Food sovereignty: Reconnecting food, nature and community* (pp. 15–31). Fernwood Press.
FAO. (1995). *Gender food security: Synthesis report of regional documents: Africa, Asia and Pacific, Europe, Near East and Latin America*. http://www.fao.org/3/x0198e/x0198e00.htm#TopOfPage
FAO. (1997). *The state of the world's plant genetic resources for food and agriculture*. FAO.
FAO. (2001). *The state of food insecurity in the world 2001*. FAO.
FAO. (2003a). *FAOSTAT: Agricultural and food trade data 2003*. FAO.
FAO. (2003b). *WTO agreement on agriculture: The implementation of experience- developing country case studies*. http://www.fao.org/3/y4632e/y4632e00.htm#Contents
FAO. (2009). *Initiative on soaring food prices: Country responses to the food security crisis: Nature and preliminary implications of the policies pursued*. FAO.
FAO. (2015). *AQUASTAT country profile- Sudan*. Food and Agriculture Organization of the United Nations (FAO). http://www.fao.org/3/i9808en/I9808EN.pdf
FAO. (2018). *Africa sustainable livelihood 2050: Livestock and livelihoods spotlight Uganda, cattle and poultry sectors*. FAO.
Fernandez. (2020). Neoliberal obesity and coronavirus in Mexico. *Al Jazeera*. https://www.aljazeera.com/opinions/2020/9/19/neoliberal-obesity-and-coronavirus-in-mexico/
Firro, K. (1990). Silk and agrarian change in Lebanon, 1860–1914. *International Journal of Middle East Studies*, *22*, 151–169.
Fischler, C. (1993). A nutritional cacophany or the crisis of food selection in affluent societies. In P. Leathwood, M. Horisberger, & W. James (Eds.), *For a better nutrition in the 21st century* (pp. 57–65). Vevey, Raven Press.
Fold, N., & Nylandsted Larsen, M. (2008). *Globalization and restructuring of African commodity flows*. Nordiska Afrikainstitutet.
Freeman, A. (2007). Fast food: Oppression through poor nutrition. *California Law Review*, 2221–2259.
Friedmann, H., & McMichael, P. (1989). Agriculture and the state system: The rise and decline of national agricultures, 1870 to the present. *Sociologia Ruralis*, *29*(2), 93–117.
Garrity, D. P., Akinnifesi, F. K., Ajayi, O. C., Weldesemayat, S. G., Mowo, J. G., Kalinganire, A., Larwanou, M., & Bayala, J. (2010). Evergreen agriculture: A robust approach to sustainable food security in Africa. *Food Security*, *2*(3), 197–214.
Gomez, A. (2010). Interview with Alberto Gomez. *Journal of Peasant Studies*, *37*(1), 226–229.
Grew, R. (2018). *Food in global history*. Routledge.
Guthman, J. (2004). *Agrarian dreams: The paradox of organic farming in California*. University of California Press.
Guthman, J. (2011). *Weighing in: Obesity, food justice, and the limits of capitalism*. University of California Press.
Harrington, J., Fitzerald, A. P., Layte, R., Lutomski, J., & Molcho, M. (2011). Sociodemographic, health, and lifestyle predictors of poor diets. *Public Health Nutrition*, *14*(12), 2166–2175.
Harvey, D. (2003). *The new imperialism*. Oxford University Press.
Hawkes, C. (2006). Uneven dietary development: Linking the policies and processes of globalization with the nutrition transition, obesity and diet-related chronic diseases. *Globalization and Health*, *2*(4), 1–18.
Holt-Giménez, E. (2009). Linking farmers movements for advocacy and practice. *Journal of Peasant Studies*, *37*(1), 203–236.

Holt-Giménez, E., & Shattuck, A. (2011). Food crises, food regimes and food movements: Rumblings of reform or tides of transformation? *The Journal of Peasant Studies*, *38*(1), 109–144.
Hyder, A. A., Maman, S., Nyoni, J. E., Khasiani, S. A., Teoh, N., Premji, Z., & Sohani, S. (2005). The pervasive triad of food security, gender inequity and women's health: Exploratory research from sub-Saharan Africa. *African Health Sciences*, *5*(4), 328–334. https://doi.org/10.5555/afhs.2005.5.4.328
Issawi, C. (1988). *The Fertile Crescent, 1800–1914: A documentary economic history*. Studies in Middle Eastern History. New York: Oxford University Press.
James, C. L. R. (1989). *The Black Jacobins: Toussaint L'Ouverture and the San Domingo Revolution*. Vintage.
Jane, H. (2011). Food security in the Middle East and North Africa (MENA) and sub-Saharan Africa: A comparative analysis. *Journal of Clinical Nutrition*, *87*, 1107–1117.
KARAT. (2011). Rice land grabs undermine food sovereignty in Africa. *Development*, *54*, 31–34.
Labadarios, D., Steyn, N. P., & Nel, J. (2011). How diverse is the diet of adult South Africans? *Nutrition Journal*, *10*(1), 33.
Lamartine Yates, P. (1959). *Forty years of foreign trade: A statistical handbook with special reference to primary products and under-developed countries*. Allen & Unwin.
Lang, T., & Heasman, M. (2004). *Food wars: The global battle for mouths, minds and markets*. Earthscan.
Lee, H. (2011). Inequality as an explanation for obesity in the United States. *Sociology Compass*, *5*(3), 215–232.
Levenstein, H. (1980). The New England kitchen and the origins of modern American eating habits. *American Quarterly*, *32*(4), 369–386.
Levenstein, H. (1993). *Paradox of plenty: A social history of eating in modern America*. Oxford University Press.
Martiniello, G. (2015). Food Sovereignty as praxis: Rethinking the food question in Uganda. *Third World Quarterly*, *36*(3), 508–525.
Mayén, A. L., Bovet, P., Marti-Soler, H., Viswanathan, B., Gedeon, J., Paccaud, F., Marques-Vidal P., & Stringhini, S. (2016). Socioeconomic differences in dietary patterns in an East African country: Evidence from the Republic of Seychelles. *PLoS One*, *11*(5), e0155617.
McLaren, L. (2007). Socioeconomic status and obesity. *Epidemiologic Reviews*, *29*, 29–48.
McMichael, P. (2000). *Development and social change: A global perspective*. Pine Forge Press.
McMichael, P. (2005). Global development and the corporate food regime. In F. H. Buttel & P. McMichael (Eds.), *New directions in the sociology of global development*. Elsevier Press.
McMichael, P. (2008). Peasants make their own history, but not just as they please. . . . *Journal of Agrarian Change*, *8*(2–3), 205–228.
McMichael, P. (2009). The world food crisis in historical perspective. *Monthly Review*, *61*(3), 32.
McMichael, P. (2013). *Food regimes and agrarian questions*. Fernwood Publishing.
Mintz, S. W. (1986). *Sweetness and power: The place of sugar in modern history*. Penguin Books.
Monteiro, C., Moura, E., Conde, W., & Popkin, B. (2004). Socioeconomic status and obesity in adult populations of developing countries: A review. *Bulletin of the World Health Organization*, *82*(12), 940–946.
Moore, J. W. (2010). The end of the road? Agricultural revolutions in the capitalist world-ecology, 1450–2010. *Journal of Agrarian Change*, *10*(3), 389–413.
Moss, M. (2013, February 24). (Salt + fat2/satisfying crunch) × pleasing mouth feel = a food designed to addict. *New York Times Magazine*, 34–41, 46–48.
Murphy, A. (2017). *The roots and repercussions of Moroccan soft wheat consumption, production and import patterns*. Portland State University Honors Theses. Paper 364.
Nestle, M. (2002). *Food politics*. University of California Press.
Njelekela, M. A., Liu, E., Mpembeni, R., Muhihi, A., Mligiliche, N., Spiegelman, D., Finkelstein, J. L., Fawzi, W. W., Willett, W. C., & Mtabaji, J. (2011). Socio-economic status, urbanization, and cardiometabolic risk factors among middle-aged adults in Tanzania. *East African Journal of Public Health*, *8*(3), 216–224.
Otero, G., Gürcan, E. C., Pechlaner, G., & Liberman, G. (2018). Food security, obesity, and inequality: Measuring the risk of exposure to the neoliberal diet. *Journal of Agrarian Change*, *18*(3), 536–554.
Otero, G., Pechlaner, G., & Gürcan, E. C. (2013). The political economy of "food security" and trade: Uneven and combined dependency. *Rural Sociology*, *78*(3), 263–289.
Otero, G., Pechlaner, G., & Gürcan, E. C. (2015). The neoliberal diet: Fattening profits and people. In S. Haymes, M. Vidal de Haymes, & R. Miller (Eds.), *Routledge handbook of poverty and the United States* (Chapter 44, pp. 472–479). Routledge.

Patel, R. (2009). Food Sovereignty. *The Journal of Peasant Studies*, *36*(3), 663–706.

Patel, R. (2012). *Stuffed and starved: The hidden battle for the world food system*. Melville House Publishing.

Patel, R. (2013). The long green revolution. *The Journal of Peasant Studies*, *40*(1), 1–63. https://doi.org/10.1080/03066150.2012.719224

Patel, R., & Moore, J. (2017). *A history of the world in seven cheap things*. University of California Press.

Pechlaner, G., & Otero, G. (2008). The third food regime: Neoliberal globalism and agricultural biotechnology in North America. *Sociologia Ruralis*, *48*(4), 351–371.

Pechlaner, G., & Otero, G. (2010). The neoliberal food regime: Neoregulation and the new division of labor in North America. *Rural Sociology*, *75*(2), 179–208.

Pollan, M. (2008). *In defense of food: An eater's manifesto*. Penguin.

Pretty, J., Hine, R., & Twarog, S. (2008). *Organic agriculture and food security in Africa*. United Nations Environment Programme.

Reardon, T., Timmer, C. P., Barrett, C. B., & Berdegue, J. (2003). The rise of supermarkets in Africa, Asia, and Latin America. *American Journal of Agricultural Economics*, *85*(5), 1140–1146. Retrieved May 13, 2013, from http://www.who.int/healthinfo/global_burden_disease/GlobalHealthRisks_report_full.pdf

Riachi, R., & Martiniello, G. (2023). Manufactured regional crises: The middle East and North Africa under global food regimes. *Journal of Agrarian Change*, *23*(4), 792–810.

Richards, A. (1982). *Egypt's agricultural development, 1800–1980: Technical and social change*. Westview Press.

Richards, C. (2013). *Utilizing a modular approach to gamification to improve nutrition and fitness in children*. Graduate Theses and Dissertations. https://scholarworks.uark.edu/etd/872

Scrinis, G. (2007). The emerging nano-corporate paradigm: Nanotechnology and the transformation of nature, food and agri-food systems. *International Journal of Sociology of Food and Agriculture*, *15*(2), 22–44.

Shiva, V. (2016). *Who really feeds the world*. Zed Books.

South Asia Partnership. (2011, May 22). *Poor farmers*. SAP-Pakistan Blog.

Taube, G. (2016). *The case against sugar*. Penguin Random House LLC.

Van der Ploeg, J. D. (2013). *Peasants and the art of farming: A Chayanovian manifesto* (Vol. 2). Fernwood.

Wallerstein, I. (1983). *Historical capitalism*. Verso.

Weis, T. (2007). *The global food economy: The battle for the future of farming*. Zed Books.

Weis, T. (2013). *The ecological hoofprint: The global burden of industrial livestock*. Zed Books.

WHO (World Health Organization). (2009). *Global health risks: Mortality and burden of disease attributable to major health risks*. WHO.

Wilson, J. (2010). Creating movements and momentum: A reflective piece on NGO sustainable agriculture support to farmers in East and South Africa. *Journal of Peasant Studies*, *37*(1), 215–220.

Winson, A. (2013). *The industrial diet: The degradation of food and the struggle for healthy eating*. UBC Press.

Wittman, H., Desmarais, A., & Wiebe, N. (2010). The origins and potential of food sovereignty. *Food Sovereignty: Reconnecting Food, Nature and Community*, 1–14.

World Bank, FAO, & IFAD. (2009). *Improving food security in Arab countries*. http://www.fao.org/family-farming/detail/en/c/294448/

Yamo, V. (2019). *Consumer perceptions on animal welfare and food safety across East Africa*. World Animal Protection.

4

LABOR, UNIONS, AND THE TRANSFORMATION OF WORK

Introduction

> He who does not work, neither shall he eat.
> Paul the Apostle, *New Testament*

The quote above is an aphorism attributed to Paul the apostle and that was famously reprised by Lenin in the early days of the Bolshevik revolution in Russia and that had two functions. First, it posited a key principle of socialism that is the necessity to be productive. Second, it decried the contrast between the lavish lifestyle of the idle royals and aristocrats and the harsh living of the poor peasants and workers. Most importantly, the Bolshevik revolution became a symbol of the rise to power of those who defend those who work.

The photograph after the quote shows a street in Taqadum (Figure 4.1), meaning "development" in Arabic, a neighborhood that is the heart of the working class community of Morocco's capital city, Rabat. There you can hear an uninterrupted click-clack of working hands, and you can catch a whiff of boiling tagine on almost every street corner. This neighborhood is just a couple miles away from the industrial zone of Rabat, also called Taqadum, where many of the residents used to work in textile manufacturing. The industrial zone had been abandoned like a sinking ship for over a decade now, and many of those residents lost their jobs and some opted to try their luck migrating outside the country. Part of the reason behind the death of textile manufacturing in the Taqadum industrial zone was the workers' strikes that very legitimately contended increasing demands for more productivity with little to no salary raise in the early noughties (Joffé, 2013). The struggle led most of the factories to shut down and production moved to Southeast Asian countries where salaries remained lower. This also happened because there was a logistics revolution: bigger ships were built making the cost of transportation lower even when products were shipped from far-away geographies (Khalili, 2021). As such, the strikes failed, and the jobs were lost.

The quote and the photograph are ways to think about the power and the powerlessness of labor, this factor in economic output that comes from people's work. Work has been crucial to

DOI: 10.4324/9781003264255-4

FIGURE 4.1 Taqadum neighborhood in Rabat

Source: Zaynab El Bernoussi.

unlocking production potentials that not only define the Anthropocene, or humans' increasing control of their living environment, and it is with labor that we may best see the extent of unequal distribution of resources, factors of production and cost and benefits in the global economy. Labor is central to thinking about IPE because its power and powerlessness can determine costs, prices, flows of products, services, and capital, home and abroad. To think about labor in connection to IPE and the Global South, let us be guided by the following questions:

- How does labor impact markets?
- How does labor impact politics?
- How are those impacts operating at both the local and international levels through policy making?
- How does society impact labor?
- What makes labor in the Global South distinct?

This chapter focuses on how labor has been oscillating between power and powerlessness through times and geographies. The evolution of work encompasses changes in whose work is recognized and waged, changes in working conditions and changes in rights. One big story we have so far of labor is that it remains very unequal, despite many uprisings led by those who defend work, like the example of the Bolshevik revolution. However, time and time again, workers rise to defend their interests.

Labor Markets and Labor Politics

In this section, we start with the story of an entrepreneur who adjusted to his country's national strategy of export-led industrialization. The story helps us understand how labor, capital and politics shaped the story. The key point in this section is to examine the link between labor economics and labor politics.

The story of Azzouz is a story of labor, capital movement and changing market needs. Azzouz[1] comes from a family of carpenters, which goes back at least since the nineteenth century, and based in the mountainous region of Taza. As a young man, Azzouz worked with his hands, cutting, polishing, carving, varnishing and delivering the finished wood pieces around Morocco. Azzouz and his family decided to move to Rabat, the capital of the country on the Atlantic Ocean, to seek a better economic opportunity for growing their business as Taza was a place of little market growth. This was in the early decades of postcolonial Morocco, in the 1970s, when the Late King Hassan II launched a program of "Moroccanization" (*marocanization*), which forced European business owners to sell their companies to Moroccan buyers. Azzouz's father, Ahmed, bought an atelier in Rabat and he was told that it used to be the property of Mr. Aliotta, an Italian entrepreneur who established his carpentry business in Morocco. Ahmed renamed the site and established his company as SOMMEFA (*Société Marocaine de Menuiserie ébénisterie Ferronnerie Aluminium*). The atelier in Rabat was larger than the one in Taza, and the equipment was much better. It was Azzouz who came up with the name SOMMEFA and he had an idea behind his mind. He wanted to do more than carpentry, and especially get into the growing aluminum construction industry back then, which was supported by bauxite extraction that came mostly from Jamaica as we saw in the first chapter. About a decade later, due to a family dispute, Azzouz left SOMMEFA and founded AMIN (*Aluminium Menuiserie INdustriel*), that aimed to specialize in aluminum-based construction but the political economy dynamic in the country was moving to an export-led growth. Azzouz thus shifted to textile manufacturing because the government encouraged him to do so. Textile manufacturing was a sector that relied on "low-skilled" labor in a country that had a growing population and lacked in educational and training means to produce high-skilled labor. For Azzouz, textile manufacturing was very different from carpentry. He was no longer working with his hands at the workshop and in construction sites, dangling his tape measure and surrounded by male craftsmen, architects and engineers. He was instead in his closed office, handling all sorts of paperwork, dealing with the customs office and overlooking the working lines of female workers on the sewing machines. Azzouz's new factory, in Taqadum Industrial Zone, on the outskirts of Rabat, was much bigger than the SOMMEFA atelier on Tadla Street, near the City center. AMIN factory had a deafening noise from those many lines of sewing machines, cutting tables and steaming equipment, and there was plenty of skill from the workers. Izza, who barely spoke to anyone and only in the Amazigh language, was one of those embodiments of those skills. She adorned a beautifully embroidered hijab and finished piece after piece with impressive dexterity and speed. Mr. Patrice, the technician partner who came to the factory every quarter period from the subcontracting firm in Belgium, had repeated several times that in his decades of experience in textile manufacturing factories in France, he never saw a quicker handling of complex garment compositions like that of Izza. In AMIN, most of the production was of uniforms for workers in heavy industries and the military in Europe, which included several safety accouterments, making the pieces complex to sew together.

The workers of AMIN were employed from March 1986 to November 2011, when AMIN went bankrupt. In 25 years, AMIN contributed to Morocco's exports and the country's total production. Most of AMIN's labor force was composed of young women with a few years of primary to middle school education. The workers were unionized and they went on strike against AMIN in its final years. This was around the notable time of the 2011 Arab uprising that swept across the region. The situation in AMIN, like in many other factories, was untenable: workers demanded higher wages and foreign subcontractors demanded lower prices. After its bankruptcy, many AMIN workers remained jobless and a few others migrated.

Based on this story, let us identify elements of labor, capital movement and changing market needs (Table 4.1):

Now let us explain some basics to understand the role of labor in the political economy, including at the international level. Labor is defined as the grouping of workers who rely upon their own work to provide themselves with the resources necessary for existence (O'Brien, 2013). Labor is one of the factors of production for economic output, along with capital and land. In labor economics, we see that wages can be set by the market dynamic, that is, the intersection of supply and demand, which should optimize the use of labor to an equilibrium level between demand for labor and supply of labor. However, in many contexts, labor gets involved in politics by pushing for its interest, that is, better working conditions. In many countries, there are policies and rules for price floors for wages (minimum salary) not to let salaries drop too low, even if it is at the market equilibrium level, as this is not in the interest of labor. The rationale behind the demand for a minimum salary is that we have rising standards of life (because of inflation, see Chapter 7) that make a wage from the market equilibrium not enough. From a

TABLE 4.1 AMIN's and the transformation of labor, capital movement and market needs

Labor	*Capital movement*	*Changing market needs*
- Male carpenters (like Azzouz, cutting, carving, varnishing wood). - Delivery of finished wood pieces. - Female textile workers (like Izza on the sewing machine). - Workers of heavy industries and military personnel, mostly in Europe, whose uniforms were sewn in AMIN. - Former AMIN employees migrating for work. - Jobless/unemployed former AMIN workers. - AMIN workers' union/strike. - Factory workers in the region joining the 2011 Arab uprisings.	- Ahmed moving the carpentry business from Taza to Rabat. - National economic policy of "Moroccanization" forcing foreign owners out of the country (Mr. Aliotta's capital moving out of Morocco). - Morocco's trade policy of export-led growth, that is, giving financial advantages to entrepreneurs. - Customs office accumulating revenue from imported garments needed for AMIN's production. - Belgian textile business subcontracting in France then subcontracting in Morocco. - AMIN's bankruptcy and remaining capital used to pay off government and workers.	- Larger atelier in Rabat, compared to Taza, because of the bigger market for wood furniture. - Growing demand for aluminum furniture (sometimes instead of wood furniture). - Textile manufacturing production decreasing in Morocco after two decades. - Demand for female textile workers decreasing in Morocco (unemployment). - Supply of female "low-skilled" workers increasing abroad.

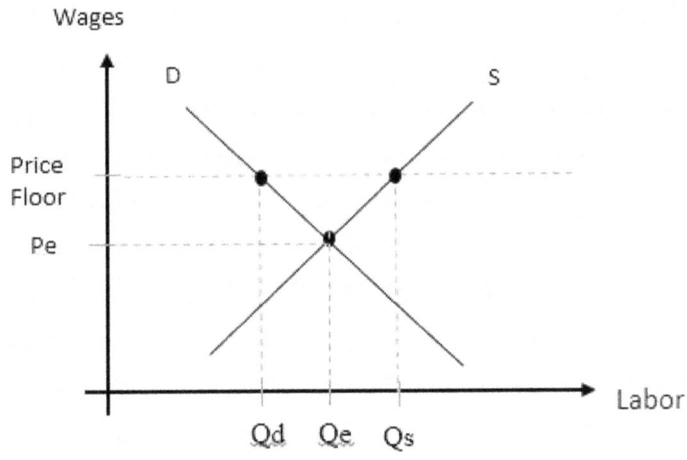

FIGURE 4.2 Labor market with the introduction of price floor (minimum salary)

classical economic standpoint, a policy for a minimum salary seems to distort a possible market equilibrium and leads to accepting a natural rate of unemployment due to a surplus of labor (Figure 4.2). This distortion also creates a black-market opportunity for informal labor. Informal employment is a work engagement not subjected to labor regulation, meaning labor laws, labor rights and labor dues, and labor protections guaranteed, in principle, by the state. Workers who cannot get jobs at the government rate because firms are not recruiting at such prices anymore, accept salaries below the price floor in the black market. Once in the black market, the workers become exposed to high levels of precarity, including exploitation, criminality and various forms of violence.

In addition to the distortions of the labor market because of a surplus or shortage of workers, we also find an issue of social stratification of labor, according to determinants such as age, gender and race. For example, anti-Blackness in the United States is an entanglement between a so-called race attribute and economic marginalization of a particular group of people. Groups that are marked by a particular social attribute, say race, and that fall behind in the labor structure in a marginalized position such as low-paid, or informal labor, or labor involved in criminal activities, then garner social resentment and stigma that becomes connected to their race and translates as structural discrimination, that is, racial bias in recruitment, pay and even in legal prosecution. Critical race theory analysis convincingly contends here that racial discrimination in society is not just the result of a market distortion because this group of people falls behind in the informal economy, but the very result of the capitalist production model which keeps a low-paid vulnerable group at hand for exploitation (Kendi, 2019). This argument also reflects a Marxian logic of alienation of workers, which is more convincing than the classical economics one of market distortion, because we see throughout history and in different countries the recurrent problem of economic marginalization of different groups with the adoption of policies that help capital growth. This means that blaming social problems such as anti-blackness on the inability of the black people group to catch up with the capitalist economy is erroneous; rather, it is the capitalist economy that reinforces the economic marginalization of black people and the ensuing social resentment toward that group (Kendi, 2019). As such, thanks to a combined view of labor politics with labor economics, one can make a better assessment of social issues in the labor market.

Industrial change also had an impact on the evolution of labor dynamics, creating even more inequality between workers and capital holders as the scale for such exploitation grew. Modernizing communities around the world have been adopting various industrial strategies as part of their development. The industry is the secondary economy, which means that there is a transformation of raw material extraction, that is, the primary economy. Processing foods that come from farming is an example of industry. Transforming minerals, wood and other natural or human-made components into cars, furniture and clothes is also an industry. Indeed, many countries dedicate ministries to industrial development both for local consumption and for exports. Some countries are more industrialized than others, particularly in terms of industrial development. Economies of the Global North have dominated several industrial sectors, such as auto-manufacturing and energy. Some countries of the Global South, such as the BRICS (Brazil, Russia, India, China and South Africa) and the GCC (Gulf Cooperation Council) countries have been chipping away from the Global North dominance on many of those industrial sectors (Hanieh, 2024). In other cases, some economies of the Global South have been falling behind in their industrial development, going through a process of de-industrialization like Morocco (Akesbi, 2022). All these industrial changes have a direct impact on labor as workers need to adapt by changing jobs, remaining unemployed, or migrating to find jobs. Because of the constant industrial transformation (sectorial change or technological change), work is also constantly transformed. As such, in our industrialized global economy, labor, despite its ability to bargain for its interest, is constantly threatened to be disposed of or/and replaced by technology. It is because a capitalist model creates a gap in bargaining power between workers and capital owners that we see the phenomenon of commodification of labor. When commodified, labor becomes disposable to market needs. As such, workers can lose their jobs because of the market, even if they still desire/need to work to sustain themselves and/or their dependents.

A workers-led production corrects this issue by factoring out labor from the production function, which means production is reduced by other means, but not by reducing labor.

A workers-led production can limit the gap in bargaining power between capital holders and laborers. Notable examples of workers-led production emerged with deindustrializing Argentina, Uruguay, Brazil and Venezuela, when workers occupied abandoned factories in a practice dubbed recuperation. This phenomenon has also risen in post-industrialized Europe after 2011 with Greece, Italy, France, Spain, Croatia and Bosnia Herzegovina in similar self-management practices (Kotari et al., 2019; Karyotis, 2020). Such democratic self-management replaced rigid hierarchies of the horizontal decision-making process (similar discussion in chapter 9). The top-down governance in dominant capitalist models around the world produces surplus labor, because a portion of the workforce will be deemed "inefficient" and "uncompetitive", and which then structurally creates an economy of the poor, those who will be pressured in the precarity of the informal economy (Paczynska, 2007; Kotari et al., 2019). It is also the top-down approach of neoliberal development projects, usually commanded by the highest authorities in the states of the Global South, that has been triggering resistance movements which often go back to anti-colonial rhetoric, particularly as seen with the Zapatistas in Mexico, a workers' movement in the Chiapas region, a poor, rural and originally unindustrialized province that has been exploited for its cheap labor. The Zapatistas have been leading a war against the Mexican government to counter its rigid governing style in terms of industrial development and have put women and land at the center of production and progress, and not in the margins bearing the costs (Solano, 2017).

The revealed struggles when looking at labor economics are not new and explain the inherent political nature of labor. In addition to workers' movements of all sorts and with different agendas, often such groups are triggered by different forms of violence. Evidence shows that the first labor strike was likely to have taken place in ancient Egypt under the reign of Ramses III, the last ruler of the New Kingdoms, over a millennia BC. Even if slave work was common at the time, the strike was led by some of the better paid artisans, when increasing pressures of trade and rampant corruption made the work balance for those artisans unappealing even if their pay was considered good. A first attempt to quash the strikers involved distributing free pastry, to no avail.[2] Egypt today, like many places in the world, has remained a troubled context for laborers, notably amounting to the experience of the *fellahin*, or peasants in Arabic, who have been repeatedly disenfranchised by colonial powers and postcolonial military elites. However, the resistance of the *fellahin* has kept a long tradition of struggle and, similarly to the Zapatistas' case, also kept women at the center stage. Indeed, the late Egyptian activist Shahenda Maqlad, is a case in point, as she led a movement that successfully fought for the land rights of dispossessed peasants of the Nile Delta village of Kamshish. This shows that a pyramid of power model cum a capitalist interest comes at the expense of the wellbeing of laborers and that labor politics, as in the fight for workers' rights, is needed to correct the loss.

Liberal economic development depends on an exploitative relationship toward labor that has repeatedly led to abolitionist movements as we see with strikers (Shilliam, 2021). The exploitation of labor, even though it serves the purpose of economic growth, perpetuates violence against the workers, who try to resist, while capital owners seek more power (Goldsmith et al., 2006).

Workers around the work and through times have been subjected to the whims of markets. However, unlike land and capital, workers are a strategic actor in politics and as such deserve more attention in IPE (O'Brien, 2013). Therefore, when we try to understand labor markets, it is not enough to rely solely on economic analysis of the labor resource. The labor resource is an actor that can, on its own, determine the markets and production.

Unions, Inequality, and Transforming Work

Unions are workers' front in labor politics and can be key advocates against wage discrimination (on the basis of race, gender, age, physical attributes, lookism, etc., see Fuller, 2006) and setting up/raising a minimum wage. Unions' favoring of a minimum wage and other workers' benefits is an important sign of institutionalism of labor (Harrod & O'Brien, 2002). Workers also tend to be paid less because labor markets tend to be monopsonies, meaning one single major buyer of labor (employer) has disproportionate control over prices that are then driven down. In addition to low-paying jobs, we also have widespread informal labor, including children's work. However, neoliberal development has come at a cost to unions' work. Part of the reason is how union's attempt to increase the price of labor is an affront to capital growth. Recent transformation of work, particularly with the increasing numbers of front-line workers in shipping and other cheap price services, has created a new wave of unionization demands, in the United States,[3] for example, and that can inspire other parts of the world where there has been a retracting of unions, including in socialist political systems such as in China (Elfstrom, 2021). In the United States, Amazon's pushback on unionization has also become a fight for dignity, particularly as the K-shaped recovery post-pandemic, resulted in disproportionate absorption of profits made during the pandemic by Amazon CEO, Jeff Bezos, at the expense of workers, particularly middle-class black workers in the United States.[4]

The role of the bourgeoisie, or middle-income earners, is key to understanding a paradox in labor politics as this group of people is powerful enough to organize a fight for its interests and powerless enough to be marginalized by the elite in power. The middle-income earners' group, as such, swings between powerfulness and powerlessness. This group, because of its large size, can significantly impact the overall labor dynamic. The growing bourgeoisie with the growth of capital has been creating both an opportunity for the group to seize more power and also to be further exploited by capitalism. Interestingly, the institutionalization of labor since the post-Cold War era has been marked by more solidarity among workers across borders creating a form of societal imperialism, challenging state imperialism (Harrod & O'Brien, 2002; Palan, 2013). Even before the Cold War era, sociologist Nicos Poulantzas described a form of transnational solidarity in protest from Europe to the United States visible (1974). Indeed, students' movements took to the streets in 1968 across the world to protest state support of all sorts of capitalist interests (including colonial/imperialist ones) of a few actors, at the cost of the wellbeing of a large portion of society, falling behind in economic progress (1974). The protests were often quashed with little to no improvements to the conditions of the destitute. A Gramscian analytical approach to this problem prompts us to ask about the politics behind keeping the status quo, that is, inquiring about who is benefitting (Cox, 1977). At the surface, it seems that elite interests dominate; however, one can also argue that, with the growth of our communities, both the power scale grows, but also the counterpunch. And failings can pave the way to wins. Indeed, unions and anti-discrimination, anti-war, and anti-colonial militants around the world continue their work despite the defeats. Even, in the marking case of the global riots of 1968, one interesting legacy was an increase in the preference for conservative political parties, which tend to be more protective of the local communities against liberal trade (Barone et al., 2022).

The labor force, through a process of negotiating its collective interests, is an important non-state actor that drives regulation and promotes civil rights (Mattli & Woods, 2009). However, the increasing societal diversity in globalizing contexts may create hurdles to the global labor force in its capacity to coalesce its interests. In this debate, one side views the New Internationalism of the post-Cold War as a force of labor solidarity capable of bridging differences, and another is skeptical that workers from all around the world can unite. Only the future can tell us which side will be right, but labor is most definitely likely to continue shaping the shifting demands for political expression and institutionalization in the context of changing global capitalism (Pakes & Pitts, 2022). Concrete institutionalization of global labor had already been taking place with the founding of the International Labour Organization (ILO) at the end of World War I, in 1919, many years before even the birth of the United Nations in 1945. The ILO is, therefore, an earlier push for global societal cooperation from below, unlike governments' leadership in the United Nations. The ILO has been established as a result of mounting pressures from various social movements in the nineteenth century, particularly in Europe. Today, the ILO continues its mission to fight for the right to work, to encourage decent working conditions, and, importantly, to push forward wage advocacy. The

ILO collects data on workers' salaries and rights and gives a platform for different unions to benchmark their labor status. With the rise of the ILO, we have also seen the rise of the field of human resources management. Human resources management is an academic discipline concerned with the transformation of work with scientific management to promote productivity. Human resources management has also become an increasingly interdisciplinary field of study, though more anchored in business studies and relying on psychological approaches to incorporate the workers' wellbeing.

The gender issue of labor, particularly women's disproportionate precarity as workers, is closely related to women's status as primary caregivers, which is often unpaid or low paid. Women's bodies are the major site of reproduction and reproductive care, and when they invoke and seek a right to work, this often needs to happen with more reproductive care assistance (such as the help of a nanny), and even more so to rise in rank in one's chosen profession – when possible, making those who then assist reproductive care (women, predominantly) also limited in their own reproductive and professional capabilities (Briggs, 2017).

There is also the aspect of feminization of labor, meaning that certain sectors of work may be more likely to employ women. By employing more women, these sectors are more likely to have precarious working conditions, including lower wages and informal structures, because of the little bargaining power that women workers have. This is more noticeable in cheap labor markets as the one of textile manufacturing we talked about. Indeed, the story of AMIN that we opened with was the story of the factory by a male boss employing mostly younger women, with minimum salaries, working full time in garment sewing lines. Such aspect of the feminization of labor has also amplified stereotypical tropes that devalue feminine characteristics and that have dire consequences on further marginalization of concerned groups, which entrenches hierarchical inequalities.

Another important transformation of work has been triggered by increasing digitization and artificial intelligence, which increased the productivity of workers, or replaced workers by other workers in other geographies – deterritorialization of work or disposed of the need for labor altogether (Terranova, 2000). The digital industrial revolution is the fourth wave of industrialization (after mechanization, electrification and electronics) of the global economy and is marked by a phenomenon of jobless growth, meaning there is capital growth but not much growth in employment, as workers are increasingly replaced by software and logarithms.[5] As a result, it is likely to see an increase in workers' protests and strikes around the world.

Work in the Global South and the International Division of Labor

In this last section of the chapter, the aim is to look a bit more specifically at the political dynamics of work in the Global South. These characteristics are the product of structural constraints of work in the Global South as they result from marginalization and precarity. We explore one case study of dockworkers in Hong Kong, a microcosm for emerging economies of the Global South (Box 4.1). Lastly, there is an overview of a few proposals for the improvement and labor conditions in the Global South.

In scholarly work, understanding labor has relied on social theory that tends to be much Eurocentric, and which has been difficult to adapt to Global South contexts. French sociologist Émile Durkheim argued that the division of labor in industrializing communities in Europe gives both economic and moral benefits (1984). First, the stratification of work and wages helps the growth of the economy. Second, the stratification of the status of workers is mitigated by laws that regulate and formalize labor, consolidating solidarity between people. The result of such a logic is that industrialization is promoted as a solution to poverty and informality. If in the industrialization experience of the Global North, we have seen the growth of formal labor, it is not necessarily the case in the Global South. For example, South Africa is an emerging Global South economy, yet many jobs are still non-standard jobs, which goes counter to the classical theoretical expectation that with capital growth we should be seeing the shrinking of informal labor (Ferguson, 2015). Indeed, unlike European industrialization in which the proletariat was mostly uniform and urban to semi-urban, the proletariat in the Global South is less uniform, less organized and less powerful and as such can be defined as a precariat (Žižek, 2012). Much of the labor in the periphery is also wageless and rightless, such as for destitute, illegal migrants and refugees (Denning, 2010; Chatterjee, 2011). Such political society also allows the state to confront a fragmented political front compared to a compact one if it was to be collectively organized.

Despite these different historical backgrounds for the Global South versus the Global North, Economist Dani Rodrik describes a future of economic convergence because poor nations seek to industrialize to capture economic growth (2011). However, this economic growth has expanded capital far more than employment, deepening income inequalities everywhere, and increasing precarity, including in the Global South. There is also an international division of labor, meaning a global distribution of work, with more high-paying jobs in the Global North, leading to a phenomenon of brain drain (see Hasselbalchm, 2019). With this brain drain, highly skilled workers of the Global South leave for the Global North, creating a shortage in skills in Global South economies and allowing for an abundance of skills in Global North economies, which exacerbates the difference in economic performance/innovation between North and South. In addition, economic growth in the Global South becomes a race to the bottom in terms of wage earnings (Neilson, 2021). The international division of labor also means that cheaply manufactured goods tend to come from economies in the periphery that supply advanced economies such as the United States with cheaper consumer goods, due to a form of social dumping.[6] Interestingly, because of the race to the bottom for wage earnings in the Global South, meant to supply cheaper goods in international markets, low-skilled production or extraction in Global North economies is no more competitive. Coal miners' protests in the United States are a case in point of this consequence of the international division of labor that also harms workers' interests in the Global North (see Gaventa, 1982).

We have already talked about the feminization of work, which is more likely to happen at the periphery given the looser institutionalization of workers' rights. Feminist researcher Elizabeth Armstrong documented the impact of neoliberalism on women's movements and, more specifically, women's labor movements in India (2013). The precarity that women workers in India suffer from is double. First, they are marginalized compared to male workers in India. Second, all workers in India, including women, are already marginalized in the international division of labor, because India has more low-paying jobs than many other countries. Given the said structural limitations on workers' rights and particularly the emancipation of women's work in the Global South, many important labor movements have focused on becoming social networks, revealing different tools of negotiation and struggle of labor in the Global South, which can also be inspiring to the rest of the world given pressures on traditional methods of labor resistance such as unions (Armstrong, 2013).

In terms of considering solutions to the issues of work in the Global South, one interesting proposal is limiting the widening inequalities through a focus on protecting domestic markets, instead of export (Neilson, 2021). Such a process may rely on an attempt to delink the Global South from the global economy, particularly with local policies such as food sovereignty (Chapter 3) that can alleviate several issues of precarity in the Global South such as poverty, malnutrition, health issues and environmental degradation (see special tribute to Samir Amin's work in the *Review of African Political Economy* published in 2021.

Production led by workers can upend the conceptualization of work as a force of destruction, and reinstitute work as a force of production and sustainability of life (Kurz, 2013). Indeed, the creative evolution of warfare in capitalist contexts has both shaped the creation and application of new technologies as they also serve industry, and the relationship between the state, businesses as they transform production (Pitts, 2021). Geopolitical strategies in the current global economy have also reinforced a colonial and imperialist mindset, instead of a focus on local wellbeing, which is another argument in favor of delinking Global South economies from global trade to improve labor conditions.

To conclude, the experience of work in the Global South represents a more acute concern about capitalist development and colonial exploitation that needs to be solved by de-peripheralizing the South. Also, such a model may inspire other economies, particularly in the Global North to further the gains of socialist democratic development that builds systems of production rather than systems of destruction.

BOX 4.1 HONG KONG DOCK WORKERS' FIGHT FOR DIGNITY

Hong Kong, a former British colony handed over to the People's Republic of China, is an example of multiple convergences. Indeed, it is where East meets West culturally and where South meets North economically. The economy of Hong Kong both attracts capital and highly skilled labor, yet also features high levels of precarity and inequality.

In the Spring of 2013, tents and posters of the Hong Kong Dock Workers Strike including the demonized photograph of Li Ka-shing, the Hong Kong real estate tycoon mushroomed around the Cheung Kong Center of the Central District in Hong Kong. A caption read "Ruthless Exploitation – Dock Workers Strike for Dignity".

The Chinese word for dignity is *zūnyán*, 尊嚴, with the first character, 尊, meaning respect and the second character, 嚴, meaning strict (can also refer to rules) (see Figure 4.3). As such, by demanding dignity, the workers demanded stronger rules to protect them.

These Hong Kong protests emerged at a time of a significant global labor dynamic against a global economic and political order in which inequality and precarity became too rampant. Indeed, the Arab revolutions at the time were still unfolding. Those uprisings and revolutions emerged as a labor struggle and relied on an anti-colonial rhetoric and connected their demands to the past and also to other uprisings in the Global North such as the Occupy Wall Street in the United States or the Indignados in Spain, to name a few (El Bernoussi, 2015, 2021).

FIGURE 4.3 Photograph of Dock Workers (with their consent) Strike for Dignity near Cheung Kong Center, April 28, 2013

The anti-colonial nature of some of these protests is closely related to the anti-capitalist motive of the labor force involved. Indeed, capitalism expands in other geographies, whether it is through direct control of the territories or indirect one, like "preferential" trade relations between a powerful core and a powerless periphery. The labor force in such protests seeks to re-establish the agency of workers and their right to defend their interests. In other words, the right of workers to dignity.

The Kwai Tsing Container Terminal dock workers went on strike on March 28, 2013. They demanded better pay and better working conditions, a common union demand worldwide, and they chose to focus on dignity to give gravitas to their call. They focused on the humiliation arising from their work conditions, especially not having bathroom breaks.

Financially, the dock workers in Hong Kong were not doing so badly: they were averaging monthly salaries up to HK$ 20,000 ($ 2,580) which was what research fellows get in Hong Kong universities. Indeed, several dock workers did not join the strike as they were quite satisfied with their pay and did not want to lose their jobs.

More than the "low" pay, what shocked public opinion was the abject working conditions that dock workers had to go through: up to 72-hour shifts with no toilet breaks. A dock-worker recounted that many used bottles and newspapers to relieve themselves when up on the crane.

The solidarity with the demands of the Union of Hong Kong Dockers (UHKD) was very strong: Hong Kongers and even Australian maritime workers took to the streets denouncing the leadership of the Hong Kong International Terminals Ltd. (HIT). HIT is a subsidiary of Hutchison Port Holdings Trust (HPHT), led by Li Ka-shing, Hong Kong's richest man. The protest paraders wore donkey costumes to portray the inhumane and undignified working conditions at Kwai Tsing Container Terminal, which boosted public indignation.

The strike ended on May 6 when the union accepted a 9.8% pay rise along with the guaranteed right to take bathroom breaks as officially announced by HIT. A win.

Conclusion

In this chapter, we have seen the convergence between labor economics and labor politics in the context of the history of global economic integration. On the political front of labor dynamics, unions are a key force that promotes workers' rights but that have been repeatedly neutralized in their actions, which prompts a need to look for new ways to advance workers' rights and wellbeing. The COVID-19 pandemic added more concerns about labor, notably because of exacerbating the trend of the casualization of the workforce, meaning extended hours of work. But Labor is central to IPE as it shapes our global economy and can take us from models of the destruction of our ecosystems and communal livelihoods to systems of sustainable collective living. A Global South focus on IPE can bring back attention to labor in its central role to usher transitions to more social justice and peaceful living. Lastly, it is very likely that the future of work is one of further transformation given technological advances and increasing precarity of living due to climate change. Labor, as a counterforce to capitalist development, is a strategic actor for a more sustainable future.

Notes

1 A family story from Morocco.
2 https://www.worldhistory.org/article/1089/the-first-labor-strike-in-history/
3 https://www.hrw.org/news/2020/12/22/amazon-unionization-effort-spotlights-need-us-labor-reform
4 Perry, A. https://www.brookings.edu/blog/the-avenue/2021/03/16/the-amazon-union-battle-in-bessemer-is-about-dignity-racial-justice-and-the-future-of-the-american-worker/
5 https://www.weforum.org/agenda/2014/11/will-2015-year-jobless-growth/
6 Rodrik, D., & Stantcheva, S. (2021, July). *Project syndicate*. https://www.project-syndicate.org/commentary/inequality-report-of-macron-commission-by-dani-rodrik-and-stefanie-stantcheva-2021-07?barrier=accesspaylog

Bibliography

Akesbi, N. (2022). Maroc: Une économie sous plafond de verre. *Revue Marocaine des Sciences Politiques et Sociales*, Hors-Série 4, *XXII*.

Alan, R., Waterbury, J., Cammett, M., & Diwan, I. (2013). *A political economy of the Middle East*. Westview Press.

Armstrong, E. (2013). *Gender and neoliberalism the all India democratic women's association and globalization politics*. Tulika Books.

Barone, G., de Blasio, G., & Poy, S. (2022). The legacy of 1968 student protests on political preferences. *Economic Letters*, *210*, 110198.

Briggs, L. (2017). *How all politics became reproductive politics*. University of California Press.
Chatterjee, P. (2011). *Lineages of political society: Studies in postcolonial democracy*. Columbia University Press.
Cox, R. W. (1977). Labor and hegemony. *International Organization, 31*(3), 385–424.
Denning, M. (2010). Wageless life. *New Left Review, 66*, 79–97.
Durkheim, É. (1984). *The division of labor in society*. The Free Press.
El Bernoussi, Z. (2015). The postcolonial politics of dignity: From the 1956 Suez nationalization to the 2011 revolution in Egypt. *International Sociology, 30*(4), 367–382.
El Bernoussi, Z. (2021). *Dignity in the Egyptian revolution: Protest and demand during the Arab uprisings*. Cambridge University Press.
Elfstrom, M. (2021). *Workers and change in China: Resistance, repression, responsiveness*. Cambridge University Press.
Ferguson, J. (2015). *Give a man a fish: Reflections on the new politics of distribution*. Duke University Press.
Fuller, R. (2006). *All rise: Somebodies, nobodies, and the politics of dignity*. Berrett-Koehler Publishers.
Gaventa, J. (1982). *Power and powerlessness: Quiescence and rebellion in an Appalachian Valley*. University of Illinois Press.
Goerres, A., & Vanhuysse, P. (2021). *Global political demography: The politics of population change*. Palgrave Macmillan.
Goldsmith, A. H., Hamilton, D., & Darity, W., Jr. (2006). Shades of discrimination: Skin tone and wages. *American Economic Review, 96*(2), 242–245.
Grant, M. (1992). *A social history of Greece and Rome*. Charles Scribner's Sons.
Hanieh, A. (2024). *Crude capitalism: Oil, corporate power, and the making of the world market*. Verso.
Harrod, J., & O'Brien, R. (Eds.). (2002). *Global unions? Theory and strategy of organised labour in the global political economy*. Routledge.
Hasselbalchm, J. A. (2019). Framing brain drain: Between solidarity and skills in European labor mobility. *Review of International Political Economy, 26*(6), 1333–1360. https://doi.org/10.1080/09692290.2019.1626755
Hobsbawm, E. (1965). *Primitive rebels: Studies in archaic forms of social movement in the 19th and 20th centuries*. W. W. Norton.
Joffé, G. (2013). The Arab spring in north Africa: Origins and prospects. In *North Africa's Arab spring* (pp. 3–28). Routledge.
Karyotis, T. (2019). Beyond hope: Prospects for the commons in austerity-stricken Greece. In J. Holloway, K. Nasioka, & P. Doulos (Eds.), *Beyond crisis: After the collapse of institutional hope in Greece, what?* PM Press.
Kendi, I. X. (2019). *How to be an anti-racist*. One World.
Khalili, L. (2021). *Sinews of war and trade: Shipping and capitalism in the Arabian Peninsula*. Verso.
Kotari, A., Saleh, A., Escobar, A., Demaria, F., & Acosta, A. (2019). *Pluriverse: A post-development dictionary*. Tulika Books.
Kurz, R. (2013). The crisis of exchange value: Science as productive force; productive labor; and capitalist reproduction. *Mediations*, 27(1–2).
Kvangraven, I. H., Styve, M. D., & Kufakurinani, U. (2021). Samir Amin and beyond: The enduring relevance of Amin's approach to political economy. *Review of African Political Economy, 48*(167), 1–7.
Mattli, W., & Woods, N. (2009). *The politics of global regulation*. Princeton University Press.
Moore, P. V. (2012). Where is the study of work in critical IPE? *International Politics, 49*, 215–237. https://doi.org/10.1057/ip.2011.40
Neilson, D. (2021). Reversing the catastrophe of neoliberal-led global capitalism in the time of coronavirus: Towards a democratic socialist alternative. *Capital & Class, 45*(2), 191–213. https://doi.org/10.1177/0309816821997114
O'Brien, R. (2013). Labour shapes the global political economy. In R. Palan (Ed.), *Global political economy* (pp. 46–57). Routledge.
Paczynska, A. (2007). Confronting change: Labor, state, and privatization. *Review of International Political Economy, 14*(2), 333–356. https://doi.org/10.1080/09692290701203714
Pakes, A., & Pitts, F. H. (2022, March). *Labour and the past, present and future of work*. Progressive Britain Paper pb002.
Palan, R. (2013). *Global political economy: Contemporary theories*. Routledge.

Pitts, F. H. (2021, November 3). Editorial: Welcome to an age of workplace geopolitics? *Futures of Work, 20*. https://futuresofwork.co.uk/2021/11/03/welcome-to-an-age-of-workplace-geopolitics/

Poulantzas, N. (1974). Internationalisation of capitalist relations and the nation-state. *Economy and Society, 3*(2), 145–179.

Rodrik, D. (2011). *The future of economic convergence* (Working Paper w17400). National Bureau of Economic Research.

Shilliam, R. (2021). The past and present of abolition: Reassessing Adam Smith's "liberal reward of labor". *Review of International Political Economy, 28*(3), 690–711. https://doi.org/10.1080/09692290.2020.1741425

Solano, X. L. (2018). Geopolitics of knowledge and the neo-Zapatista social movement networks. In J. Sen (Ed.), *Movements of movements: Part 1: What makes us move?* PM Press.

Terranova, T. (2000). Free labor: Producing culture for the digital economy. *Social Text, 18*(2), 33–58.

Žižek, S. (2012). *Less than nothing: Hegel and the shadow of dialectical materialism*. Verso.

5

SEX WORK AND GLOBALIZATION

Why Sex Work and Globalization?

Sex work, like globalization, seems as old as human history and as pervasive as the idea of money. Sex work is highly stigmatized, and the topic often brings up concerns over human rights, religious morality and economic exploitation. Forms of sex work such as erotic dancing or massage are legal in some parts of the world, but in general most sex work remains informal and is considered illegal in most human societies, particularly in the Global South. Because of the precarity and stigma involved in this type of work, it is hard to quantify the contribution of sex work in our economies and ultimately impossible to know the total number of sex workers in the world or how much profit they produce, with many countries refusing to display or even to generate data on sex work. As such, domestic policymaking often ignores sex workers, including cooperative endeavors between states. Sex work exists everywhere, yet it is usually cited as evidence of the failures of a given society, challenging dominant narratives about the good and moral paternalistic state. Sex work is also associated with other societal problems such as the AIDS epidemic and drug abuse. Karl Marx himself considered sex workers as the most exploited of the lumpenproletariat, or those having a socioeconomic status beneath that of the working class. As we will explore in this chapter, however, globalization foregrounds labor concerns across different forms of marginality and precarity, in ways that may not be as visible or as fetishized as sex work but are structurally connected to it as a marginalized form of labor.

Focusing on sex work as a global formation of labor reveals the centrality of the body in day labor markets and in the informal economy more broadly (e.g., construction, sex work and domestic labor), which in most countries represent a significant part of the economic sector. In this chapter, we explore globalization and sex work in parallel, while highlighting their intersections in terms of the underlying precarities of informal labor and the exploitation of vulnerable groups of people. We are moved by the urgent questions raised thereby, including the following: how have globalization and neo-liberalization changed notions of work around the world? Who is most vulnerable to labor exploitation? And what is the role of informal economies in the IPE of the Global South?

DOI: 10.4324/9781003264255-5

Informal Labor and Sex Work

It is not only the formal labor market and legal economic spheres that have become globalized. Informal labor markets and underground economies or illicit economic spheres have also grown in significance alongside and are not separate from the formal economy. This is so much the case that scholars have argued convincingly that "the illicit and illegal economy is intimately related to, not separable from, the functioning of the 'formal' global economy" (Smith, 2011). While informal labor generates value out of unacknowledged social elements, bodies and persons, or from disavowed aspects of political, cultural and socioeconomic life, it is nonetheless integral to the functioning of the formal economy. The aim of this chapter is to show the pervasiveness of globalization as a material experience that is embodied in individuals, markets and structures of informal labor over time through a sustained emphasis on *sex work* as a global formation of labor. We define sex work as the sale of sexualized labor time.

Like all work, sex work is inherently exploitative in that it takes the form of necessary human creative activity (in this case, sexuality) and turns it into simply a means to gain a wage. Our definition focuses on the economic aspect of sexualized labor that is sold and bought, but the sociological picture is more complicated, given that sex work is often connected to both intimate relations of care or exchange between consenting adults and violent spheres of social and political life that include sexual slavery, child sexual abuse and rape as a weapon of war.

Although people of all genders may engage in sex as work, sex work is feminized labor regardless of the sex worker's gender or sexuality because it is a marginalized form of service labor premised on embodiment. This form of sexual labor is also connected to *care work* (work that is based in caring for the customer), a form of service labor or work that involves serving another person, which is itself normatively understood as an inherently feminine form of labor (Cooper, 2007). While sex itself need not be thought of as a form of service, understanding the dimensions of sex work labor that are connected to care can help us to see beyond the category of sex to comprehend that the labor involved in sex work is not merely coitus.

Although sex work is highly stigmatized, it is not always informal and is instead in many places regulated by civil law. Some societies have allocated resources to regulate or legalize some types of sex work while continuing to criminalize other forms and markets. In these cases, legal sex work is part of the formal labor economy, but informal or illicit modes of sex work may and often do endure alongside the legal. While often dangerous and sometimes coerced, in some contexts performing sex work can be a strategy that facilitates survival in dire circumstances.

Sex work economies manifest differently in different places, legal contexts and gender economies. And sex work is carried out by particular people making constrained choices within their complicated lives. Yet, the availability and feasibility of sex work as a survival strategy always function within gendered structures of domination, and it is often connected to racialized experiences of poverty, migration, violence and displacement shaped by large historical forces such as colonialism and imperialism. Individual-level and group-level societal factors shape sex labor markets and their expressions, logics and ways of functioning within cultures.

While sex workers might find themselves in challenging economic circumstances that make them more vulnerable to exploitation, it is important to differentiate between sex work and human trafficking, which are not the same thing. Human trafficking is a form of physical capture and coerced labor that is tied to both tourist and domestic economies and includes things such as rape, sexual slavery, child sexual exploitation and dehumanization.

The boundaries between sex work and human trafficking can be blurry and there is much debate among scholars about the character of these different forms of sexualized exploitation and state responses to them. While recognizing that sex trafficking is a real problem and a terrible experience of violence that happens to vulnerable women (especially migrant women), Juana Maria Rodriguez (2003) has argued that "In the United States and Europe, the language of sexual trafficking has been powerfully marshaled to make all sex work subject to increased state and public surveillance" (10). Others put greater emphasis on the need to differentiate between chosen and forced sexual labor in discussions of sex work.

Since our purpose is to re-contextualize globalization and IPE through the stigmatized form of informal labor known as sex work, and while recognizing that sex work is a form of work that takes place in secret, thus creating greater risk, here we are focused on sex work rather than on sex trafficking, which we see as a separate (though related) problem (Kempadoo et al., 2015).

Sex Work as a Global Formation of (Mostly) Informal Labor

Unlike most accounts of the globalization of late capitalist production and consumption processes, we endeavor in this chapter to tell the story from a different perspective, one that centers informal and marginalized forms of work as major aspects of economic organization in the Global South. One important expression of globalization as a phenomenon that relies on informal labor markets and generates marginalized forms of economic survival strategies is the expansion of sexuality as a commercialized site for the production of value. Feminist IPE has paid attention to this question, as it stages some of the most important and enduring problems within the political economy (see, e.g., Butler, 1997; Fraser, 1997; Bedford & Rai, 2010).

While sexuality is everywhere fundamental to human and social reproduction, sex work as a stigmatized category of labor includes a wide array of activities ranging from physical sexual encounters to Internet-based or phone-based exchanges that remain in the digital or virtual sphere and everything in between. All of these are significant, but we emphasize the role of physical sex work encounters in the Global South, rather than the many virtual modalities that also exist. The reason for our emphasis is that in the intimate exchanges that constitute the Global South sex work economy, the materiality of the body matters. We dedicate a box to the research of anthropologist Svati Shah on sex work in India (2014) as a layered sphere of work within the informal labor market. Crucially, Shah analyzes sex work in India as part of migrant labor and so-called day labor sectors that both rely on and exceed modes of caste, gender and racialized domination (2014, p. 3). Like Shah, we highlight the significance of forms of oppression and resistance to oppression that co-exist within spheres of marginalized, precarious or informal labor, including sex work.

Roads, Slums, Bases, and Hotels

Sex work sites and labor markets emerge along predictable routes that are ultimately linked to capitalist development and processes of globalization. There are four primary veins through which sites of sex work are generated: (1) the construction and development of new access roads, highways or sea routes, and the existence of hubs and thoroughfares linking workers to labor and leisure sites such as construction jobs and bars, respectively; (2) displacement and migrant flows leading into spaces of economic and social marginalization such as slums and migrant camps; (3) military bases; and (4) hotels. Sex work is differentiated from care work and domestic work as follows:

TABLE 5.1 Characteristics of sex work, care work and domestic work

Intimate labor type	*Characterized by*	*Example*	*Usual pay*
Sex work	Sexualized interaction	Selling nude digital photographs or videos	Not waged
Care work	Home health care and nursing	Bathing, grooming and dispensing medication	Waged
Domestic work	Performing chores at home	Cleaning, cooking and child-rearing	Not waged

New means of economic and material access to sites of extraction and mass employment such as petroleum wells and mines in the Global South give rise to or intensify care and sex work economies as they mobilize, and aggregate different types of laborers based on or organized through gender, racialization, ethnicity, status and socioeconomic class (Shah, 2014). Likewise, the displacement of vulnerable social groups through forms of migration-under-duress based on dispossession, displacement, gentrification, social marginalization, or ecological destruction produces waves of precarious migrant workers who may come to rely on intimate forms of labor to survive (Luna, 2020). The topic of migration is an important dimension of globalization that we will delve more deeply into in the next chapter. For now, suffice it to say that the historical and contemporary role of military bases and tourism in the creation and maintenance of sexual marketplaces is well known and established in the scholarly literature (Enloe, 2014; Padilla, 2007).

Intimate labors are forms of service work that require intimate knowledge of and contact (either virtual or physical) with another person who is a paying customer. These include sex work, care work and domestic work (i.e., work traditionally performed in the home such as cleaning, cooking and child-rearing). Intimate labor manifests interpersonally in complicated ways in the post-industrial contexts of the Global North, as, for example, with the phenomenon of so-called sugar daddies who finance students in university and college campuses around the world while demanding or expecting time, intimate attention, affection and/or sexual favors from them. While there may be many varieties of intimate labor, it can be broadly defined as labor that "sustains the day-to-day work that individuals and societies require to survive – and flourish" (Boris, 2010, p. 1).

This chapter makes note of the significant role of intimate or feminized labor and of gender and sexuality as conflictual sites of potential social empowerment or disempowerment. They are also sites of self-reproduction under global capitalism as they articulate localized modes of gendered and sexualized domination and social stratification in places around the world, particularly in the Global South where the price of both formal and informal labor is often cheaper. Sex work is just one example of the kinds of marginalized, gendered and racialized spheres of economic life that may appear marginal but are central to understanding both IPE and the effects of globalization in or from the Global South. There are other economic spheres, such as those for trades of illegal substances and materials, or even for essential things such as access to fuel and clean water.

As we reflect on these aspects of the informal economic sphere, we invite you to identify examples around you. Consider what kinds of informal economic activity, intimate labor or underground are familiar to you. Do people in your community rely on informal economic networks for essential things like water, food, fuel, health care, or communication? Are you familiar with places in your town or city where you can go to hire informal laborers or purchase illicit goods and services? Who cooks, cleans, or cares for children in your home? What kinds of care work do you personally rely on?

Experiences of Globalization

Adjacent to IPE debates, other social sciences, notably (but not only) anthropology and sociology, have examined how social groups have resisted, been subsumed within or adapted to varying trends and culturally specific, local manifestations of globalization that complicate any understanding of globalization as either one-dimensional or an easily defined phenomenon (Bilge, 2022; Tsing, 2000).

In the Global South, which we remind the reader includes marginalized areas and populations physically located in the Global North (as noted in the introduction), globalization is an ongoing, multilayered process that integrates workers into a global production and consumption process, and it occurs at the same time as people are being introduced, re-admitted, expelled, kept out of and/or forced into localized forms of wage labor. Further complicating the picture, neoliberal modes of corporate and state governance generate and rely on unstable or precarious forms of minimally paid, subcontracted, individualized labor to minimize production costs, producing degraded jobs that shift costs to laborers and are unreliable from the perspective of the worker, often requiring total availability from the worker without guaranteeing adequate pay, dignified working conditions, nor stable compensation for their time.

Globalization is a concept that may be difficult to grasp all at once because it is so broad and has so many different manifestations. Often, globalization is historicized as part of Western economic domination of the world organized by a discovery of the so-called New World and the partitioning or dividing up of the Americas between the Spanish and Portuguese empires through the fifteen-century Treaty of Tordesillas. This timeline matches the historical chronology of the modern era, within which there has occurred an increasing objectification and systemization of life and labor through the mechanization of bodies and social structures, particularly through the centralization and polarization of political power in states. While indeed this chronology may correspond to the dominant understanding of globalization as an economic phenomenon in late capitalism, we contend that in other ways, processes of globalization predate European hegemony (Gunder Frank, 1994).

We could even say it goes as far back as 100,000 years ago to the various early human musings on cosmology and astronomy through different practices of navigation and of reading the skies. The striking resemblance of the myth of the seven sisters (a cluster of seven stars also known as the Pleiades) as recounted by people in different parts of the world, which communities are unlikely to have heavily communicated with each other about, if at all.[1] The seven sisters myth is commonly narrated as the story of the daughters of Atlas who were fleeing the Greek god Orion, centering thereby a European mythic interpretation and view of the cosmos. However, concomitant to this early account, and dating to even earlier human societies, we find other narratives about this cluster of stars, which were also known as Subaru to early Asian cultures. Stories about these stars are found in Amazigh cultures of Northern Africa, Iroquois legend and Aboriginal Australian myth, among others. In other words, the experience of globality or planetarity predates globalization and need not be strictly tied to the European colonial period, nor to the late twentieth century.

Nowadays, however, globalization is understood as a transformation of local communities through external or global influences, ideas and the wider circulation of consumer goods such as iPhones or the Big Mac. One useful conception of globalization in IPE is seeing it as a simultaneous project of international cooperation and nominal free trade among states, heightened in the aftermath of World War II, and the economic incentive or perhaps even the imperative to become integrated into the global economy (Scholte, 2017). In what seems to be an increasingly interconnected world, connections grow not only through communication technologies but also through the creation of new organizations and platforms for cooperation. Particularly among nation-states, global governance may be seen as a threat to states' interest in exercising control over communities and their resources. In IPE, the state/globalization debate is already a relic from the past, as it has been established that the two are not anathema but instead coexist quite well despite the state and its legal apparatus undergoing a series of crises brought on by globalization (Arrighi, 2010; Cerny, 1997; McMichael, 2005; Palan, 2013). The fact remains that our global economy relies on the legal and cultural particularities of local labor markets, which are themselves regulated by nation-states. Globalization is therefore an ambivalent phenomenon when it comes to nation-states, both threatening their hegemony and exclusive use of violence as legitimized through their regime of border imperialism and simultaneously relying on its continuous imposition.

The study of globalization has also become a discipline in and of itself through which we can better understand our changing world particularly as it is becoming a complex ecology wherein we constantly interact with economic value through media, finance, culture, science and technology.[2] Such a planetary human social ecology presents a problem for its description in the form of potentially essentializing and totalizing or limiting and artificially reducing an experience of the global economy by looking through only one of these lenses, for instance, attempting to capture the worldwide experience of poverty by essentializing it through a racialized and racializing ethnological lens. Poverty as a social experience is not limited to any ethnic or cultural group and is instead mostly the result of economic policies.

Importantly, technology is doubly transformative in our societies as it both enables connections and flows in the exchange of ideas, bodies, goods and services, but it also builds in, inscribes and executes more rigid processes of exclusion and discrimination against marginalized groups of people based on algorithms, quantified experiences and coded data, particularly as it feeds into the development of new Information and Communication Technologies (ICTs) (Benjamin, 2019; Castells, 1996).

In sum, the notion of globalization has been described through six main narratives as follows and in order of popularity: (1) a state-led process of globalization championed by a quest for more power; (2) a market-led globalization marshaled by profit-making corporations; (3) a united front comprised of variegated socialist groups projecting a more cooperative globality; (4) an ethno-nationalist lament about the harms of globalization; (5) what can be perceived as a mixed message from glocalization advocates, that is, advancing an ambivalent globalization that enhances local experiences; and (6) an urgent ecological crisis that emerges out of economic globalization and yet is politically sidelined as a global imperative (Lairson & Skidmore, 2017). These narratives necessarily paint a picture where some are winners and other losers in the brutal game of globalization, thus creating an overly simplistic view of the phenomenon, while the "wins" can also be simultaneous losses and vice versa.[3]

Contextualizing Globalization

To better appreciate the expanse of time involved, we must incorporate a historical perspective, which also allows for a consideration of diversity and differences in experiences of globalization (Abu-Lughod, 1989; Coleman & Sajed, 2013). A historical approach allows us to observe an important accomplishment of globalization; galvanizing outraged activists against abuses of power, as we will discuss briefly in the following section (Graeber, 2002; Glasius & Pleyers, 2013). Yet, experiences of abuse and marginalization, particularly those that are the result of the precarity of the contemporary informal and gig economies, are also intensified by globalization and they do not necessarily produce solidarity across time and space, nor will they necessarily produce revolutionary change without intentional organizing, visionary leadership and inter-communal support. Lived experiences of globalization can be quite paradoxical and their outcomes uncertain.

A notable inspiration for us in this project is the late Puerto Rican scholar and feminist Maria Milagros Lopez' (1993) definition of globalization as a transformation in the social division of labor and the collapse of the wage labor structure through history. This transformation in the ways people worked to sustain themselves had to do with the collapse of the hacienda plantation model in the Caribbean colonies, the end of the mid-century manufacturing boom and the collapse of the welfare state in the United States and its peripheries.

This transformation can be observed in the example of Puerto Rico, a group of islands in the eastern Caribbean governed under an imposed US sovereignty. The archipelago was colonized by Spain in 1493, but these islands had other names before that. Borikén and Bieke in the indigenous language of the Taíno people who lived there before Christopher Columbus and his genocidal mafia all but eradicated their societies within 20 years of their arrival (Walvin, 2024). On Columbus' second voyage to the Americas he arrived on the shores of what is now known as Guánica Bay, the same deep harbor and town that was to witness the US American invasion of July 1898 at the end of the Spanish–American War – the beginning of a second and ongoing colonial period. From Puerto Rico's beginnings as a modern political entity, the islands have been a subordinate economy; first to Spain and subsequently to the United States.

During this long colonial era, which again has yet not ended, Puerto Rico's labor structure was rooted in a palimpsest of slavery, indentured labor and brutal subordination to the imperative to produce surplus value in the form of profit for private entities and corporations based in the reigning metropole, whether that be Castille (Spanish Colonial Empire) or Washington DC. As the Black American political scientist Cedric Robinson argued (1983), "slavery was a critical foundation for capitalism" (160). In Puerto Rico, that foundation was set under Spanish colonial rule. After 1898, wages were established by US American corporate interests who saw in captive colonial laborers a way to recover some of the losses suffered by former slaveholders after emancipation and the formal end of slavery in the Americas. Since 1898, US American companies operating in Puerto Rico have been granted tax exemptions central to the failed local economic development strategy and that in combination with public assistance funds like food stamps spurred the growth of a protected industrial labor market under US American imperial power, generating what legal scholar Efren Rivera Ramos (2001) termed the "modern colonial welfare state". Legislation known as "the 936 laws" established tax incentives that led to the growth of the industrial workforce on the islands but did little to foster or sustain economic stability and independence. Subsequent reforms to social benefit programs in the United States have generated additional crises for poor people in the archipelago.

In a sense, the development model implemented by the United States in Puerto Rico was an early version of the offshoring of manufacturing operations, a practice that involves the dispersal of the process of production around the world and that became emblematic of globalization as a phenomenon in the late twentieth century under the doctrine of free trade. Once the corporate protections created by the 936 laws ended, it became more lucrative for companies to reorganize and parcel out different production processes to other (international) shores, rather than investing in the reproduction of the more expensive Puerto Rican labor force. Thereafter, the wage labor structure collapsed, and Puerto Rico lost its brief economic edge, eventually leading to an unprecedented fiscal crisis that has buried three million people living on the islands under more than 78 billion dollars of governmental debt (Garriga-López, 2020b).

Once production shifted to sites beyond the nation and its fragments, or in the case of the United States, its territories and imperial possessions, the division of labor was no longer national, or even supranational (accounting for internal or liminal tax havens like Puerto Rico). The new international division of labor became clear. In broad strokes, the Global North was to design and consume what the Global South worked to produce and assemble, rendering some national and supranational workforces in excess or obsolete, while tying together the economic fates of many disparate places through a de-territorialized and globalized production process that redistributed grueling work and industrial pollution to the Global South, while sending cheaper goods and greater profits to the Global North. While there is a deep and broad scholarly debate about these North/South dynamics, as well as different interpretations of the categories and why they matter, it is important to note that these processes generated large-scale migrations as people left their homes seeking work and a better life in other places, thus dispersing populations and creating concentrations of productive age laborers in some places, while leaving children and elderly folks amassed in others.

Resisting Globalization

The late twentieth century and specifically the decade of the 1990s witnessed political developments that began what is often referred to as the anti-globalization movement, itself a global phenomenon. The first of these was the Zapatista uprising of 1994 in Chiapas, Mexico, which began the same day that the North American Free Trade Agreement (NAFTA) went into effect; an extraordinary rebellion that showed the world what anarchist indigenous revolutionaries were capable of in defense of their lives and communities at a moment in history when not just revolutions, but history itself had been declared by some critics to be over (Fukuyama, 1992); history was outdated it seemed to some, but not to the Zapatistas.

The second major event was a week-long protest of the World Trade Organization (WTO) that took place in 1999 in Seattle, Washington (The United States). The WTO, headquartered in Geneva, is the world's largest intergovernmental organization. It sets the rules of international trade, and it enforces international trade agreements. The 1999 protests in Seattle manifested the wide and multi-sectorial opposition that existed to the free trade agreements that undergirded the process of globalization. They also highlighted the presence of the long-muted anarchist and international socialist left in the United States, and they galvanized a whole generation of activists, including thousands of college students who took on globalization and free trade agreements as key economic drivers of global, regional and local socioeconomic inequality. The protesters highlighted frequent labor abuses perpetrated through the model of sweatshops and maquiladoras, and they rebuked the environmental destruction resulting from the large-scale dependency on fossil fuels that underpinned globalization's planetary transportation infrastructure.

Since the 1990s, the movement has continued but has changed and transformed, at times blending with other social, environmental and economic protest movements. What we might recognize today as the global movement for social justice owes a great deal to these early manifestations of resistance against the assumed benefits of free trade, though the terms of struggle and loci of engagement have changed along with transformations and changes in the effects and mechanisms of globalization itself.

Contesting the State, Alternative Globalizations and Evolving Understandings of Sex Work

In this section, we will explore alternative explanations for processes of globalization as they help us understand issues of the global economy, particularly labor structure, neoliberal tendencies and precarity. Here, it is also crucial to observe the assertion of state power and the resistance to it while experiencing phenomena tied to globalization. Thereafter, we move to a discussion of sex work and its critique within the Marxist analytical tradition to consider how we can help make sense of the historical evolution of sex work as a marginalized economic activity in the global political landscape.

The old contrast of imperialist countries versus dominated nations, or the juxtaposition between industrialized and predominantly agrarian states, or even the binary of developed and underdeveloped countries that served as the hallmarks of a particular imagination and understanding of our globalized world do not suffice anymore to understand how some communities reap the benefits of globalization at the expense of the others. Indeed, we are witnessing emerging globalization leaders from the Global South, as well as failing economies based in post-industrial contexts. There are various paths to global power.

A large part of the change in the forms globalization takes is the result of a gradual centralization of advantages associated with what the late Egyptian–French economist Samir Amin called the "five new monopolies of imperialist countries", those being: the control of modern technologies, natural resources, the global financial system, means of communication and weapons of mass destruction (2017). It is important to understand such contrasts as have emerged from global capitalism and which prompt Global South economies to build sovereign and popular economic and political projects for their own development and the means they employ to this end.

There has also been a widespread idea that globalization leads to a homogenization of human societies, cultures and even psychic dispositions[4] and, ultimately, to a convergence in policymaking, of which this last point has been consistently disproved (see Drezner, 2001; Radice, 2000; Stiglitz, 2019). Indeed, the Global North/South divide persists and not only inequalities but also different forms of radicalism, ethnonationalism and fundamentalism are increasing.[5]

Globalization as a continued phenomenon of transformation of societies and institutions has been challenging to the growing role of states in the very control of societies and institutions. We are seeing not only an empowerment of states through greater control of more complex and entrenched institutions thanks to globalization, but also a retreat of states, to use Susan Strange's words (1996), because of the rise of new non-state global actors, such as global social justice movements, global labor movements, transnational corporations and global charity actors, among others.

To see how globalization challenges states, colonialism serves as a good example because while colonization allowed for imperialist states to gain more power, it also multiplied the forms of resistance to these states both from within and without the metropoles and across continents. With our focus on sex work in this chapter, we can see how such activities have been both criminalized or limited, and licensed or allowed to happen by states, most notably in their colonies and military outposts. For example, the British Empire established an act in 1864, the British Contagious Disease Act, which was meant as a eugenicist law to regulate the work of European sex workers in African and Asian colonies to avoid racial mixing. Sex workers were then monitored with the stated intent of reducing the spread of sexually transmitted diseases like syphilis (Manjapra, 2020). Such preventive measures in fact backfired, as these very European sex workers became more unruly as a reaction to the rigidity of the colonial power control (Manjapra, 2020, p. 212). This example also helps us see the early days of a growing global sex industry tied not only to imperial geographies in the nineteenth century but also to the masculine imagination of desire that was triggered by the experience of modernity. French poet Charles Baudelaire not only is credited for inventing the term modernity but also presents an iconic portrayal of the imagination of desire as encapsulated in the body, spirit and role of the prostitute as the ultimate source of desire for men, rendered possible as such by a modern society in which states regulated sex work as a form of care work and "feminine singularity" unencumbered by domesticity (Chatterjee, 2016).

Regarding a Marxist approach to sex work as a form of labor, Karl Marx, in his *Economic and Philosophic Manuscripts of 1844* described sex work as being "only a *specific* expression of the *general* prostitution of the laborer", one that evidenced a particularly extreme form of alienation of the worker from her own embodiment, and he viewed the abolition of prostitution as a necessary part of ending capitalism. Similarly, in *The Communist Manifesto*, he called prostitution the "complement" of the exploitation of women ensconced in the bourgeois family structure, the premise of which was precisely women's reproductive labor and predicted that both institutions (sex work and marriage) would one day vanish. His collaborator Friedrich Engels even wrote about the continuity of prostitution with marriage as a contractual relationship, which also suggests a sexual or gendered difference (feminization) at the heart of the social contract and social division of labor (Pateman, 2016).

Given the persistence of capitalism and its pervasiveness, we are also seeing the endurance of the sex industry as part of a market dynamic in which the consumption and the performance of sex work have become extremely multifaceted and include things such as stripping or erotic dancing, escort services, intimate massages, phone sex lines, live webcam shows and websites where sex workers sell exclusive images and videos, as well as old-fashioned public solicitation on the street. The violence of sex work as a form of the alienation of the laborer, as expressed by Marx, is also reflected in Joy James' (2021) concept of the "captive maternal", meaning that sex laborers within this widely variegated sphere are "through their non-transferable agency to care for another" intimately tied to the state's racialized, classed and gendered violence (as the official regulator of work). Indeed, capitalism as a model of production was founded on the exploitation of the surplus value produced through the labor of the working class. Concurrently, the undervaluation of feminized labor is best observed with regard to domestic labor, itself a form of care work often performed by racialized migrant laborers that relies heavily on affective labor (Tadiar, 2013). Domestic labor and sex work are not necessarily very distant from each other in that the same worker can perform either or both, but also because they are both normatively forms of feminized labor that are mostly unremunerated because they are assumed to be in some way "natural" to women's existence. The global reality that mostly poor migrant women perform this work across so many diverse cultural contexts, however, should illuminate the ways that they are often left out of conversations about labor organizing precisely because these are considered marginalized forms of labor or "women's work".

Although sex workers and domestic workers have largely been sidelined by the global labor movement, there is a storied history of feminist organizing around these issues and there are even some incipient labor unions such as the International Union of Sex Workers (based in the UK), the Sex Workers Industry Movement in Quebec and the National Domestic Workers Alliance (The United States). These organizations are working to help generate better working conditions for domestic workers and sex workers, recognizing that their work is work and that they deserve the same protections from exploitation as other workers. For sex workers, the stigma of their work often has repercussions that lead them to be secretive or to hide what they do. But it is important to recognize that poverty, as well as lack of access to legal citizenship or residency status, safe housing, clean water, electricity and stable nutrition are in fact the most significant reasons leading people to engage in sex work. While sex workers may feel empowered by being in control of their labor, or others might see sex work as a temporary strategy for wealth accumulation or to pay off debt, the reality is that most sex workers are engaged in sex work as a strategy for survival.

Conclusion

Globalization is a complex phenomenon that can be understood in multiple ways and across different temporalities. However, its predominant forms involve the interweaving of economies and communities existing at great physical and cultural distances from each other. Despite the seeming contradiction of national-state and global economic interests, global power and state power are engaged in a productive exchange of resources, modalities and devices. This global economic form has produced new forms of work and new experiences of the body that articulate older modalities of work (like sex work) with contemporary technologies in ways that continue to generate profit, but that require minimal investment and resources to maintain the health and wellbeing of workers. Sex work is a global formation of labor that manifests differently in different contexts and places, but one which is always responding to the routes, mechanisms and displacements created by global (patriarchal) power. Globalization puts pressure on unstable or marginalized social groups, and it produces mass migrations toward centers of capital, as well as the circulation of desire for exoticized goods and services, or particular people and places, even as it requires participation in precarious forms of labor for women and for people living in poverty. It also sometimes creates escape routes and opportunities for advancement, solidarity or evasion, but even then, it often comes at the expense of the workers' own bodily or psychological safety or integrity.

BOX 5.1 SEX WORK IN INDIA

Intimate labor pervades public spaces but is either discreetly ignored or criminalized. In *Street Corner Secrets: Sex, Work, and Migration in the City of Mumbai* (2014), anthropologist Svati Shah presents ethnographic examples of the lives of sex workers in three different sites within Mumbai: brothel houses, street sidewalks and day-wage labor markets. Through carefully orchestrated and thoughtful interviews with sex workers, Shah shows how sex work is an integral part of India's informal economy, given its centrality as a survival strategy, especially for migrant women from rural areas.

Shah documents the web of violence and struggle that enmeshes sex workers, while simultaneously demonstrating the structural similarities between sex work and other forms of day-wage or hourly wage labor in Mumbai and the agentive choices women make within their constrained possibilities. Shah highlights the experience of one woman named Shubha who had migrated to Mumbai from a rural area and who, like other women, often sought out construction work in the local day labor market or *naka*. Shah emphasizes that most sex workers she interviewed "reported looking for construction work from their local laborers" *naka* in the morning.

"If we don't find work there, we come here", they said, adding, "it has to be done for the stomach". I asked Shubha what she thought about this "for the stomach" argument for doing sex work. She replied, "Yes, for honor, a person could sit inside their house" (83).

Consequently, Shah explains that it is wrong to think "sex workers and day wage laborers are worlds apart". Instead, she argues, "sexual commerce is properly understood as one of many livelihood strategies that landless migrants engage, where all strategies bear attendant risks" (40). To clarify, Shah states that "all women at the construction workers' *naka* were not identified as sex workers all the time. On the other hand, having proximity to large groups of men, being unchaperoned by a family member in public areas, and visibly using public space to seek out paid work are all necessary to be hired for a day job by a contractor for women soliciting work at the *naka*" (83). This analysis highlights the connections between sex work and other forms of marginalized or precarious labor rather than isolating sex work as a completely different sphere of the sale of labor power. As the labor of sex workers is an open secret at the margins of state and public discourse, and given the issues of morality so often attached through culture, sex workers are usually not counted as day laborers even though they are engaged in an activity that is fundamentally economic, is bought and sold in the same labor markets, and constitutes the main income generating activity for the workers and despite the significant overlaps with other formal, informal and/or care work commonly procured in street markets. While the discourse of sex trafficking posits that sex workers are victims of traffickers, sex workers may instead engage in sex work as part of a strategy for survival. Sex work procurement is not separate from other kinds of informal or precarious labor but is instead often a form of transitional labor that can give way to other means of work. Migrants are particularly vulnerable to sexual exploitation, especially by the police.

Notes

1 See https://theconversation.com/the-worlds-oldest-story-astronomers-say-global-myths-about-seven-sisters-stars-may-reach-back-100-000-years-151568. For Arabic speakers (with English subtitles): https://www.youtube.com/watch?v=HNNvzAgcLzo. For Spanish readers: https://noticierouniversal.com/cosas-que-pasan/pleyades-las-leyendas-sobre-esta-constelacion-podrian-ser-las-mas-antiguas-del-mundo/
2 See "Globalization" by Lauren Miller Griffith, Texas Tech University, and Jonathan S. Marion, University of Arkansas. In *Perspectives: An open invitation to cultural anthropology* (2nd ed.). Society for Anthropology in Community Colleges, 2020, under CC BY-NC 4.0.
3 See https://aeon.co/essays/there-are-six-main-narratives-of-globalisation-all-flawed
4 See Librett's discussion of Lacanian psychoanalytic approaches to thinking about the effects of globalization (mondialization or world-formation) on adolescents today: https://www.taylorfrancis.com/chapters/edit/10.4324/9780367809560-5/subject-age-world-formation-mondialisation-jeffrey-librett
5 See Adrien Abecassis' analysis on increasing populism and radicalism. https://epicenter.wcfia.harvard.edu/blog/turnout-and-voter-insecurity-french-elections

Bibliography

Abu-Lughod, J. L. (1989). *Before European hegemony: The world system AD 1250–1350*. Oxford University Press.
Amin, S. (2017). The sovereign popular project; the alternative to liberal globalization. *Journal of Labor and Society*, *20*(1), 7–22.
Arrighi, G. (2010). *The long twentieth century: Money, power and the origins of our times*. Verso.
Bedford, K., & Rai, S. M. (2010). Feminists theorize international political economy. *Signs: Journal of Women in Culture and Society*, *36*(1), 1–18.
Benjamin, R. (2019). *Race after technology: Abolitionist tools for the New Jim Code*. Polity Press.
Berg, H. (2021). *Porn work: Sex, labor, and late capitalism*. University of North Carolina Press.
Bhattacharya, M. (2016). Neither "free" nor "equal" work: A Marxist-feminist perspective on prostitution. *ANTYAJAA: Indian Journal of Women and Social Change*, *1*(1), 82–92.
Bilge, F. (2022, July). Geopolitics as an ethnographic object and agenda. *Geography Compass*, *16*(7), e12649.
Boris, E., & Salazar Parreñas, R. (Eds.). (2010). *Intimate labors: Cultures, technologies, and the politics of care*. Stanford University Press.
Butler, J. (1997). Merely cultural. *Social Text 52–53*, *15*(3–4), 265–277.
Castells, M. (1996). *The rise of the network society* (Vol. 12). John Wiley & Sons.
Cerny, P. G. (1997). Paradoxes of the competition state: The dynamics of political globalization, *Government and Opposition*, *32*(2), 251–274.
Chatterjee, R. (2016). Baudelaire and feminine singularity. *French Studies*, *70*(1), 17–32.
Coleman, W., & Sajed, A. (2013). *Fifty key thinkers on globalization*. Routledge.
Cooper, D. (2007). "Well, you go there to get off": Visiting feminist care ethics through a women's bathhouse. *Feminist Theory*, *8*(3), 243–262.
Cruz, K. (2018). Beyond liberalism: Marxist feminism, migrant sex work, and labour unfreedom. *Feminist Legal Studies*, *26*(1), 65–92.
Drezner, D. W. (2001). Globalization and policy convergence. *International Studies Review*, *3*(1), 53–78.
Enloe, C. (2014). *Bananas, beaches, and bases*. University of California Press.
Fraser, N. (1997). Heterosexism, misrecognition, and capitalism: A response to Judith Butler. *Social Text 52–53*, *15*(3–4), 279–289.
Fukuyama, F. (1992). *The end of history and the last man*. Free Press.
Garriga-López, A. M. (2020a). Compounded disasters: Puerto Rico confronts COVID-19 under US colonialism. *Social Anthropology/Anthropologie Sociale*, 1–2. European Association of Social Anthropologists.
Garriga-López, A. M. (2020b). Debt, crisis, and resurgence in Puerto Rico. *Small Axe*, *24*(2(62)), 122–132.
Glasius, M., & Pleyers, G. (2013). The global moment of 2011: Democracy, social justice, and dignity. *Development and Change*, *44*(3), 547–567.
Graeber, D. (2002). The new anarchists. *New Left Review*, *13*(6), 61–73.
Gunder Frank, A. (1994). The world economic system in Asia before European hegemony. *The Historian*, *56*(2), 259–276. Taylor and Francis Ltd.

James, J. (2016). The womb of Western theory: Trauma, time theft, and the captive maternal. *Carceral Notebooks, 12*.
James, J. (2021). The captive maternal and abolitionism. *TOPIA: Canadian Journal of Cultural Studies, 43*, 9–23.
Juno, M., &Smith, M. (2020). *Revolting prostitutes: The fight for sex workers' rights*. Verso.
Kempadoo, K., & Doezema, J. (Eds.). (1998). *Global sex workers: Rights, resistance, and redefinition*. Routledge.
Kempadoo, K., Sanghera, J., & Pattanaik, B. (2015). *Trafficking and prostitution reconsidered: New perspectives on migration, sex work, and human rights*. Routledge.
Lairson, T. D., & Skidmore, D. (2017). *International political economy: The struggle for power and wealth in a globalizing world*. Routledge.
Lenin: Capitalism and female labour. (n.d.). Retrieved December 8, 2021, from https://www.marxists.org/archive/lenin/works/1913/apr/27.htm
Lopez, M. M. (1993). The crisis of political discourse: Globalization of the social division of labor and the collapse of wage labor. In *Polifonía Salvaje: Ensayos de cultura y política en la postmodernidad*. Editorial Postdata.
Lowthers, M. (2018). On institutionalized sexual economies: Employment sex, transactional sex, and sex work in Kenya's cut flower industry. *Journal of Women in Culture and Society, 43*(2). University of Chicago.
Luna, S. (2020). *Love in the drug war: Selling sex and finding Jesus on the Mexico-US border* (1st ed.). University of Texas Press.
Manjapra, K. (2020). *Colonialism in global perspective*. Cambridge University Pres.
Marx, K., & Engels, F. (1998). *The communist manifesto: A modern edition*. Verso.
Marx, K., & Engels, F. (2009). *The economic and philosophic manuscripts of 1844 and the communist manifesto*. Prometheus Books.
McClanahan, A., & Settell, J.-D. (2021). Service work, sex work, and the "prostitute imaginary". *South Atlantic Quarterly, 120*(3), 493–514.
McMichael, P. (2005). Globalization and development studies. *Critical Globalization Studies*, 111–120.
Padilla, M. (2007). *Caribbean pleasure industry: Tourism, sexuality, and AIDS in the Dominican Republic*. University of Chicago Press.
Palan, R. (2013). *Global political economy*. Routledge.
Pateman, C. (2016). Sexual contract. In *The Wiley Blackwell encyclopedia of gender and sexuality studies* (pp. 1–3). Wiley Blackwell.
Radice, H. (2000). Globalization and national capitalisms: Theorizing convergence and differentiation. *Review of International Political Economy, 7*(4), 719–742.
Rai, S. M., & Waylen, G. (Eds.). (2008). *Global governance: Feminist perspectives*. Palgrave Macmillan.
Rivera Ramos, E. (2001). Deconstructing colonialism: The "unincorporated territory" as a category of domination. In C. D. Burnett, B. Marshall, G. M. Joseph, & E. S. Rosenberg (Eds.), *Foreign in a domestic sense*. Duke University Press.
Robinson, C. (1983). *Black Marxism: The making of the black radical tradition*. Zed Books.
Rodriguez, J. M. (2003). *Puta life: Seeing Latinas, working sex*. Duke University Press.
Scholte, J. A. (2017). *Globalization: A critical introduction*. Bloomsbury Publishing.
Shah, S. P. (2014). *Street corner secrets: Sex, work, and migration in the city of Mumbai. Next wave: New directions in women's studies*. Duke University Press.
Smith, N. J. (2011). The international political economy of commercial sex. *Review of International Political Economy, 18*(4). Routledge.
Stiglitz, J. (2019). *People, power, and profits: Progressive capitalism for an age of discontent*. Penguin UK.
Strange, S. (1996). *The retreat of the state: The diffusion of power in the world economy*. Cambridge University Press.
Tadiar, N. X. M. (2013). Life-times of disposability within global neoliberalism. *Social Text, 31*(2), 19–48.
Tsing, A. L. (2000). The global situation. *Cultural Anthropology, 15*(3), 327–360.
Tsing, A. L. (2005). *Friction: An ethnography of global connection*. Princeton University Press.
Van Der Veen, M. (2001). Rethinking commodification and prostitution: An effort at peacemaking in the battles over prostitution. *Rethinking Marxism, 13*(2), 30–51.
Walvin, J. (2024). *A world transformed: Slavery in the Americas and the origins of global power*. University of California Press.
Williams, E. L. (2013). *Sex tourism in Bahia*. University of Illinois Press.

6

BORDERS, MIGRATION, AND THE GLOBAL SOUTH

Just as none of us is outside or beyond geography,
none of us is completely free from the struggle over geography.

Edward Said, *Culture and Imperialism*, 1994, p. 6

A Fact of Life

Like monarch butterflies and many other species that travel with the seasons, humans move across vast terrains and the seas on planet Earth. Thought of in this way, migration as movement is simply part of what human beings do. We live on planet Earth. Every human society benefits in some way from migration, while also potentially being negatively affected by factors related to migration. From an anthropological perspective, migration and the dispersal or movement of humans over the globe are not the exception, but rather the rule in deep historical time. Through our present system of international borders and interrelated but separate states, humans have created barriers to movement and obstacles to well-established routes of human movement and non-human animal migration (see the image above that suggests a yearning for freedom of movement for both animals and humans across borders). Yet across the globe migration persists (see Figure 6.1). And as the epigraph above in the voice of the late Palestinian critic Edward Said reminds, the predicament of geography envelops all of us – we are all concerned with our ability to move and migrate for work, survival, or to be with kin. Undoubtedly, there are distinctly contemporary modes of migration that are specific to our era, but the phenomenon of migration (or the movement of humans, animals and ideas) is the very stuff out of which social life is made. Migration is natural and a fundamental feature of our communities, markets and societies. In other words, migration is simply a fact of life. One might even say that migration is beautiful.

The central arguments we make in this chapter are that (1) migration is an important economic engine for state economies; (2) the political context of such economic needs fundamentally shapes their expression in migration policy; (3) migration is not limited to the working poor,

DOI: 10.4324/9781003264255-6

FIGURE 6.1 Painted mural at the Mexican border with Guatemala. The inset text in Spanish reads: "May nothing on Earth stop us"

Source: Photograph by Adriana María Garriga-López, June 2016.

meaning that people of all socioeconomic backgrounds engage in migration; (4) legal limits to migration often respond to racial tensions, nationalist ideologies and ethnocentric anxieties; and (5) when it comes to the sexualized violence of migration, women and feminized subjects are particularly vulnerable. These dynamics of migration are hegemonic, meaning that they affect the experience of migration for all migrants within the international state system and even shape the migratory experiences of migrants who move within states (internal migration) or regions.

The link between migration, economy and the political struggle for control over border zones between different socio-political agents, notably between states, but also non-state actors such as drug trafficking and human smuggling organizations. Big corporations specializing in securitizing the border are also invested in increasing their profits through successively intensive waves of militarization and fortification of border zones and migrant facilities. Migration's entry point into IPE is that migration is fundamentally a question of managing the availability of human labor, which means that the bodies of migrants can be sourced, calculated, or disposed of by thinking of migrants as an input in production rather than as individual people with rights, dreams and aspirations.

Yet, the phenomenon of migration, as well as the lived experience of migration and everything that politicians, economists, journalists and social commentators say about its consequences often reflect attitudes about language, religion, race, ethnicity and culture. Nationalism, bourgeois cosmopolitanism and capitalist market formations articulate with and through borders and the work they perform to designate territories and organize them under specific forms of value production and distribution. The ability of social theory to describe these phenomena and assess their dynamics and interrelations is an important part of IPE analysis.

As an alternative perspective, internationalist or glocalist coalitional approaches that do not completely subjugate popular sovereignties or localized forms of politics to the logic of the global production process can also function to sustain a more migrant-friendly approach as well as recognize the already existing reality that all human societies are interconnected and that most contemporary economies could not function without a steady influx of new migrants and without the seasonal labor of migrants and nomads. The ability of people with varied skills and life experiences to contribute to the development of industry and the economy is fundamental for its vitality, and this is one of the most important contributions that migrants can make.

The experience of migration and of living in a border zone is its own kind of country. The testimonies of those who have survived treacherous journeys or struggled to overcome severe culture shock or trauma related to the experience of migration serve as a unique human experience that is only fully understood by those who know what it means to live a life traversed by a border, or in the philosopher Gloria Anzaldúa's words to be "a turtle" – to carry home on your back (1987, p. 21). Anzaldúa, recognized as one of the salient voices in philosophical thought about the border theorized borderlands as being, "physically present wherever two or more cultures edge each other, where people of different races occupy the same territory, where under, lower, middle and upper classes touch, where the space between two individuals shrinks with intimacy" (1987, p. 19). From the perspective of Anzaldúa's philosophical outlook, the border is much more than just a boundary between states.

The immediate space of the border itself can be a space where underground or informal economies swiftly emerge and disappear in response to the needs and pressures of a given moment. This creates situations of interpersonal violence, risk and dehumanization that do not affect all migrants in the same way. As we discuss later, national origin, race, sex, gender, religion and most of all socioeconomic class determine whether migrants are exposed to such violence or not. Nevertheless, border cultures are the stronghold of generative hybridization processes and borderlands all over the planet produce unique cultural artifacts – eclectic musical styles (Chavez, 2017), experimental performance art like that of the self-styled "border brujo" (Gómez Peña, 2000), and special hand-crafted goods that are unlike anything that is mass produced or sold in big box stores, and different from predictable and aesthetically bland commodities that conform to the standards and bounds of hegemonic (Western or simply) national cultures and aesthetics (Sperry García & Sotomayor, 2025).

People who grow up in border areas and longtime denizens of border zones tend to be comfortable not just with the two societies, languages and cultures existing on either side of the border, but with the experience of hybridity, multiplicity and human diversity itself – of not being only one thing – what co-author Garriga-López calls "border epistemologies" or border ways of knowing. These border epistemologies from around the world offer lessons on ways of thinking about the border and about border culture that can help us understand something about the adaptability and resiliency of human cultures, economies and societies. In this alternative version of borders, border thinking and learning about border zones can be a source of great energy, vitality, adaptation and creativity (both in the aesthetic sense and in the sense of how much creativity it takes to be a migrant surviving the process of precarious migration). In this way, studying borders can show us how the global economy works and helps us articulate how migration and capitalism continually shape each other.

To guide us through this discussion of IPE and migration, we consider the following interrelated questions: why is it important for someone studying IPE to consider migration? How is migration related to economic policy and the global economic system? Why are some migrants celebrated while many others are reviled? What are some examples of migratory conflict and struggle that are happening in the world today? How does the push and pull of migration affect countries of the Global South?

Global Borderlands and Migration

Migration is a human right. Article 13 of the Universal Declaration of Human Rights (UN General Assembly, 1948) establishes "the right to freedom of movement and residence within the borders of each state" and the "right to free movement in and out of a country" (UNDHR). This provision has the specific intent to protect migrant laborers and people's inherent freedom of movement as a human right around the world.

Migration can be defined as the movement of people from one place, area or country to another. When migration happens between different areas that are within states or countries, it is called internal migration or is sometimes referred to as internal displacement, depending on the circumstances of the migration. When residents of one country depart and move to another country permanently or temporarily, it is called emigration. Emigration, or people leaving a country, is an aspect of migration that is of particular significance for countries in the Global South. This is because Global South societies are often so-called "sending countries" that act as important (licit and illicit) sources of labor for more industrialized and diversified economies in the Global North. Immigration refers to the phenomenon of people entering a country to establish a new residence there. While all migration is sometimes erroneously referred to as immigration, this is technically incorrect, as specific terms exist for the types of movement considered.

Migration between states or countries often involves complicated, time-consuming and expensive paperwork and bureaucratic procedures that may take migrants many months or even years to complete. Although in our contemporary world most migrants arrive in their new places of residence via jet airplane and enter their new countries through an airport, many migrants also undertake treacherous and desperate journeys to reach their intended destinations. Specific countries and regions are more desirable than others and certain migration routes are extremely dangerous for migrants. For most people who leave their homes in search of a new life, the decision to migrate is not taken lightly, as it is one that bears many possible setbacks and dangers for the potential migrant.

For IPE, migration is one of the fundamental elements of the economic and political life of a country. Most industrialized countries are heavily dependent on large numbers of migrant laborers who routinely take on temporary work in sectors such as agriculture, meat processing, construction, health care, childcare and domestic work. Without the presence of these migratory populations, many of the current socioeconomic structures that undergird everyday life would simply fall apart. These structures are also the basis of productivity measures such as gross domestic product (GDP) or gross national product (GNP) and are determinants of non-migrant workers' ability to fulfill their roles in the wider labor force, as illustrated in art by the 2004 film, "A Day Without a Mexican" (directed by Sergio Arau, Paramount Pictures). This "mockumentary"-style film explores what a day in California would be like if all Mexicans who lived there suddenly disappeared and communications with the outside world were cut off. As you might expect, the film suggests that Californian society would decompose without Mexicans because their labor is so central to the functioning and fabric of everyday life of the state. While the film is fictional and not an actual documentary, it uses this pseudo-science-fictional scenario to posit the question, what would happen if this group of people so often vilified in public discourse in the United States were to suddenly disappear from the body politic? The film's response is that California would not be California without Mexicans. It would be something or someplace else. In this regard, it's helpful to remember that the place we now know as the State of California was part of the country of Mexico until the signing of the Treaty of Guadalupe Hidalgo of 1848. California is no longer part of Mexico, but the idea that Mexicans don't belong in California becomes much harder to sustain when we consider this historical context. We discuss the US/Mexico border situation in more detail below, particularly as it includes a steady flow of migrants from Central and South America, the Caribbean, and increasingly from more distant parts of the world such as Russia, India and China.

A significant portion of migrants leave their homes in search of asylum in other countries from violent situations, political persecution, or other situations of violence in their homes, and these are known as political migrants, refugees or asylum seekers. The UNHCR (the United Nations agency tasked with tracking refugees) estimated there would be approximately 117.3 million refugees by the end of the year 2023. Normative understandings of migration parse these dynamics as reflecting strong states versus weak ones in the international order, but this is a reductive and overly simplistic way of seeing the matter, as many more factors determine the movement of people and populations than the relative strength of a state's machinery.

Yet not all migrants are fleeing political instability, war or persecution. Most migrants simply seek a better life for themselves and their descendants, meaning they are looking for gainful employment and the chance to save some of their earnings to improve their situation in life. Migrants who are motivated to move to countries for economic reasons are often referred to as economic migrants. The distinction can be somewhat blurry, as all migrants have some hopes of improving their overall situation.

The distinction between political and economic migration is not always clear, in fact, as these domains are interrelated. However, one way to think about the distinction is that refugees and asylum seekers are commonly fleeing violence and dangerous political situations, while economic migrants might be more likely to seek an escape from poverty. How nation-states respond to the pressures created by migration in large part defines how border zones look and feel; whether it is represented by a fortified wall, a fence, a sign, a checkpoint, a river, a desert or a sea, and the precise modalities of persecution, capture and deportation that migrants might be subject to. This is why some scholars have argued that the border "is largely an act of political theater" (Akers Chacon & Davis, 2006, p. 201). This means that political borders are not part of nature and must therefore be "performed" or made manifest by the state through its actions of regulating, surveiling, policing and closing or opening its borders to migrants.

Most countries place financial expectations and economic barriers on migrants, meaning that even across different contexts, the socioeconomic class background of migrants often plays a huge role in who can acquire passports, visas, residencies, legal transportation and other means of legal migration, all of which involve substantial financial burdens on migrants and their families. The economic cost of legal migration is one of the reasons for the success of the illegal migration economy flourishing along popular migrant overland and sea routes. This situation also creates greater insecurity and danger for migrants along the journey as people become vulnerable to unscrupulous actors seeking to benefit from their desperation, their bodies and whatever valuable possessions migrants might have been able to carry. Although freedom of movement is considered a human right, migrants who do not meet set expectations of available income, professional education or other high-bar migratory standards are often criminalized. But this was not always so.

Migration has been a normal aspect of social change throughout history, yet it assumed a new form during the colonial era in Europe and the birth of the capitalist world economy. These major shifts in European society precipitated massive population movements that largely corresponded with the labor needs of the new industries developed and fed by the resources extracted from the colonized South. The formation and development of the international state system and the forms of global governance we are familiar with today are the result of prior conflicts, previous outbreaks of violence, development-induced displacement and the growth of forces of displacement within the boundaries of nation-states and throughout the world (Castles, 2010). The legacies of European imperialism and colonialism continue to shape the forces that drive migration to a large degree.

Thinking about the dynamics of globalization as a late twentieth and early twenty-first-century phenomenon, it is instructive to look at migration, especially labor migration for reflecting on IPE and the Global South. The problem with dominant approaches to understanding migration is that they tend to overly focus on the rational choices that may lead a person to migrate and thereby fail to see migration as an effect of social relationships. The developments in transportation and communication technology that have occurred since the end of the Industrial Revolution at the end of the nineteenth century made air travel and being able to communicate with almost anyone in the world completely ordinary experiences for people. As a consequence, people are more likely to travel, to imagine their lives beyond or across borders and to actually live transnational, diasporic or nomadic lifestyles. Such people routinely cross borders for tourism and for things like study, professional advancement and marriage.

The right to be mobile is now more class-specific and selective than ever, it seems, despite the growing speed and forms of physical movement, communication and transport. At the same time, national border controls have become highly restrictive political flashpoints in many countries around the world. Most people alive today have neither the economic resources nor the political rights required to achieve free movement around the world. And that reality combines with the commonly brutal indifference of migratory procedural regimes that treat migrants who are not wealthy as undeserving sub-humans to create a very difficult and often traumatizing experience of migration, which is again a human right that people have access to simply by virtue of being human. Pause here to reflect: what borders have you crossed? What kind of boundary was it: state, regional, other? What made it possible for you to travel, migrate, or study abroad? Are there places on planet Earth where you as a person are not allowed to go or countries that you are banned from traveling to? Why do you think that is?

Theories of Migration

There is no unified, transdisciplinary theory of migration, and theorizations of migration tend to be shaped by the disciplinary frameworks and methodologies employed by any given scholar. These theorizations often produce essentialist or overly simplistic analyses that focus on limited aspects of migration and lack a holistic understanding of the experience of the entire migratory process. We discuss here a few key concepts and some shared understandings about the dynamics of migration, but with the understanding that there is much more to say on the matter than could be covered in one chapter and that there is so much variation across contexts in the experience of migration that it can be hard to reduce that diversity to a monistic explanation or a single system of meaning. One of the dominant consensus ideas that exist today about migration is the notion that migration trends are the result of the push and pull of factors that drive people to migrate and that are related to phenomena, such as war and economic crisis; droughts, floods and other climate-related disasters; and dynamics of social prejudice, racism, exclusion and discrimination.

The causes of migration go beyond specific decisions made by individual people – migration is not exclusively the result of the self-directed capacity or agency of migrants because economic and political forces create the conditions leading to these decisions. On the other hand, the predominance of this idea of a push and pull often reflects bias coming from Global North observers and commentators with regard to the purported desirability and good quality of life available in one place or country over another. Who can forget the disrespectful and dehumanizing phrasing of Donald J. Trump, forty-fifth President of the United States of America when he referred to Haiti and other Global South countries as "s***hole countries", for example?

This kind of attitude toward the Global South reflects an obsolete paradigm of thought and analysis for migration that dates to the industrial era and focuses on legal approaches to migration based on neo-classical economics frameworks that center rational actors making free choices in accordance with given factors as well as the primacy of the relative desirability of wealthy Europeans and white Americans over any other kind of migrants. Reductive approaches to migration of this sort may name different factors that affect the flow of migration but do not fully explain or account for the interactions between them, nor the relative weight of each factor in the equation. They also reproduce common logics and tropes within white supremacist discourse and other modes of racism and discrimination that like to paint or portray non-white people as being less intelligent, capable, organized, strategic and methodical than white Americans and Europeans.

Migration as a state bureaucratic process is largely based on inequality and discrimination. It is controlled and limited by the punitive arms of the state, including the prison system, detention facilities, courts, procedures and fortifications. In the political discourse, so-called skilled migration (i.e., the movement across borders of highly educated or specialized people) is celebrated as professional mobility and seen as enhancing the local economy that receives them, while the movement or arrival of workers without professional degrees and who do not have big bank accounts is condemned as unwanted migration regardless of the fact that many agricultural economies and construction sectors around the world are severely dependent on migrant labor.

The mobilization of workers and their classification at the international level through differing criteria of gender, race, ethnicity, national origins, religion, language, wealth, education and legal status is a crucial part of the global economic order. This results from a powerful interplay between market forces that require workers to migrate in service to the whims of a globalized productive process on the one hand; and political forces demanding control over national territories and borders on the other. This tension can be seen as highly effective in creating a global labor market stratified not only according to differing characteristics of human resources or capital (i.e., the possession of certain skills, educational background, training and experience) but also in accordance with the power differentials implicit in a host of categories and demographic characteristics.

Gender, class and racialization are particularly powerful characteristics shaping dynamics and experiences of migration as they produce spheres of extreme vulnerability, victimization and precarity within the migration economy. The international labor market is thus an expression of a global class hierarchy that is racialized and gendered, one in which people with high human capital from rich countries or family backgrounds enjoy almost unlimited rights of mobility, while others without such privileges are singled out, differentiated and controlled, as well as often maligned or blamed for problems existing within receiving countries or are excluded from participating fully in society in a variety of ways.

Ecologies of Migration

In this section we examine the environmental aspects shaping contemporary migration in our world. It might seem strange for one of the major themes of this chapter to be the ecologies of migration, but as we will see, ecology and human movements are deeply interconnected. Ecologies of migration are the result of the interaction between the socioeconomic, political and historical pressures that generate migratory movement and the environmental conditions that shape their expression. Ecological change, destruction and instability affect migration patterns in significant ways. Harsh or significant ecological features such as deserts, rivers, mountains and seas, as well as their relative levels of danger, exposure and pollution are weaponized. This is the case of the New River, for example, which runs along the US/Mexico border within and beyond the US border state of Arizona. This beleaguered river abuts working class residential neighborhoods along the US/Mexico border zone, and it is filled with sewage and toxic pollutants. Despite the health risks to the surrounding community posed by the river, its imperiled state is considered an asset, at least in terms of its purported capacity to enact border deterrence through the threat of environmental risk and harm to human health, although there are many video-documented cases of migrants wading across the New River to enter Arizona.

Analyzing how processes of climatological and ecological change lead to and shape human migration requires attunement to the enmeshment of human and non-human fates. Considering, for example, the plantation regime established in much of the Global South under European colonial domination, we can observe that it spawned the transatlantic slave trade that made humans into chattel, as well as numerous other forms of indenture, servitude and other forms of labor exploitation. But it also established agricultural regimes, geographies and spatializations, and it subjugated indigenous ecologies that flourished through specific forestry and horticultural practices tied to diverse human cultures. Some scholars have started to look at ecological change through the analytical frameworks developed to study the effects of colonialism on the planet. Political scientist Gustavo García López, for example, argues that climate colonialism has expanded through logics of extraction, experimentation and disposability (García López, 2024).

Conclusion

Migration is a major factor within IPE, particularly as it marks and it is shaped by the dynamics of interrelation between states in the global order. Why some migrants are welcome while others are seen as invaders, illegal aliens, or traitors has everything to do with the sociohistorical and cultural context of migration. The economics of migration tell the story. If you have money and power, there are hardly any borders closed to you. If you are poor and without influence, you may never be able to travel outside of the boundaries of your immediate environs. The lack of equality and fairness in open movement across national territories is evidenced by these differential barriers to human movement that also impinge on non-human animal migratory corridors.

While politicians and state narratives often paint the borders of a national territory as a given or as a transcendental reality that has always existed, borders are produced, performed and must be made manifest on the skin of the Earth and on the bodies of migrants so that the state can appear to be materially as dominant as it is ideologically. But the deeper we investigate our geographic and cultural histories, and the more we think about what it means to be human and for humanity to be a single species that is spread out all over the planet, we might feel the urge to ask ourselves, why and for whom are borders truly necessary? In response to this question, you or any other reasonable reader may decide that you do indeed find borders to be necessary and within this world that we inherited and live in now they are almost unavoidable. But even if that be so, migrants have human rights, including the right to live and the right to dignified asylum.

BOX 6.1 THE US/CENTRAL AMERICAN MIGRATION CORRIDOR

One of the most well-known examples of the criminalization of migration and militarization of a border zone is the area known as the United States/Mexico border. Looked at in strict terms, this border comprises 3145 kilometers of frontier zone between the countries of Mexico and the United States. Considered historically, the border did not signify an actual obstacle to movement until 1917, when "regulated crossing points were established to monitor Mexican migration" and unregulated crossings continued well into the mid-to-late twentieth century.

Instead of speaking about the United States/Mexico border as the primary border zone in this area, it is more precise to speak of a Central American migratory corridor. Contextually, the United States/Mexico border is not just the zone of encounter between two territorial sovereignties. Through the application of the federal policy known as the Plan Colombia, this highly militarized border zone extends south over most of Central America and across the Darien Gap into South America, as well as extending deep into North America and out into the oceans, as in the border fence in Tijuana, Mexico, that literally extends into the sea (Álvarez Velasco & Cielo, 2023).

As such, the expanse of the United States/Mexico border zone enacts a form of border imperialism that is not strictly relegated to the actual space of the frontier, and which is a process that is never finished, as the border must continue to be performed lest it cease to exist. Jason De León's work is particularly illuminating in showing how even the natural elements of the border, such as the desert, the heat and animals, are in a way weaponized in addition to the border patrols to keep migrants out of the United States (2015). The result is in many cases the death of the migrant and that becomes the cost of the criminalization of migration.

Bibliography

Akers Chacon, J., & Davis, M. (2006). *No one is illegal: Fighting racism and state violence on the U.S.-Mexico border*. Haymarket Books.

Álvarez Velasco, S., & Cielo, C. (2023). Circulations and solidarities in the Darién. *NACLA Report on the Americas*, *55*(4), 345–349. https://doi.org/10.1080/10714839.2023.2280318

Anzaldúa, G. (1987). *Borderlands/La Frontera: The new Mestiza*. Aunt Lute Book Company.

Castles, S. (2010). Understanding global migration: A social transformation perspective. *Journal of Ethnic and Migration Studies*, *36*(10), 1565–1586. https://doi.org/10.1080/1369183X.2010.489381

Castles, S. (2011). Migration, crisis, and the global labour market. *Globalizations*, *8*(3), 311–324. https://doi.org/10.1080/14747731.2011.576847

Chaar López, I. (2024). *The cybernetic border: Drones, technology & intrusion*. Duke University Press.

Chavez, A. E. (2017). *Sounds of crossing: Music, migration, and the aural poetics of Huapango Arribeño*. Duke University Press.

DeGenova, N. (2010). *The deportation regime: Sovereignty, space, and the freedom of movement*. Duke University Press.

De León, J. (2015). *The land of open graves: Living and dying on the migrant trail* (Vol. 36). University of California Press.

Fukushima, A. I. (2019). *Migrant crossings: Witnessing human trafficking in the U.S.* Stanford University Press.

García-López, G. A. (2024). Decolonial encounters and autogestion. In Undisciplined Environments Collective (Ed.), *Insurgent ecologies: Between environmental struggles and postcapitalist transformations*. Fernwood Publishing.

Gómez Pena, G. (2000). *Dangerous border crossers*. Routledge. https://doi.org/10.4324/9780203360682

Lowe, L. (2015). *The intimacies of four continents*. Duke University Press.

Massey, D. S., Arango, J., Hugo, G., Kouaouci, A., Pellegrino, A., & Taylor, J. E. (1993). Theories of international migration: A review and appraisal. *Population and Development Review*, *19*(3), 431–466.

Pötzsch, H. (2015). The emergence of iBorder: Bordering bodies, networks, and machines. *Environment and Planning D: Society and Space*, *33*(1), 101–118. https://doi.org/10.1068/d14050p

Pötzsch, H. (2018). iBorder/ing. In *Routledge handbook of interdisciplinary research methods*. Routledge.

Rosas, G. (2023). *Unsettling: The El Paso massacre, resurgent white nationalism, and the US-Mexico border*. Johns Hopkins University Press.

Soto, L. (2018). *Girlhood in the borderlands: Mexican teens caught in the crossroads of migration*. New York University Press.

Sperry García, C., & Sotomayor, L. C., II (2025). *Art borderlands in theory, practice, and teaching* (1st ed.). Routledge.

UN General Assembly. (1948). *Universal declaration of human rights (217 (III) A)*. UN General Assembly.

Undisciplined Environments Collective. (2024). *Insurgent ecologies: Between environmental struggles and postcapitalist transformations*. Fernwood Publishing.

7

IPE OF FINANCE

Regulation and Crisis

Introduction

The picture above Figure 7.1 is of the headquarters of the Argentine subsidiary of the Chinese bank, ICBC (Industrial and Commercial Bank of China). The location and the building are very symbolic. The location of the bank is on Florida Street, which is the very heart of the city of Buenos Aires, at the intersection between the government district and the financial district. Before ICBC Argentina took those grounds, the building inhabited the subsidiary of the US bank, First National Bank of Boston, which now lost all its Latin American branches. The building is a prime example of the Spanish neocolonial architecture style in Latin America and reminds us of the Spanish control of many territories in Latin America. The foreign control of the very building in different stages is also telling about the financial imbalances discussed in this chapter.

This example of a historical building hosting different foreign banks is an insightful starting point to the chapter's discussion of IPE of finance. IPE of finance is a story of takeover and crisis. To talk about the world of financing is to talk about the role of money. Money enables the control of resources. If money supply is in shortage, that is, there is not enough funding for the economy's sustenance or growth, we get into a crisis.

The word finance originates from the Latin word *finis*, that is, to end, which is quite telling about the meaning of the word itself. Indeed, finance is defined as the allocation of funds to complete and end a transaction. Finance is a powerful tool for actors in an economy as it allows them to secure resources for production, now and in the future. Finance is about money. Money can be held by people and institutions. Banks often secure money transactions, and as such, they are a symbol of power and wealth.

As one can see from Figure 7.2, IPE of finance is the allocation of financial resources resulting from trade. Global trade is the exchange of goods and services and there is an additional and parallel process of exchange of credit and debit of assets between financial markets that funds global trade, dubbed the international monetary system. The politics of finance involve questions such as: who gets to fund? Who gets the funding? and How is the funding made?

DOI: 10.4324/9781003264255-7

FIGURE 7.1 ICBC Argentina Casa Central (Main Branch), Florida Street, Buenos Aires, Argentina, July 2023

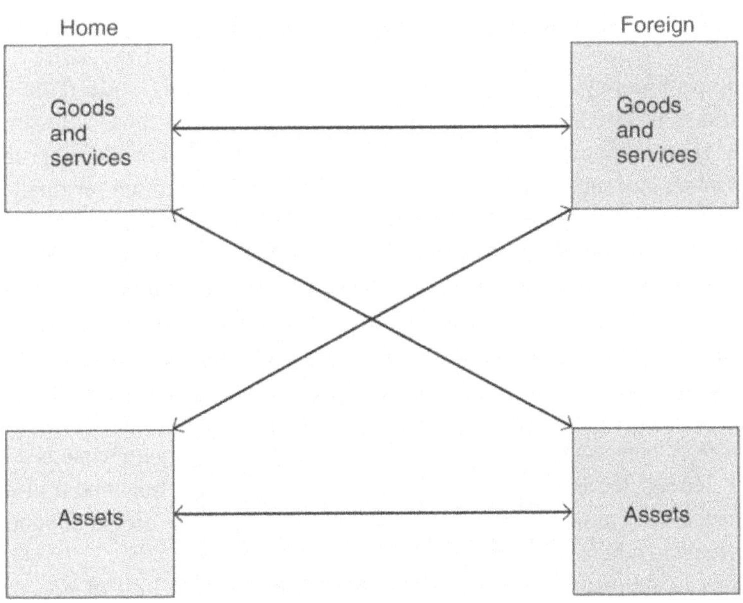

FIGURE 7.2 Financing of Trade

Regulation of finance addresses the politics of finance and sets rules to respond to those political questions. Monetary policies regulate the supply of money in markets and fiscal policies regulate money circulation. Banks can be subjected to regulation, say a cap on interest rates, and they can also be a tool for regulation, say promoting retail consumption by subsidizing loans.

The level of regulation in finance is much contested between those who want to free finance from any regulation and unleash the power of money and wealth and those who see finance as another mechanism of exploitation of workers and poorer people by capital holders. Keynesian economists see a need for market corrections, through governments regulating finance, whereas Minskyan economists would see that finance is intrinsically causing a market imbalance because some actors speculate on multiple transactions at the same time disturbing values (Keynes, 1923; Minsky, 1986).

This chapter argues that finance adds a layer of inequality to the existing imbalance in global trade between Global North and Global South (Wade, 2008; Rodrik, 2011). In fact, the financial system is highly reflective of the status of the political economy, meaning winners and losers in local markets and winners and losers in trade. Furthermore, finance, locally and globally, is systematically affected by crisis due to inherent asymmetries and paradoxes. We look at a few of them.

Some questions we touch upon in this chapter to help us examine the inequality in IPE of finance: how far back can we trace the rise of finance? How did finance and financial systems evolve? How can we identify a disparity between the Global South and the Global North in terms of finance?

The Rise of Money and the Risks With Financialization

If we take a basic understanding of finance as the allocation of resources, then finance is as old as ancient markets of barter. Enter money. The rise of money greatly helped finance by simplifying exchange or value storing, using a standardized unit, that is, coins, bills, checks or other liquid assets.

Early mentions of money can be found in the code of Hammurabi. Indeed, the code is a very early text of law that describes the rules of communal life. Often those rules include punishments in death, grain or money. The early coins of those Babylonian times had probably inspired the minting of many currencies around the world. Money was a medium for financing, yet there were other means too, such as barter, gold and slaves. The historian Niall Ferguson pins the rise of money and the beginning of the modern financial systems to the history of the West and more specifically to the expansion of the banking empire of the Rothschild family in Europe in the nineteenth century (2008). The wealth of this Jewish family from Germany grew because they established a family banking group throughout Europe in which the brothers internally offset exchanges of money, without physically transporting money, which was very risky, especially given the many wars sweeping across the continent. Ferguson highlights the story of this family in the rise of money because their family model introduced the private bank as a new player in global finance. Indeed, the Rothschild Bank allowed international financial transactions and as long as one trusted their money in this bank, they had access to the global economy, regardless of who they were and where they were.

Money brings to the economy three major functions: being a unit of accounting, a store of value and a medium of exchange – more specifically a bartering veil (Palan, 2013). These different functions engender themselves a value: value of the accounting system, value in the assessment of value and, last but not least, value in the translation of the transaction in money terms. As such money is not just a medium to get a value derived from a good or a service, money itself carries value that is then supplemented to the value of the derived good and service. What is interesting to see here is that finance also adds value to the value of the economic transaction as the value is not just derived from the financial activity itself, but also from the variance in the value of money (e.g., changes in exchange rates, which is the price of money). Indeed, political economist Anastasia Nesvetailova explains that the financial innovations that we have seen lately add to the complexity of tracking the value of money independently from the real economy which adds to the stress of predicting markets (2014).

To understand finance in the international political economy, a dominant approach in orthodox economics has been the one that predicts the impact of money supply on increasing inflation and that shows an equilibrium between money exchange and the exchange of goods and services. This approach is based on the quantity theory of money or the Fisher equation,[1] which states that money circulation depends on price levels and volume of transactions as such:

$$(M) \times (V) = (P) \times (T)$$

where,

- M = Money supply
- V = Velocity of circulation (the number of times money changes hands)
- P = Average price level
- T =Volume of transactions of goods and services

The quantity theory of money predicts that as long as the two sides of the equation are fairly equal, we have financial stability and soundness. Financialization greatly distorts this theory as money now circulates more than the exchange of goods and services resulting in a form of multiplication of money. More money is circulated in a concern to hedge the value of money and make more profit out of it. What happens is that instead of just circulating money for the end goal of supporting transactions, money is also circulated to speculate on the future value of money and to contract debt. In contrast to conceptualizing financial markets as places where stability is sought after, economist Hyman Minsky proposed the financial instability theory of capitalist economies, a theory that states that financial markets are in their nature unstable, not just because of disruptions of markets (1974). With Minsky's theory, we see that the capitalist market mechanism is flawed, "in the sense that it does not lead to a stable price–full employment equilibrium" (Minsky, 1974, p. 267). Minsky has indeed unveiled a structural issue of fragility in financial systems as they are not only separate dynamics from the real economy with their additional risks but also because they are prone to the volatility of prices and speculation (Nesvetailova, 2007).

Despite Minsky's contestation of financial stability in the early 1970s, financial markets have flourished and multiplied around the world, notably with stock markets and the frenzy to get very rich, very fast, or lose it all. Actually, since the 1980s one could trace at least two to three decades of the Wall Street golden age and expansion of stock trading around the world including in the Global South with the emerging economies of East and later South-East Asia.

Despite numerous great financial crises sweeping across the world since the rise of money and banking, the popularity of finance and financial markets is still strong. Despite the evident instability of financial markets, the prospect of growing money is winning over. And some do grow their money greatly, like Warren Buffet who was the richest man on earth just for trading stocks, and not producing anything. Interestingly, Buffet takes his advice from late financier Benjamin Graham who marketed the profession of finance as one of high intellect and analytical dexterity, and not of quick wins as commonly advertised by financial institutions around the world.[2] Benjamin Graham described the intelligent investor as a person not influenced by trends and frenzies to follow or buy a "promising" stock to trade, instead this humble investor safely saved and secured their finance kept an eye on the real economy and only traded when the real economy was clearly and assuredly projected to grow. Nothing like what bankers would tell you. Graham grew up during the Great Depression, and his investing patterns had all the hallmarks of conservatism and high awareness of the heterodoxy of the economy, meaning greater awareness of the instability of markers.

The prelude to the mortgage-based security crisis of 2007 was a time in which the advice to investors was at the polar opposite of Graham's intelligent investor. Preceding the crisis, financial institutions, which were often state-sponsored, encouraged poor people who, in principle, did not have enough money to invest in financial markets. These people were exposed to a very high risk of getting even poorer. Individuals with no income, no jobs and assets (NINJA) were enticed to buy houses and contract mortgages that swallowed any mere cash they had and forced them to pay interest to powerful financial institutions. Eventually, many of these financial institutions defaulted, some even got saved by the treasury, but the poor people entrapped in the scheme were left in greater poverty.

The crisis of 2007 was also interesting to observe as an outcome of significant financialization, meaning the expansion of financial services paralleling the real economy both domestically and at the international level. Financialization permits multiplying the financial instruments tied to a single underlying liquid asset, which gives an illusion of multiplication of money and liquidity (Alami, 2019). The 2007 financial crisis gave the phenomenon of financialization a negative reputation, however, it is worth noting that the intent with instruments such as "securities", "options" and "derivatives" was to tail-risk hedge and limit the fragility of the financial system. But instead of securing markets, what happened instead seemed to be that these new instruments allowed financial institutions to grow their market and target more clients, increasing the overall risk from financial transactions. The crisis also revealed an asymmetry in how the government protects actors in the face of crisis: first big actors, that is, banks, are saved, which leaves little for individual investors who were also exposed.

The expansion of financialization in the evolution of finance has also created a mechanism of integration of financial systems, often included in the overall experience of accelerated globalization as noted in Chapter 5 when discussing Samir Amin's new imperialist monopolies, which include a monopoly of financial systems. The monopoly in financial systems is derived from the US dollar or US dollar-based transactions. The US dollar is the most convertible currency, and unlike other currencies, it gets its value from the very large global market giving it much monetary strength, more than from its domestic market. Here we see the additional layer of inequality that is brought by financialization, one of inequality in financial systems in terms of how much multiplication of money is possible and how many safety nets guarantee the perennity of the credit system. The process of integration also means that the financial industry is now connected to virtually all industrial sectors, in addition to traditional sectors closely connected to finance, like insurance. The sector of security is a notable example. The military–industrial complex (MIC) since 9/11 has both significantly grown thanks from the rapid expansion in militarization demands of the so-called War on Terror around the world and from the parallel growth of financial institutions that specifically fund the MIC, making it more profitable (Marshall, 2015).

So far, we described the rise of money and the risks with financialization across the board. In the following box, we look at the additional costs of both money and financialization in the Global South. Both the "Original Sin" and imported inflation leave Global South economies at a higher risk of default and, as such, in perpetual crisis.

BOX 7.1 THE "ORIGINAL SIN" AND THE PAINS OF IMPORTED INFLATION

To understand the schism between the experience of the Global South and the Global North in terms of the development of global finance, it is important to shed light on two intertwined phenomena of the "Original Sin" and imported inflation.

The Original Sin

The coining of the Original Sin began in the seminal article of economists Eichengreen and Hausman (1999) regarding the consequences of volatile exchange rates (particularly between currencies of developed economies vis-à-vis those of developing economies) and the resulting financial fragility. The original sin is that poor countries are always at a comparative disadvantage when there is an overall growth of the global financial system because their debt is denominated in rich countries' currencies. When there is a healthy expansion of global money, both rich and poor countries' net foreign assets will increase but for poor countries, net foreign liabilities, that is, debt, will also increase, which causes them to have a decreased net foreign wealth. In addition, Eichengreen and Hausman demonstrate that domestic monetary mechanisms in poor economies are not helpful to counter the growth in the cost of their debt as is the case for rich countries. Unlike rich countries that increase the money supply without much lowering the value of their currency, poor countries run the risk of downward spiraling in an episode of hyperinflation.

Imported Inflation

Many of the development policies in the Global South have relied on export-led growth which often was based on commodity trade, resulting in little diversification of economic activities. This has been notably the case for the oil economies of the Gulf (Salih, 1993; Basher et al., 2012). Despite pegging their currency to the US dollar, to limit the financial fragility resulting from the "original sin" described earlier, these economies have been trapped with imported inflation that limits the competitivity of other sectors of economic activity in these contexts and limits the possibilities of diversification of the economy (also coined the resource curse). Countries in the Gulf and China, most notably, have been denouncing the issue of importing inflation, given that most financial assets are denominated in rich countries' currency and have therefore called for monetary sovereignty to control their exchange rate and use government subsidies to correct for the competitive disadvantage they have when they trade in the global market.

The rise of money and its risks is also addressed by an important school of thought in economics called monetarism. Monetarists agree that markets are monitored through the government's control of the money supply. For example, Keynesians view the possibility to limit inflation, through the increase of funding and investments. Monetarists, on the other hand, view that inflation is controlled via the circulation of money. A decrease in money movement means that the government tries to keep price levels down. An increase in money movement means that the government tries to alleviate price levels that are falling. However, in countries of the Global South monetary policy is not entirely in the hands of local governments which means that they cannot afford these corrective measures. Therefore, a troubling consequence of the monetarist approach, especially during a time of crisis, is giving much power to financial institutions in the control of the economy. Because of the dependence of Global South financial systems on the Global North ones, this means that the latter gain further power and control deepening the imbalance in the global financial system.

Fragile Financial Systems and Failing Regulation

In this section, we discuss the need for regulating money given the fragilities of financial systems. First, we explore a few major milestones in the evolution of international monetary systems, intended to promote global governance. Then, we look at the failings of regulatory mechanisms and the cyclicality of crises, particularly as the crisis is more acute in the Global South in recent decades.

International monetary systems are the context for the IPE of finance. A monetary system is an arrangement of currencies accepted for financing. An international monetary system is the interaction between different monetary systems and determines how local and foreign currencies are priced. Consequently, an international monetary system governs the allocation of funds internationally.

Governments safeguard against financial instability in several ways: with deposit insurance, reserve requirements, asset restrictions (notably, limiting risky assets), bank examination, and, last but not least, by being the lender of last resort thanks to a local central bank that can even print money if needed. However, these mechanisms are less effective in poor economies of the Global South notably because these guarantees are based on a smaller pool of available resources. Government bailouts of financial institutions are indeed less likely to be possible in such contexts, which limits the possibilities to avoid crises. Indeed, a great majority of banking crises over time had been happening in the Global South, far more than in rich countries.

Regulation is therefore needed to correct market instability and the cyclicality of crises. As discussed earlier, orthodox economists like John Maynard Keynes believe in the autonomy of markets and when it comes to the financial ones, they see a demand-driven growth that needs to be stimulated through favorable monetary policies that facilitate credit (1923). However, such approaches are likely to exacerbate the volatility of prices in poor economies as they are already impacted by imported inflation as seen earlier. Minskyan economists would see that financial transactions add up to the instability of markets and grow the potential of crisis (Minsky, 1986). In other words, Keynesian sees financing as an opportunity to help markets and make them stable, while Minskyanism establishes that financing itself is the source of disturbance of markets. One can wonder whether, in the latter proposal, there is a call to abolish money.

Monetary systems could be considered as old as finance and early forms of international monetary systems could also be seen with early forms of trade between different communities. Even if communities were different across ancient trading routes, such as the Silk Road, for example, various currencies were pegged to universally recognized commodities of value, such as gold and silver. Fast forwarding millennia and arriving to our modern times, a key milestone in the evolution of monetary systems was the inception of the Bretton Woods system. In July 1944, 44 countries met in Bretton Woods, NH, in the United States to design the Bretton Woods system, a fixed exchange rate against the US dollar and a fixed dollar price against gold. This allowed for a privileged position of the US dollar in being exclusively converted to the most important underlying commodity for the value of money, gold, in a consistent manner. As such Bretton Woods created a major asymmetry in how global money is priced: when particular financial markets were unstable, this reflected on the price of their local currencies, except for the US dollar which kept a stable price, despite its changing value. This mechanism was a vital step toward seating the hegemony of the US dollar in global finance. Bretton Woods also established other institutions such as the International Monetary Fund (IMF), the World Bank, and the General Agreement on Trade and Tariffs (GATT), the predecessor to the World Trade Organization (WTO). Bretton Woods was dissolved in 1973 and has been replaced by the IMF as an institution dedicated to supporting countries with persistent balance of payments deficits and to approving devaluation, spurring controversies of becoming a tool to limit monetary sovereignty in the Global South. The IMF is the world's bank of last resort and gives loans in US dollars, affirming still and again the hegemonic role of the United States as the major financial actor in the global economy because of its currency.

In addition, many IMF loans are conditional on the supervision of domestic policies by the IMF, which means that financial control comes with political control as well. The IMF has also systematically promoted flexible exchange rates or even the freeing of currencies in countries of the Global South which leaves poor economies with little or no control over exchange rates and thus less opportunity to redress from the competitive disadvantage they have in engaging in global finance as discussed in our box (i.e., fixing the original sin and imported inflation).

Despite the claim that the IMF aims to help poor economies, many economies of the Global South have experienced chronic financial crises. Two are worth highlighting: (1) the 1980s debt crisis due to the export-led growth in many countries in Latin America, prescribed by the IMF, and that led these economies to borrow excessively, beyond their means; (2) the 1997 Asian financial crisis that started in the stock market of Bangkok, Thailand, and was triggered by arbitrage trading of the local currency, the Thai Baht. The Baht value soared at first, but when the market (and foreign financial markets more specifically) started to panic over the matching strength of the real economy in Thailand, massive selling of the Baht led to the plummeting of the value of the currency and the impoverishment of many households in Thailand.

Paradoxes of IPE of Finance

In this section, we start first by discussing the fundamental paradoxes of financial systems. Then, we look at forms of resisting these problems in the Global South. Lastly, we look at alternative models to correct financial markets and rebuild trust in the economy.

The failings of global finance can be summarized in three paradoxes that explain the cyclicality of financial crises: (1) the paradox of liquidity in the sense that finance promotes finding new ways to create liquidity but this ends up transforming liquid assets into illiquid ones, because of the multiplication of money based on a single underlying asset (see Alami, 2019);

(2) the paradox of thrift in the sense that higher rates of saving, meant to help the economy by increasing investment tend to shrink the economy as production is reduced; (3) the paradox of debt in the sense that de-leveraging, that is, reducing debt by paying back debt, tends to lead to a higher leverage ratio because assets, or savings, shrink (see Strange, 1986; Lavoie, 2011, p. 13). These paradoxes are key to understanding how global finance magnifies problems of economic inequality because financial markets throw off the benefit of regulatory policies meant to stabilize markets. The communities that are most impoverished by the financial crises are, as a result of financial inequality, likely to desire political change and may even trust sensational populist campaigns as seen with Donald Trump and his resurrection of so-called voodoo economics, that is, supply-side economics that promote high government expenditures and little taxation to boost consumption, but that are likely to expand the already soaring debt levels (Stiglitz, 2019).

Another important dimension of financial failures can be seen with the obsolescence of traditional banking and rampant shadow banking that makes up over half of credit lines in the global financial system (Nesvetailova, 2017). Shadow banking means that financial services are provided despite regulations meant to limit them, and these services put the market actors involved, often poor individuals, at a higher risk of financial exposure, that is, money loss.

In addition, offshore financial centers (OFCs) also contribute to a precarity of the international financial structure which makes global regulation even more difficult and even less effective. These OFCs allow for tax arbitrage, meaning multinational corporations are able to select more favorable tax regimes in other countries, limiting their fiscal contribution to the global economy and allowing them to act as free riders in the global economy (Nesvetailova et al., 2021).[3]

It is important to note here that the greater loss from the international financial system in the case of the Global South reflects the continuity of the colonial order (Bernards, 2022). A case in point for the (post)colonial nature of this asymmetry of the international financial system is the Franc CFA, a regional currency in West Africa, controlled in its value by France, the former colonial power in the region. Indeed, Western regulatory institutions of global finance have a vested interest in controlling poor countries' monetary policies, specifically devaluation, as a tool of financial subordination and imperialism (Bracking, 2016; Alami et al., 2022). By controlling the value of the currency of their former colonies, the prices of goods and services imported from these countries (notably natural resources) are controlled by these powers and kept at low levels. The case of France with the control of West African financial reserves cannot be more blatant. Such predatory practices have certainly decreased trust in financial markets in the Global South. Indeed, people there, when they can, tend to flee their capital and themselves through migration. In addition, these financial markets in the Global South in which there is low trust, foreign investors are also discouraged to come, leading to low levels of foreign direct investments. In addition, poor countries have limited fiscal capacities, meaning they have difficulty collecting taxes to redress their economy (Rodrik, 1997).

The COVID-19 crisis and recession have not only worsened the already existing debt crises around the world but also ushered the need to find alternatives to the problem of debt such as sovereign debt buybacks to prevent the looming sovereign debt crisis. The problem here is that to limit the soaring levels of debt, states justify taking away needed financial resources from the health, education and climate mitigation sectors.[4] Therefore, the problems of finance have also a direct impact on the social and environmental sustainability of life itself.

Anastasia Nesvetailova and Ronen Palan describe three forms of sabotage by banking institutions in global finance: (1) banking institutions sabotaging their own clients (even the deceased ones); (2) banking institutions sabotaging the state, in other words, making sure that the state either subsidizes them by reducing tax or bails them out in times of trouble or – in better times – by using sophisticated techniques of tax and regulatory avoidance; (3) sabotaging the market by sabotaging other banking institutions (2020). These practices are at the level of more sophisticated financial markets in the Global North; however, they set a trend everywhere and show us again the huge risks with finance.

Conclusion

Global finance's asymmetries, paradoxes and predatory practices add heft to IPE problems, even more so in the Global South. The global economy suffers from the idiosyncrasies of capitalist development to which global finance adds a layer of instability. Even corrective measures such as government bailouts seem to have siphoned the meager resources from the shallow pockets of the poor to the abundant resources from the deep pockets of the rich and barely mitigate crisis. The protest campaigns of the 99% around the world decries this imbalance.

Financial instability not only causes stress on markets but also causes stress on people's nerves, jeopardizing their mental health and even their physical safety (see suicide related to bankruptcy). Exchange rate volatility can directly impact one's financial ability. A liquidity crisis can even lead to bank robberies. Crises affect all the economies of the world; however, economies of the Global South are likely to inherit external crises as well (see the US mortgage-backed crisis of 2007). The other way around, meaning Global South financial crises seeping into the Global North are less likely (see graph above of banking crisis in the developing world not affecting the Global North).

Finally, and to go back to our starting questions, IPE of Finance paints the following scheme. Funds are more likely to be directed to bigger players, banks or rich countries (who gets the funding). Money and value are siphoned from the Global South to the Global North (who gets to fund). Lastly, financing is the allocation of monetary resources following market practices, which reflect regulation, failings of regulation and lack of regulation (how is funding made).

As we saw with the opening photograph in this chapter, finance reflects politics, an international politics. Latin American countries, like many countries of the world, have been dominated by the US dollar and US banks. The United States is still hegemonic in the international monetary system. However, we start to see a small process of de-dollarization, like the takeover of that Buenos Aires building by a Chinese bank and the increasing number of trade transactions in the Chinese Yuan. As such, the story of global finance continues to unfold and money could be heading to its demise.

Notes

1 The Quantity Theory of Money was developed by Economist Irving Fisher in his book, *The Purchasing Power of Money*, in 1911.
2 Benjamin Graham published in 1949 the seminal, The Intelligent Investor, which was described by billionaire Warren Buffet in 2006 as "by far the best book on investing ever written."
3 Instances of tax arbitrage were notably popularized with the controversy surrounding the Panama Papers, a series of leaked documents in 2016 that identified major heads of state who are involved in these practices of free riding and tax evasion.
4 Stiglitz, J., & Rashid, H. (2021). The looming sovereign debt crisis in Latin America. *Project Syndicate*. See: https://www.project-syndicate.org/commentary/how-to-prevent-looming-debt-crisis-developing-countries-by-joseph-e-stiglitz-and-hamid-rashid-2020-07?barrier=accesspaylog

Bibliography

Alami, I. (2019). *Money power and financial capital in emerging markets: Facing the liquidity tsunami*. Routledge.

Alami, I., Alves, C., Bonizzi, B., Kaltenbrunner, A., Koddenbrock, K., Kvangraven, I., & Powell, J. (2022). International financial subordination: A critical research agenda. *Review of International Political Economy*. https://doi.org/10.1080/09692290.2022.2098359

Basher, S. A., & Elsamadisy, E. M. (2012). Country heterogeneity and long-run determinants of inflation in the Gulf Arab states. *OPEC Energy Review*, *36*(2), 170–203.

Bernards, N. (2022). *A critical history of poverty finance: Colonial roots and neoliberal failures*. Pluto Press.

Bracking, S. (2016). *The financialisation of power: How financiers rule Africa*. Routledge.

Eichengreen, B., & Hausmann, R. (1999). *Exchange rates and financial fragility* (Working Paper 7418). National Bureau of Economic Research. https://doi.org/10.3386/w7418

Ferguson, N. (2008). *The ascent of money: A financial history of the world*. Penguin.

Keynes, J. M. (1923). *A tract on monetary reform*. Cosimo Classics.

Krugman, P., Obstfeld, M., & Melitz, M. (2017). *International economics: Theory and policy*. Pearson.

Lairson, T. D., & Skidmore, D. (2003). *International political economy: The struggle for power and wealth*. Thomson Wadsworth.

Lavoie, M. (2011). The global financial crisis: Methodological reflections from a heterodox perspective. *Studies in Political Economy*, *88*(1), 35–57.

Marshall, S. (2015). *The Egyptian armed forces and the remaking of an economic empire*. Carnegie Endowment for International Peace.

Minsky, H. P. (1974). Can and should fed "go it alone". *The Journal of Commerce*, *1*, 17.

Minsky, H. P. (1986). Money and crisis in Schumpeter and Keynes. In H.-J. Wagener & J. W. Drukker (Eds.), *The economic law of motion of modern society: A Marx-Keynes-Schumpeter centennial*. Cambridge University Press.

Nesvetailova, A. (2007). The rise of fragile finance. In *Fragile finance: Debt, speculation and crisis in the age of global credit* (pp. 9–24). Palgrave Macmillan UK.

Nesvetailova, A. (2014). Innovations, fragility and complexity: Understanding the power of finance. *Government and Opposition*, *49*(3), 542–568.

Nesvetailova, A. (Ed.). (2017). *Shadow banking: Scope, origins and theories*. Routledge.

Nesvetailova, A., & Palan, R. (2020). *Sabotage: The business of finance*. Penguin UK.

Nesvetailova, A., Palan, R., Petersen, H., & Phillips, R. (2021). *IFFs and commodity trading: Opportunities for identifying risks in energy traders' financial conduct using groups* (CITYPERC Working Paper 2021-03). Corporate Filings.

Palan, R. (2013). *Global political economy: Contemporary theories*. Routledge.

Rodrik, D. (1997). *Globalization, social conflict and economic growth* (Vol. 24, Versión revisada). Conferencia de Raúl Prebisch, Ginebra (en inglés). http://www.ksg.harvard.edu/rodrik/global.pdf

Rodrik, D. (2011). *The globalization paradox: Why global markets, states, and democracy can't coexist*. Oxford University Press.

Salih, S. A. (1993). Determinants of inflation in oil-exporting developing countries: An empirical investigation, 1970–1990. *Applied Economics*, *25*(4), 439–445.

Stiglitz, J. (2019). *People, power, and profits: Progressive capitalism for an age of discontent*. Penguin UK.

Strange, S. (1986). *Casino capitalism*. Manchester University Press.

Wade, R. (2008). The first-world debt crisis of 2007–2010 in global perspective. *Challenge*, *51*(4), 23–54.

8

BRINGING SECURITY BACK IN IPE

For the many who lived the episode of a flight takeoff and landing, and indeed traveling by plane in general, the amount of security rules that come into play has become a standard feature of the traveling experience. The hostess has just given you the security briefing in case of an emergency landing, they have explained how to pull the mask from above the seat and the lifejacket from under it, and they come to check whether our seatbelt is well fastened, whether the seat is upright and whether there are any bags obstructing the passage between the seats and the window.

According to ChatGPT, which may well tell us what a multitude of viewpoints over the internet has coalesced into, has this to say about why bags should be under the seat: "During flight take-off, it's important for carry-on items to be stowed securely under the seat in front of the passenger for safety reasons. This helps to ensure that the aisle and exit rows are clear and unobstructed, allowing for a quick and efficient evacuation in the event of an emergency. It also prevents loose items from becoming projectiles in the event of turbulence or a sudden maneuver".

Now, emergency landings are a very rare occurrence, and the probability of them being successful is even rarer. Think about it, when was the last time you heard of one that led to the survival of the people on board of the plane? Generally speaking, the security rules that are on the plane have very little practical use if we are to believe the official reasons given. Then, why are hostesses so adamant on implementing these rules and why have we normalized these in our behaviors, even though, arguably, the most sensible thing to do at this stage, in that moment where we have very little control over "life", is to just trust hazard or a higher power that there will be no crash or malfunction?

In fact, at that moment, we are asked by the hostess to trust a process that produces a certain kind of "order", stability and predictability of behavior. This is part of a series of countless rituals we do every day that on the whole may not make complete sense but that are necessary to render the world coherent to ourselves. This sense of trust is at the heart of how an economy functions. For example, think about the trust needed in a monetary transaction. Without trust in the banking institution that issues the currency, people would not be using it. A financial crash,

DOI: 10.4324/9781003264255-8

such as what happened in 2008, was basically a crisis of confidence in the financial institutions. Recall that in Chapter 2, when we looked at the notion of value, it was argued that there must be an agreed-upon custom or "tradition of doing" so as to have a certain exchangeable sense of value which is at the basis of community life or "living together". The more the economy becomes a larger assemblage of the flow of resources, technologies and people, and that needs to be managed in a stable, predictable manner, the more producing a system of trust is essential to its effective functioning. There is no economy without a sense of order and there is no sense of order without security.

In order to understand this more fully, let's look again at why is it that airports are one of the most highly securitized and surveilled spaces in contemporary cities? According to Mark B. Salter, "airports are representative of supermodern 'nonplaces' in which social relations are based on mobility rather than fixity" (2008, p. ix). Logically, because these are places where people come and go from everywhere in the world, airports are "between" borders separating different countries. Thus, airports are the sites of humans that are the least bound by any form of communal ties. By communal, we mean that are not linked by family, clan, nationality, religion, state, etc. Even though in an airport we are under the jurisprudence of one state and abide by its rules, the rapid movement of people throughout, some not destined to stay (and thus abide by those rules and participate in this particular economy), makes it a zone which requires more "security".

In fact, this sense of order/security is the reason why "political" precedes "economy" in the discipline of IPE. But there are many kinds of "security systems" that would produce order, in turn producing exchange, wealth and management of resources. At one end, we can think of the "family" or "tribe" as the smallest unit of order, and at the other, the modern state and a whole array of affiliated institutions or institutionalized behaviors that structure "the economy" or "the market" through policies. At each of these levels there is a particular type of economic/security regime that can be put in place. For centuries, families and tribes were the main economic unit, along with princedoms and empires that played a broad administrative role in extracting a fraction of resources in exchange for regional security and facilitated the establishment of trade routes. The rise of capitalism culminated in the industrial revolution of the nineteenth century and the various technological breakthroughs that dramatically changed human and social relations. But this happened hand in hand with the formation of another form of security regime, the modern state.

The rise of the modern state is inextricably linked to that of the capitalist economy, but this process is not as straightforward as one could think. There is no working economic system without some kind of "security pact". In order to trade you need a sense of trust and for that you need to have institutions, sets of rules or conventions that ensures some kind of stability in order for production and consumption to take place. At every stage of human interaction there must be some kind of code, ritual of behavior. Family has always been the cornerstone of the most "secure" human organization, or at least kin relations. In Europe the gradual changes that started roughly in the seventeenth century witnessed a gradual transformation from a large tribal structure to the nuclear family of the Industrial Revolution and its aftermath. In that sense there is a gradual transfer of "trust" in the hands of the consolidating modern state. The functioning of the rule of law with all its affiliated institutions would not be effective without a substantial transfer of "trust" from the "private" to the "public" realm to use Hannah Arendt's terms (1998).

Borders, Security, and Economy

Up until the eighteenth century most of what became European states practiced mercantilism, which is to substitute imports for local production in an attempt to grow local industries and other sectors of the economy. This process mainly affected relationships between warring European states. This was not only significantly important to produce the strong industries and manufacturing potential of the nineteenth century, but it also was foundational to the development of the modern state. As the historian Charles Tilly argued (1993), incessant wars across centuries were the main trigger for the slow formation of the modern nation-state by forcing monarchies to seek capital, fund larger and larger armies, expand control over territory, and delineate more clearly borders. This in turn led to the birth of modern "public" debt and the banking system, the rise of a middle class that gradually held accountable the ruling powers, in turn leading to the gradual development of parliamentary democracies. Meanwhile, the colonial adventures of countries such as England ensured that a steady flow of resources and goods came in through outright exploitation of colonized areas of the world.

Today, neoclassical (and neoliberal) economists think of mercantilism as a thing of the past and that the doxa of free trade has prevailed as the best form of international economic strategy. Neoclassicalism and neoliberalism refer to a strand in economic theory that believes in minimal state intervention in the economy and less protection and tariff barriers to trade. Free trade was championed by "classical liberals" such as Adam Smith and John Stuart Mill in the nineteenth century and again by neoliberal economists, especially after the 1980s following the debt crises witnessed by many countries of the Global South. But these nineteenth-century authors also believed in the fundamental importance of state regulation and institutional building in being able to provide for a fertile ground for unfettered trade and economic activity. In his book, *Kicking Away the Ladder*, Economist Ha-Joon Chang (2002) argued persuasively that the West had built its successful economies in the run-up to the late *19th* century by pursuing aggressive mercantilist strategies yet today strongly push for global southern regions to open their economies to foreign trade and investment. Ultimately as we will discuss more below, not only do powerful countries constantly use trade and financial sanctions as a weapon of war or to extract political concessions but use them so as to direct the flow of capital in specific directions leading to economic development or its absence, and these decisions are based on security rationales.

BOX 8.1 ON THE NEXUS BETWEEN SECURITY AND ECONOMIC ACTIVITIES IN CLASSICAL LIBERALISM

The nexus between security and economic activities, order and markets, had already been identified by Adam Smith in the Wealth of the Nations. In his view, trade contributed to bringing peace, order and justice domestically, and he also wished that trade would bring more peace internationally (Smith, Wealth of the Nations, 1779). As a key figure of liberal pacifism, Smith thought that the globalization of economic activities would have gradually promoted a condition of perpetual peace. Yet, he was also worried that more trade may have increased the tendency toward war to establish and protect monopolies, given the prevailing mercantilist spirit of his time. Despite these nuances, Smith remained closely associated with his emphasis on the making of a cosmopolitical economy based on the norms of free trade, ending up naively downplaying the role of national political economies and the tendencies toward conflicts and war (List, 1847, The National System of Political Economy). Pushing the critique further from a heterodox Marxist angle, Samir Amin defined liberal political economy as an ideology of universal harmonies which conveniently underplayed the hidden role of violence, colonialism and imperialism in the making of the world economy conveniently promoting a win-win view of international trade and markets (1976, Unequal Development).

Liberal economists of the eighteenth to the nineteenth century had already argued that private property was the most vital condition for a capitalist economy to emerge. But this happened on the back of one of the largest and most impressive land-grabbing colonial processes in human history: the conquest of the Americas. When English philosopher John Locke wrote his *Second Treatise of Government* (1690) he was thinking of how a clear delimitation of land presupposes a state that can enforce the rules to respect these boundaries. In that sense one of the pillars of Liberalism is based on a security question. Toward the end of the nineteenth century, Karl Marx famously said that private property is the source of socioeconomic inequality because the state which defends it, serves the interest of those who own the means of production or capital. Nineteenth-century intellectuals were called "political" economists because the point of the discipline was to figure out what is the best "security" structure, that is the types of rules and ways of enforcing those rules, that helped manage, keep and grow wealth effectively, promoted trade, etc.

Classical economists or liberals who advocated free trade were at the forefront of British empire activities and understood fully well the "order of things". John Stuart Mill, one of the fathers of Classical Liberalism, not only wrote in the heyday of British colonial adventures, but also he himself was a colonial administrator in the East India Company, the institution that governed India until the later part of the nineteenth century. It is important to read Classical political economists as advocating for the enforcement of a "securitizing" project. It is through that lens that they thought the economy was made up of three factors of production (add a short "glossary definition"): Land, Capital, and Labor. In fact, the "Political" component here pertained to the "management" of these three variables. Managing land, capital and labor, meant securing their easy movement, transfer and preservation, that is, erecting a system of rules and regulations that allowed for a predictable and enduring security regime: the modern nation-state.

In their book *A History of the World in Seven Cheap Things*, Raj Patel and Jason Moore (2020) argued that the affluence of the modern world was possible through centuries-long elaboration of a global colonial regime that facilitated the extraction and rendering available of what were the most precious or valuable "things" in premodern times. These are nature, money, work, care, food, energy and lives. This involved a drastic re-ordering of the human condition, its relationship with its external environment, the basic necessities it survives on and how it controls its own existence. According to Patel and Moore, by occupying the various corners of the world and significantly transforming it, Western colonial expeditions developed highly sophisticated systems of political and security control and management. Think about it this way: a few centuries ago, wars were fought over salt and spices and more recently over energy and oil. Doesn't this involve a completely different *ordering* of the *economy*?

In a nutshell, the capitalist world system that gradually emerged in the last few centuries is above all a "security" regime: a way of ordering the planet through new structures and rationales of management and extraction. Apart from the nation-state, this security regime involves the formation of new institutions and organizations as well as what we call in the international politics literature non-state actors, organizations and sets of institutions, sometimes armed, that fulfill parts of the functions of modern states. While premodern economies depended more on extended kinship ties, developed less exploitative technology and had less control over the environment. The ordering elements of the modern system include as we saw, nation-states, influential transnational actors and institutions, and also the perdurance or production of new types of non-state actors as we give an example below that either function within or across the nation-state model. Moreover, the global system is built on a transnational class that owns and manages specific strategic industries such as the military, energy and digital media conglomerates.

The global and contemporary security regime is also, to echo Michel Foucault, a producer of hegemonic or dominant discursive practices. For example, the very way we think of what "economy" is has been shaped by the changing reality we live in. We've seen in Chapter 2 with the concept of value how understandings of reality can change depending on context in turn impacting on how things such as "land" matter differently. In precapitalist economies such as Ancient Greece, "economy" meant management of the household. Most political treatises since Greek times are focused on the concept of the City as the main unit of the human community. States are princedoms or monarchies, usually built around a city as a hub of economic activity. Empires are a loose assemblage of cities connected by an administrative taxation structure that highly depends on constant negotiations between various influential social groups, tribes and clans, in those various cities and regions.

Moreover, precapitalist systems were characterized by a more "enchanted" understanding of reality (Taylor, 2007, p. 25) where humans were part of a larger production that was not just of man's doing. Modern times are characterized by a secular understanding, where the incessant drive to control nature, resources and population has no place for another *ruling* actor. It is not that the premodern way of thinking has disappeared, but just that it is not anymore hegemonic. Modern Western economies stress the importance of the individual as the ultimate consumer. Families/groups, where they still matter, are subordinated to the state by law, policing, etc. Even though this way of thinking has spread everywhere in the world due to the nature of capitalism, it is in constant negotiation with other previously established forms of community life and thus develops hybrid structures everywhere.

Variations depend mainly on the particular state/society relation prevalent in different places. Take the example of Lebanon where the state has, throughout the last 50 years or so, gradually disintegrated, leaving space for the rule of clans or tribes for lack of a better term. Lebanon has been described as a "consociational democracy" a form of power-sharing between various religiously denominated sects. But without any functioning executive power, the institutions that make the state and every single other organization and institution that creates order/security in the country have been managed by one of those factions. In the absence of an overarching security regime in place, various groups are in constant negotiations to manage resources, people and territory in the (initially) colonially delimited country.

In that sense a "non-state actor" such as Hizbullah takes on many of the roles fulfilled by states worldwide while conveniently staying away from actually managing the state (Saade, 2016). It works well with a capitalist economy while socially ordering its constituency beyond the "individualism" paradigm. Such non-state actors, that are more and more prevalent in regions such as the Middle East, are not completely the state and constantly challenge Western powers. They constantly suffer from the constraint of economic sanctions, in the case of Lebanon that precipitated the latest financial crisis that started in October 2019. In Iraq, the United States limits the extent to which the Iraqi Central Bank can use its dollar reserves while forbidding it to hold Chinese Yuan currency.

BOX 8.2 THE LATEST STAGE OF CAPITALISM: SURVEILLANCE CAPITALISM, THE DIGITAL REVOLUTION AND GLOBALIZATION

In her book, *the Age of Surveillance Capitalism*, Shoshana Zuboff is among a few recent authors that studied the rise of digital conglomerates such as Google, Facebook and Apple and argued that the latter revolutionized the way the capitalist economy works. Various economic/industrial revolutions of the nineteenth and twentieth centuries produced different subjectivities and thus security regimes. Just as Fordism, through the automobile industry, transformed mass production, the latest digital revolution introduced surveillance capitalism, an economic regime that generates profit from monitoring, data production and collection from consumers worldwide. In so doing bodies of people, their preferences, wants and values are constantly molded through micro-surveillance through social media and internet use. Zuboff calls a third capitalist revolution where big tech companies produce profit through the surveillance of people, by turning them into data used for marketing purposes. Zuboff calls this the behavioral surplus that is generated through data mining and data accumulation. In that sense processes of individualization in the latest state of capitalism are at the service of a more invasive yet ambiguous security regime where self-policing becomes the norm.

The International World Order Since WWII Security and Insecurity: Globalization and Imperialism?

The Marxist approach has been key to understanding the importance of security in the making of the IPE order. Marxists argue that while the modern age is characterized on the one hand by the rise of the capitalist system as the main economic mode of production, powerful states are determined to preserve this mode of extraction and management of resources through a politics of Imperialism. And in an ever-growing globalizing world, there are three main sectors that fuel imperial strategies: financial capital, the military industry and the oil industry.

In order to understand this let's briefly look at the recent history of the modern world order.

In 1945 the "Allied Forces" won the war, and the Nazis were defeated. Soon enough, this alliance broke down and two regional blocs emerged that would shape the politics of most of the rest of the twentieth century. The Soviet Union that was key in helping defeat the fascists ended up becoming the main enemy of the United States and Western Europe. Two main economic regimes emerged, Capitalism and Communism, with the world split between both or for some sitting in between. To this effect, in 1948, and in an effort to rebuild Western Europe, the United States enacted what became called as the Marshall Plan, which was a series of substantial foreign aid that helped jump-start the economy of Germany and the rest of war-destroyed Europe. What the Marshall Plan tells us is that there is no "economic development" prior to the establishment of a "security agreement" or "vision". These are shaped by a clear-cut understanding of boundaries, of who is in and out of the political structure benefiting from a particular economic activity or transaction.

Capital moves in selective directions and based on security concerns. In that sense, US foreign policy imperatives were the main shaper of the structure of IPE. Understanding the expansion of US capital is key to understanding the shape of the global system today and reveals the importance of the security regimes that were put in place in order for this global economy to emerge. What was dubbed as "the economic miracle" of South-East Asia is a case in point. The discipline of IPE often compares developmental progress in several regions of the global south such as the MENA region, Latin America and South-East Asia as examples of failed or successful strategies. Post-WWII economies reverted back to import-substituting policies in order to develop industries and another sector of their economies as Keynesianism became the prevailing method for economic growth. Keynesianism is an economic school of thought based on British Economist John Maynard Keynes who challenged the liberal idea that a free market would produce full employment. For Keynes economies could get endlessly stuck in downward spirals of depression hindering consumption and production with no natural adjustment unless the state intervened through fiscal and monetary policies.

By the 1970s, many countries of the Global South found themselves struggling under the weight of unmanageable external debts that were increasingly crowding out other economic productive activity, thereby raising inflation and slowing down the economy. Organizations such as the World Bank and the IMF were given new, more intrusive roles that involved lending capital on the condition of "restructuring economies" through a list of standards that in effect involved privatizing, inviting foreign investment and multinationals and accelerating in that sense the globalization process.

Meanwhile, in other parts of the world there still were a few "growth success stories". Southeast Asia, and namely South Korea as the prime example of it, developed into a fully-fledged industrial economy and opened up to international trade and finance after a long period of privileging local production. The prevailing narrative is such countries benefited from a different "Asian" state-run capitalist culture that caused its success. But in reality, the security pact between the United States and other countries such as South Korea or Taiwan also played an important role in directing the flow of capital in a particular direction and for military and imperialist reasons as argued by economist Ali Kadri (2018):

> the developed Asian countries serve as part of a Cordon Sanitaire hedging the advance of China . . . , to develop as such, or to grow wealthy and sustain a pro-imperialist working class consciousness, a given country has to supplement US-led imperialist hegemony.
>
> *(viii)*

For Kadri, the opposite dynamic took place in the Arab world: the Arab states have been subjected to incessant imperialist assault that eroded their role in promoting development as part of their security structure (.). Arab ruling classes "compromised the mechanisms that address social redistributive pressures and cemented the objective grounds for militarism as a principal domain of accumulation" (Kadri, 2018, p. 11).

Capitalism and the Securitization of the Gulf Region

Another example of the nexus of security and economy are the various transformations that occurred in the Gulf region since oil became a precious commodity to the functioning of the capitalist modern order. The perdurance of specific political regimes in the Gulf regions, centered around dynastic monarchies, such as the Saudi ruling family was necessary for a steady supply of oil. The energy sector required the strictest forms of control and security structure in order to insure economic profit. While the relationship between capitalism and democratization has been vaunted for decades, other authors argued that capitalism contains some very fundamental undemocratic elements built into it in order to ensure the stability of the global economic system (MacEwan, 1999).

More importantly, as argued by Timothy Mitchell, oil companies themselves dictated the rules of the game, structuring the overabundant oil sector and deciding on the pace of infrastructural development and rate of supply production, going as far as to delay the process of extraction in the early twentieth century when common economic theory would predict the opposite (Mitchell, 2013). These companies worked in tandem with the prevailing colonial powers of the time mainly Britain.

The very presence of the precious resources of oil and gas pushed Colonial powers to shape the boundaries and formation of the states that made up the Gulf region. Countries like the UK carved out territory at the periphery of imperial realms into separate states for oil production as empires needed states to operate the economy – production of security and order (Mukoyama, 2024). There were local pressures to establish federations but "Oil-rich protectorates avoided forming a larger entity because a merger would mean sharing their wealth with others, and the local ruler had a strong political incentive to remain independent for fear of losing his power in a larger state" (Mukoyama, 2024, p. 13).

Borders and the notion of space are so important to the functioning of the capitalist economy. While we do live in an increasingly globalized world, the latter depends on a series of regional orders that enable wealth accumulation. The Gulf region is an excellent example of this. Political Economist Adam Hanieh builds on the notion that space (here we can think of the nation-state as an example of it) is a product of social forces, as in a relationship between different social classes. These groups of people have a shared interest in controlling production in the economy, say oil, or finance, etc., and in so doing carve out bordered spaces. "Capitalism depends upon the production of territorial complexes such as factories, transport routes, urban environments, communications networks and regulatory institutions in order to expand and circulate capital" (Hanieh, 2011, p. 25).

Securitization and a "Political Economy" of the Environment

In the enormously influential Atlantic Monthly Essay, "The Coming Anarchy: How Scarcity, Crime, Overpopulation and Disease are Rapidly Destroying the Social Fabric of Our Planet", Robert Kaplan inaugurated a new environment–security nexus. In his paper, Kaplan described Africa as the "Dark Continent" in a state of apocalyptic crisis: overpopulated, undernourished and driven by barbaric acts of violence. Yet this coming anarchy would not be confined to Africa alone, but all the developing world fueled by "surging populations, spreading disease, deforestation and soil erosion, water depletion, air pollution – developments that will prompt mass migrations and in turn incite group conflicts" (1994, p. 58). Within a few weeks from its publication, Kaplan was invited to the White House and Al Gore championed "The Coming Anarchy" as a model of green thinking he had tried to promote in the 1990s. Later on, President Clinton put the paper at the center of a new sensitivity to environmental security. Within one year, James Woolsey Director of Central Intelligence and William Perry, Secretary of Defense, were singing the praises of an aggressive environmental program as critical to the Defense mission.

Neo-Malthusian notions about the possible consequences of demographic growth were again at the center of the debates and agendas of international development and security. In an international context characterized by the fall of the Berlin Wall and the end of the Soviet Union, the idea of environmental security, of green wars, fills a historical void and contributes to situating environmental questions in the geostrategic context. The question of environmental security merges with the issue of national security, and these security disquietudes diffuse among many members of NATO. The cycle of simple causal relations starts with demographic growth, which contributes to natural resources scarcity and depletion, deteriorating economic activity, which in turn triggers mass migrations, fragilizes the state, and causes conflicts.

And yet, Peluso and Watts criticize the series of simplistic causal and mechanical links, offering a political economy and political ecology analysis of violence in their pioneering Violent Environments (2001). They criticize the notion of scarcity as something natural, trying to repoliticize the debate connecting violence to processes of material transformations and power relations. They argue that the capture of resources happens in a context of social class relations which constitute the political economy, and which are forged by environmental changes and modes of accumulation. They analyze conflicts in a mechanical manner, trying instead to take into consideration the ways in which specific environments and natural resources (tropics, forests and oil reserves) and environmental processes (e.g., deforestation and conservation of resources amelioration) are constituted by and in part constitute the political economy of the access to water, soil and natural resources.

They stress therefore the importance of (1) situating this violence in the context of the modes of accumulation, the unequal spatial distribution and the displacement generated by the accumulation of capital; (2) understanding the forms of access and control of natural resources (entitlements and modes of imposition); (3) the actors (enterprises, workers peasants and institutions of the state) which emerge from the social relations of production.

From Traditional Security to Human Security: Implications on the World Economy

A key function of modern states is to ensure the security of the community. This sense of security is commonly perceived as the protection of a defined territory, a permanent people and a government, which are the defining features of a recognized state in international law. As such, security has been traditionally concerned with strengthening the defense apparatus, or in other terms, the military capability. From its early origins with the Westphalian treaties, the modern state's obsession with military capability as a means of national security has evolved to capture other dimensions of security such as economic security and human security. *The Westphalian treatises* were a series of peace treaties signed in the region of Westphalia, Germany, in the seventeenth century that highlighted principles of mutual recognition of the sovereignty of numerous European kingdoms to ensure peace and end the Thirty Years' War. The particular shift in human security about 30 years ago marked an important turn of policymaking evolution concerned with the individual and not just the aggregate. Such a shift has implications on the management of resources as it presupposes to be concerned with the distribution of resources at the micro level. In this section on the shift from traditional security to human security, we will start by defining some contextual elements for traditional approaches to security, before delving into the rise of human security. We will then attempt to reveal some of the limitations of human security, including the problems with the "security-development nexus". We will end this section with a brainstorming exercise inviting the reader to think about sources of insecurity, particularly in the Global South.

As stated earlier, the seventeenth-century evolution of the modern state in Western Europe was concerned with security, in the sense of defending the sovereignty of governments to end conflict. This model for security has become a yardstick model beyond Europe and centuries later on in other parts of the world, particularly in the mid-twentieth-century era of independence for the postcolonial world. Such a traditional approach to security was still very relevant during the Cold War in shaping security approaches. The Cold War was a period of indirect military confrontation between the United States and the Soviet Union, often fought in proxy wars around the world from the end of World War II to the fall of the Berlin Wall in 1989.

The traditional understanding of security comes from the Realist approach that takes the state to be the referent object of security. In this sense, international stability relied on the premise that, first, state security must be maintained, to, second, ensure the security of citizens (i.e., one follows the other in that order). By the 1980s, with the waning of the Cold War, it became clear that the security of citizens was also threatened by internal state activities, shifting the referent object of security from the state to the people. Indeed, some of these internal state activities led to civil wars, in addition to rising poverty, disease, hunger, human rights abuses and environmental problems. What came out of this new realization is that focusing solely on state security leads to neglecting basic human rights.

Political Scientist Rudolph Rummel even coined the term "democide" to reveal that even in the case of modern democracies, one can see the incidence of state violence and murder of people even at times of peace (1998). The shift away from strictly state-centric views of security to human dimensions of security brought in more holistic approaches to security, integrating into human needs the quality of institutions, culture and social norms. Some of these founding principles were laid out in the seminal 1994 Human Development Report (HDR), published by the United Nations Development Programme (UNDP), an organism concerned with promoting development policies, particularly in the Global South where issues of poverty are more acute. The 1994 HDR is credited with the rise of the human security concept and metric in development. The 1994 HDR that championed human security built on the major strides achieved by the first HDR that introduced the metric of the Human Development Index (HDI), which already shifted concerns of growth from the market aggregate, captured by the gross domestic product (GDP), to individual wellbeing, captured by the HDI in the form of income per capita, literacy rate and life expectancy.

The rise of "human development" concerns in the 1990s is a context for the rise of human security. In addition, the increased transnational nature of threats such as global terrorism, climate change and cyberwarfare prompted the need to go beyond traditional approaches to security. The 1994 HDR emphasized the importance of human rights and humanitarian intervention to uphold human security. The increasingly integrated approach to both national and human security defined that the state has both the responsibility not only to protect citizens from violent death and protect its sovereignty (defining as such a *narrow* sense of human security) but also to ensure resources and wellbeing for its citizens (defining as such a *broad* sense of human security).

The 1994 HDR's narrow sense of human security was also coined freedom from fear and garnered the support of Canada and Norway. The freedom from fear principle was a way to emphasize security as conflict resolution and pushed for policies that support humanitarian intervention. The 1994 context was particularly marked by these concerns for humanitarian intervention as the Rwandan genocide was under way and that period was particularly marking given that there was little intervention, particularly from superpowers to stop the genocide. Middle powers such as Canada and Norway had an opportunity to fill such a void by promoting the International Commission on Intervention and State Sovereignty (ICISS), which laid the foundations of a somewhat formal protocol to intervene in cases of major state violence like genocide. However, despite a just cause to stop violence, the ICISS and the principle of the Responsibility to Protect (R2P) have become obsolete protocols for humanitarian intervention as cases of intervention were more likely to be politically motivated than driven by humanitarian goals, particularly in the African continent (Branch, 2011).

Regarding the broad sense of human security, which the 1994 report coined as "freedom from fear and freedom from want", the emphasis was on dealing with broader social issues as they create conflict and insecurity. The policy implications here are to fund and promote human development programs that will improve the HDI metric. UNDP and Japan have been key actors in promoting this broad sense of human security. However, there has been here as well a critique of the consequences of such an intervention to push human development. This critique became well known as the security–development nexus which shows that even development programs that target poverty-fighting come with belligerent tones that normalize forms of violence and give authority to external actions (e.g., international organizations, private charities) over local actors (Duffield, 2007). Critical theorist Noam Chomsky had already warned us that development programs can be seen as new tools for imperialism and forced neoliberal globalization (Chomsky, 1998).

In that vein, even knowledge production, research and thus policy recommendations regarding climate change have been ideologically charged involving specific politics toward the African continent. For example, Harry Verhoeven (2014) argues that Africa has for decades been framed as a security-sensitive continent and as a source of environmental problems that end up spreading to the rest of the globe. "[H]istorically established paradigms of thinking about Africa, its ecosystems and notions of disorder, danger and violence" (Verhoeven, 2014, p. 787) have seeped into the prevailing understanding of climate change and other environmental problems. He argues that "[s]ecuritisation is the result both of a specific moment in the post–Cold War era with its particular geopolitical configuration and of deeply embedded modes of imagining the African continent, its peoples and their relationship with the environments they inhabit" (Verhoeven, 2014).

The issue with this kind of thinking is that it has concrete political implications. By thinking of the African continent not as made up of different countries and political regimes, economic structures, and so on, but as being plagued by overarching climate-related and environment-related issues, it "deprive[s] Africans of agency" and restricts a better understanding and acknowledgment of "how African governments, especially through extraversion, instrumentalise environmental narratives that help them stay in power and continue processes of concentrating wealth and power" (Verhoeven, 800).

Bibliography

Amin, S. (1976). *Unequal development: An essay on the social formations of peripheral capitalism*. Monthly Review Press.
Arendt, H. (1998). *The human condition*. University of Chicago Press.
Bilgin, P. (2016). *The international in security, security in the international*. Routledge.
Branch, A. (2011). The irresponsibility of the responsibility to protect in Africa. In P. Cunliffe (Ed.), *Critical perspectives on the responsibility to protect*. Routledge.
Chang, H.-J. (2002). *Kicking away the ladder: Development strategy in historical perspective*. Anthem Press.
Chomsky, N. (1998). *Profit over people: Neoliberalism and global order*. Seven Stories Press.
Duffield, M. (2007). *Development, security and unending war: Governing the world of peoples*. Polity.
Hanieh, A. (2011). *Capitalism and class in the Gulf Arab states*. Palgrave Macmillan.
Hanieh, A. (2018). *Money, markets, and monarchies: The Gulf cooperation council and the political economy of the contemporary Middle East*. Cambridge University Press.
Kadri, A. (2018). *The cordon sanitaire, a single law governing development in East Asia and the Arab world*. Palgrave Macmillan.
Kaplan, R. D. (1994, February 1). *The coming anarchy*. The Atlantic. https://www.theatlantic.com/magazine/archive/1994/02/the-coming-anarchy/304670/
MacEwan, A. (1999). *Neoliberalism or democracy: Economic strategy, markets, and alternatives*. Fernwood Publishing.
Mitchell, T. (2013). *Carbon democracy: Political power in the age of oil* (1st edition). Verso.
Mukoyama, N. (2024). *Fuelling sovereignty: Colonial oil and the creation of unlikely states*. Cambridge University Press.
Patel, R., & Moore, J. W. (2020). *A history of the world in seven cheap things: A guide to capitalism, nature, and the future of the planet*. Verso Books.
Peluso, N. L., & Watts, M. (Eds.). (2001). *Violent environments*. Cornell University Press.
Peoples, C., & Vaughan-Williams, N. (2010). *Critical security studies: An introduction*. Routledge.
Rummel, R. J. (1998). *Statistics of democide: Genocide and mass murder since 1900*. LIT Verlag.
Saade, B. (2006). *Hizbullah and the Politics of Remembrance: Writing the Lebanese Nation*. Cambridge University Press.
Salter, M. B. (Ed.). (2008). *Politics at the airport*. University of Minnesota Press.
Taylor, C. (2007). *A secular age*. Harvard University Press.
Tilly, C. (1993). *Coercion, capital and European states, AD 990–1990* (New Ed edition). Wiley-Blackwell.
Verhoeven, H. (2014). Gardens of Eden or hearts of darkness? The genealogy of discourses on environmental insecurity and climate wars in Africa. *Geopolitics*, *19*(4), 784–805.
Zuboff, S. (2019). *The age of surveillance capitalism: The fight for a human future at the new frontier of power*. PublicAffairs.

9

RURAL SOCIAL MOVEMENTS IN THE GLOBAL SOUTH AND IPE

Introduction: Rural Social Movements in the Global South

On November 29, 2018, 35,000 farmers and agricultural workers from all over India organized under various umbrella groups, among which was the All India Kisan Sabha (AIKS), and marched to Parliament in Delhi in a two-day protest against soaring operating costs and plunging produce prices. In one of the largest farmers' mobilizations that Delhi has ever seen, demonstrators chanted slogans against Narendra Modi's right-wing government's false assurances and unfulfilled promises, demanding a special parliament session to discuss the persistent agrarian crisis in India, for example, a progressive deterioration of agricultural livelihoods. The social reproduction crisis manifested into generalized levels of poverty fueling vast levels of indebtedness – a dynamic that many considered being behind the suicide crisis, which claimed the lives of three million farmers in the last 20 years (Nilsen & Roy, 2016).

Far from being epiphenomenal, these mobilizations represent the culmination of a decade of agrarian struggles between farmers' organizations and the Indian state around issues of farmers' rights, livelihoods and voices, especially in Rajasthan and Maharashtra states – the latter known as the "graveyard of farmers." Rural discontent generated by agricultural stagnation, unemployment and state-sponsored elite-driven land grabs, manifested into various forms of large-scale protests. These grievances culminated in a 200-km long march from March 6 to 12, 2018, which began in Nashik with 25,000 people and concluded in Mumbai with over 50,000 protesters, and a mass demonstration of 100,000 people (Dhawale, 2018, p. 261). The vigorous, democratic and unprecedented Long Kisan March, which saw hundreds of women marching barefoot, with bruised and bleeding feet, succeeded in putting the agrarian crisis at the core of the political debate, capturing the imagination of many and symbolically stirring the consciousness of the nation. To the astonishment of those who have been espousing grand narratives of modernity and industrialization within the Indian society, and those who had theorized the demise of peasants and their agency (see, e.g., Hobsbawm, 1995 on the disappearance of peasants), the resurgence of rural social movements had shaken the edifice of consensus of Modi's government at its foundations. By providing opposition leaders and other civil society organizations, who

DOI: 10.4324/9781003264255-9

joined the farmers in protest, with a common ground and rallying point, rural social movements significantly contributed to opposing Modi's neoliberal and authoritarian political project.

These dramatic events and symbolic protests point to the resurrection and lasting relevance of rural social movements and peasants' collective action both as terrain of analysis and as an alternative political project to authoritarian populism in the Global South (Martiniello, 2022). As shown in a recent study by Jung (2022) about anti-systemic movements in the Global South from a historical perspective, popular protests against exclusion have been peaking in the last decade and have taken precedence over struggles against exploitation. Struggles over land in particular have reflected the "responses from below" and repertoires of resistance to large-scale land acquisitions and enclosures in the periphery of the global system, what scholars have termed "global land grabbing" (Borras & Franco, 2013; Martiniello, 2015). Enclosure is a process of privatization of land and other resources held as common property rights, whether that process happens *de facto* (in practice) or *de jure* (with legal status). These agrarian contestations built upon previous waves of rural protests that have characterized the neoliberal epoch as shown in the cases of Brazil with the emergence of the *Movimiento dos Trabajadores Rurais* – and its campaign of land re-appropriation; Zimbabwe with growing rural mobilizations around land reclamation against colonial land dispossession; and South Africa with the emergence of numerous rural-based organizations which to a lesser extent than in Zimbabwe elaborated similar claims against apartheid-driven land expropriation, land redistribution and restitution (see Moyo & Yeros, 2005).

What is the place of rural social movements in the contemporary politics in the Global South? How do they help us understand the character of national and international political economy? What do they tell us about political agency and social change within international political economy?

Agrarian struggles occurring in India are not an isolated phenomenon; there exists, in fact, a myriad of instances of contestation in the countryside of the Global South which do not necessarily take the shape of organized collective action that reaches the public sphere. In some cases, localized episodes of resistance do not automatically translate into broader social movements at the national and regional levels. Historically, peasants have made their presence felt on the political scene by engaging in a multitude of different forms of struggle vis-à-vis externally posed threats to their moral economies and attempts at surplus extraction, in the form of labor, taxes and commodities, by state and accumulating classes (Scott, 1975; William, 1976). Social analyses from different disciplinary perspectives focused on rural politics explored the significance of peasant political actions in revolutionary struggles of the twentieth century (Shanin, 1971; Wolf, 1969) and national liberation anti-colonial movements in Africa (Davidson, 1974; Fanon, 1967).

To Franz Fanon (1967), peasants represented the quintessence of the revolutionary subject. James C. Scott (1975) defined their actions as mainly oriented to "minimize risks". The literature further bifurcates into those who became interested in the study of social revolts as moments that revealed the existence of a separate political domain which elite domination and hegemony have been unable to supersede or suppress (Arnold, 1984; Guha, 1983), and those who maintained that peasants' agency and dissent was largely manifest in low-intensity, everyday, hidden practices of resistance of a non-confrontational nature (Scott, 1985). Land struggles are more likely to embody "uneasy and erratic, contradictory and shifting alliances of different class elements and tendencies than to express the interests of some unambiguous and unitary class subject" (Bernstein, 2009, p. 253). However, recent critical agrarian scholarship has returned to unpacking land struggles, motivated in part by the need to understand the stubborn persistence of peasants and small farmers in the face of a developmental model geared toward their extinction (Desmarais, 2007, 195).

Studying rural social movements and transnational agrarian movements (TAMs) allows us to understand the global character of contemporary rural social struggles and the responses from below to processes of neoliberal agricultural restructuring put in place by Western states, global financial institutions and food empires. Mainstream IPE theories have left little space for the study of collective social and political agency. Caught in the dichotomy of state and markets, they have ignored the ways in which both are shaped by the underpinning social structures, ecologies and agencies. While realist theories of IPE have narrowed down the space of the "political" to the state, liberals have contributed to reducing the "social" to an assemblage of individuals competing for resources in free markets. In doing so, they have participated in anesthetizing the potential for an analysis about the role of social forces in driving meaningful political change from below.

Analyzing rural social movements in the Global South allows opening the spectrum of the debates within the discipline paving the way for a dialogue between critical IPE, political sociology and political ecology. Doing so is key toward an understanding of the way in which existing social and political forces from the periphery of the global system challenge, organize and resist state, capital and global development agencies, interrogating, the contentious character of politics, the class, race and gender determinants of economic structures, the role of hegemonic ideologies and the praxis of resistance, their visions of ecologies. Analyzing rural social movements involves asking questions about the existing material and political conditions as well as the levels of political, class and collective consciousness that spearheaded the emergence of these networks, coalitions and mobilizations. It allows identifying the key elements that contributed to the rise of peasants' agency, including questions of class composition, organization and communication, ideology, the praxis of struggle and so on. It also assists the comprehension of the internal dynamics of any given movement, the critical role in advocating change played by peasant organizations and the content of social struggles to gain greater access and control over productive resources.

Rural social movements analysis helps us in highlighting and informing the importance of IPE to decenter its analytical focus from central industrial economies and urban spaces toward agrarian economies and rural ecologies which are still the home of almost half of the global population. It allows re-evoking the continuing centrality of the agrarian questions, for example, the privatization of land, the commoditization of labor and social reproduction, the commercialization of agricultural production in the countryside, the resistance to this transformation and the ecological implications of the process, to the study of economies, polities and societies of the Global South. We mean by agrarian questions the classical theory regarding the structural transformation of agriculture subjected to capitalism and the political-economic fate of the peasantry.

Studying rural social movements also allows framing the emergence of these movements in the context of the impact of neoliberal capitalist restructuring in the countryside, and the obstacles that pre-existing land-based social relations pose to the fully fledged development of capitalist relations. Inquiries into the role of rural social movements also allow an understanding of the linkages between changes in the political economy of a specific country, for example, the growing transformation and commercialization of the agri-food sectors or the adoption of a specific law on land property or the environment, and the implications they have for the emergence and development of agrarian movements. There is, in fact, a trend within social sciences to situate the rise of social movements in the context of the growth of civil society activism, often at the expense of an analysis of capitalism, class struggle and conflict (Hetland & Goodwin, 2013). And indeed, the changes in global political and economic structures of capital accumulation which have major implications for local economies, ecologies and social relations because of the ways these spaces are integrated into the global capitalist economy, contribute to shaping the emergence of rural social mobilizations. There is thus a need to analyze how global forces impact the local since it is at the local level that rural social movements are most often engaged in concrete struggles, as we will see in our two case studies. It is impossible to understand the politics of rural social movements in the absence of an in-depth analysis of the class-based division of labor in the countryside (large commercial farmers, rich peasants, small peasants or landless laborers). Understanding the class composition and differences among rural social movements also allows us not only to plan alliances between various social constituencies that compose rural social movements but also to underscore some contradictions and differences among them.

Yet an analysis that considers only class relationships alone is no longer a sufficient toolbox to explore the diverse terrains of the unfolding rural politics in the Global South. Class relations intersect and combine with other forms of social difference and division, among which gender and other oppressive relations such as race, ethnicity, age, religion and caste are among the most important (Bernstein, 2010). These sources of social contradiction, which predate the spread of capitalism, contribute to the complex and contradictory nature of capitalist social relations. Deepening social differentiation and intensifying competition over land, which result from the penetration of capitalism in agricultural production and social reproduction, take many forms including generational, gender, ethnic and religious confrontations. Yet as Pauline Peters has argued: "proliferating tensions and struggles between generations and genders, or between groups labelled by region, ethnicity or religion are intimately tied up with the dynamics of division and exclusion, alliance and inclusion that constitute class formation" (2004, p. 305). In what follows, the chapter will provide an overview of critical debates around the origins, emergence and development of rural social movements. We will later discuss two selected case studies – the *Movimiento dos Trabahadores Rurais Siem* Terra (MST) and the Korean Peasants League (KPL). Finally, it will explore the political and economic dynamics of change in the neoliberal era that have pushed them to coalesce into transnational agrarian movements.

Debating Rural Social Movements

Rural social movements are networks, coalitions, assemblages of peasant and other popular organizations, community-based and human rights organizations, women and youth associations and trade unions, struggling for a radical transformation (or reform) of the existing structures of political, social and economic power (Desmarais, 2007). Their main objective is to produce political mobilizations, advocacy campaigns and social struggles that aim at democratizing the political space and radically contesting state policies (Moyo & Yeros, 2005). They have developed diffused and elaborated repertoires of collective action and contention (Tilly, 1978) though mobilizations and public protests remain the most important strategies of struggle that radical agrarian movements use in their battle for greater access and control over productive resources. Some of them claim to be representative of the disenfranchised, dispossessed and excluded by global capitalism. At the same time, their vision takes inspiration from principles of economic and social justice, which include gender and ethnic equality.

Rural social movements do not represent newness. Massive peasant-based insurrections have informed revolutions in China (1949), Bolivia (1952) and Cuba (1959) (see Wolf, 1969); the anti-colonial, liberation and anti-imperial movements in Vietnam, Algeria, Portuguese Africa and Rhodesia (see Cabral, 1965; Fanon, 1967); and the rise of guerrilla movements in Malaysia, the Philippines and Colombia (Edelman & Borras, 2016, p. 28). These events also coincided with the emergence of a new field of enquiry, "peasant studies", which aimed at understanding the role of the peasantry as an important historical actor and protagonist of social and political change (Shanin, 1990).

In the last couple of decades, there has been a renewed interest in social movements and civil society activism which emerged as a result of deepening processes of economic globalization. The birth of multiple and diversified sets of collective practices and networks, such as those coalescing in the World Social Forum (WSF)[1] and the "alter-mondialization" movement, contributed to the articulation of demands about the environment, human rights, Indigenous populations, women's rights and structures of governance (Della Porta & Tarrow, 2005; Della Porta et al., 2006). This school of thought mostly saw new social movements emerging out of the weakening and fragmentation of the state and the ensuing growth of civil society networks and activism. Most of the contemporary scholarship heavily focused on urban social movements (Edelman & Borras, 2016). Scholarly work on rural social movements in the Global South also increased in part because some of the social organizations that spearheaded these mobilizations had a rural character and were among the largest in the world.

Critical agrarian scholarship significantly contributed to the study and mapping of the resurgence of rural social movements in the Global South as a response from below to the profound socioeconomic and political changes brought about by neoliberal globalization in the 1980s and onwards. This represents an important entry point into IPE debates around the role of the state, capital and global development agencies. Studies from around the globe have shown how agrarian restructuring, structural adjustment programs and growing state authoritarianism contributed to the dramatic deterioration of the conditions of social reproduction for millions of peasants and rural workers pushing them to the desperate search for political and economic alternatives (Moyo & Yeros, 2005; Borras et al., 2008a; Edelman, 2008; Peluso et al., 2008). Others have pointed to the rise of new social movements born out of local resistance to seed multinationals, the degradation of ecosystems and the threats to livelihoods because of agricultural modernization, especially in Latin America (e.g., the Zapatista) and in India (e.g., the Chipko) emerging in defense of agricultural policies favorable to traditional agro-ecological methods (Guzman & Martinez-Alier, 2006).

This scholarship contributed to squarely situating the question of rural social movements within the frame of the political economy and political ecology of agrarian and environmental change, reintegrating debates over capitalism, class and gender conflicts, and nature as crucial elements in the analysis of the dynamics of capital accumulation, social composition, political ideologies and praxis of resistance in the contemporary world system. Such reintroduction is particularly welcome given the not-so-surprising absence of notions such as capitalism, political economy and class struggle from most of the studies of social movements (Hetland & Goodwin, 2013) with priority given to concepts such as global networks and global civil society, which may obscure hierarchies and power relations within civil society itself (Desmarais, 2007).

However, not every corner of the world where economic and social conditions have worsened has witnessed growing contestation. It would be therefore erroneous to link protest mechanically to the worsening of socioeconomic conditions; so how do we explain thus these cycles of protest (Tarrow, 1988)? How do we understand the recrudescence of these forms of social mobilization and collective action? A good starting point is to distinguish between objective conditions and their subjective perceptions. It is only when rural subjects collectively define the actual terms of exploitation and oppression as unjust and subject to change, and a translation from objective to subjective interests occurs, that the process of becoming a class for itself begins, as Marx would have put it (Shin, 1994). Class, collective or other social forms of consciousness do not depend strictly on one's position in the division of labor of the capitalist economy but are historically and collectively constructed through struggles (see Thompson, 1978). Yet consciousness alone without the mobilization of material, symbolic and cultural resources cannot succeed in sustaining long-term mobilizations. There is, therefore, a relationship between past protests, processes of consciousness formation, the mobilization of material and symbolic resources and the current phase of rural protest which needs to be identified if we intend to grapple with the complexities shaping peasants' collective action.

And yet, a focus on the position occupied in the formal capital/labor relationship does not facilitate, for example, grappling with the multiple forms of informal, non-monetary, social reproductive labor undertaken within rural households (Razavi, 2009). Nor does it help us disentangle the work and power differentials in control, access and use of land within rural households and the implications for the political agency of rural subjects (Bezner-Kerr, 2017). Recent studies on large-scale land acquisitions have highlighted their gendered effects and how they differentially affect men and women, exasperating gender inequalities in control, access and use of land (White & White, 2012). In other words, gender shapes how women respond to large-scale land acquisitions and their politics (Park, 2019). By the same token, how do we explain the character of specific rural mobilizations such as those led by Dalits and Adivasi in India without incorporating caste and ethnicity in the analysis? It is therefore of paramount importance to integrate class, gender, ethnicity, age, caste, religion and other social cleavages to unpack the dynamics of agrarian change and rural political agency.

Critical agrarian scholarship on agrarian movements allowed us to capture the dynamics, origins and forms of a new wave of peasant activism, intersecting at local, national and transnational levels (Edelman, 2008; Desmarais, 2007; Borras, 2008; Peluso et al., 2008). In what follows, I will provide a discussion of some of the critical elements (origins, class, ideology and praxis) of some of the most influential rural social movements such as the MST and Korean Peasant League. These organizations have been vital promoters in the making of broad coalitions of transnational agrarian movements such as La Vía Campesina, an umbrella organization which gathers more than 170 peasant organizations around the world (Desmarais, 2007; Borras, 2008). We locate their emergence in the context of variegated national and regional experiences, mixed political cultures and historical memories whose convergence shaped the making of a genuinely transnational peasant movement.

MST and Korean Peasant League: Case Studies

In the 1960s, the massive peasant agitations which erupted in Central and South America against uneven landholding patterns inherited from colonialism and plantation society spurred several left-wing governments to implement a variety of redistributive agrarian reforms (De Janvry, 1981). However, under pressures from the US government, land reforms were also embraced by more conservative and authoritarian governments as instruments to quell rural unrest, pacify the countryside and remove support for armed rebellions (McMichael, 2006). In Brazil – a country with one of the most uneven landholding patterns in the world (along with

South Africa) – land reforms and struggles have threatened the interests of large latifundio (large-scale estates) proprietors and landed elites whose interests triggered a coup d'état and the instauration of a military dictatorship (1964–85). In such a context, the agrarian reform then became a highly strategic and security issue to both promote capitalist development and industrialization through large-scale schemes in order to reduce the dependency on smallholder production and undermine class struggle in the countryside, transforming potentially revolutionary peasants into conservative, individual-minded small-scale farmers (Martins, 2006; Baletti et al., 2008, p. 125).

With the restoration of democracy, the MST, founded in 1984 with the support of grassroots religious organizations, the Confederation of Workers (CUT) and the Workers Party (PT), started challenging the classical agrarian reform model and legislation of the Brazilian state, campaigning more vigorously for redistributive land reforms and the rights of smallholder peasants and landless workers to (re)productive resources. The MST first became popular on the national and international scene through land occupations in the state of Rio Grande do Sul, denouncing the problem of land concentration and latifundios, and successfully forcing on the political agenda of the country the question of redistributive land reforms and cooperative settlements. Exploiting legal caveats and taking advantage of constitutional provisions, which permit confiscation of unused land in cases of labor and environmental violations, the MST increased the number of land occupations from 119 in 1990 to 2210 in 2005 (Martins, 2006). Despite repressive measures, and incarceration of MST activists, defamatory campaigns and attempts at co-opting the leaders of the mobilizations, the MST campaigns and struggle contributed to putting into question the sanctity of property rights: a core value in the capitalist and neoliberal ideology.

According to Baletti et al. (2008), the reasons for this spectacular rise and success include leadership, occupations and autonomy. In terms of leadership, the movement has been able to maintain an essential base of peasant leadership. Nourished in various cooperative settlements resulting from land occupations and agrarian reform, young peasants and tenants of these settlements have progressively become the base of the leadership of the movement. The *acampamentos*, the sites where two million people settled in government-funded land reform settlement schemes, have become the focus of cooperation and the center of a new radical praxis which contributed to molding new social relations based on the social ownership of the means of production (Martins, 2006). Others such as Martins have emphasized the role of settlements as pedagogic units based on the work-and-study methodology and the intense process of political and ideological formation through study groups on radical theories (Martins, 2006, p. 265). In the political language of the MST land redistribution is not a means to incorporate smallholders within the circuits of the capitalist economy; it instead involves a radical shift in the production and power relations embedded in the agrarian social structure of the country.

According to João Pedro Stédile, leader of the MST, agrarian reforms are a means

> to take land and other productive resources off the market and to practice the principle of social ownership of land, whereby families who work on it have usufruct right. . . . We want an agricultural practice that transforms farmers into guardians of the land, and a different way of farming that ensures cultural heritage, genetic diversity, ecological equilibrium and also guarantees that land is not seen as private property.
>
> *(Stedile, 2002, p. 100)*

Rather than strive for inclusion into existing political structures, radical social movements struggle to transform the institutions in which they operate (Alvarez et al., 1998). In doing so, they engage with the broader cultural politics, striving to create alternative political identities and solidarities and new spaces of social interaction (Eschle, 2001).

Capitalist restructuring of agriculture and the trade liberalization of agricultural commodities at other latitudes spearheaded the emergence of another influential farmers' organization in South Korea, the Korean Peasant League (KPL). Established in a period of agrarian distress in the 1980s by the current president Lee Gwangsuk, the organization has grown into an intricate network of village-level, city-level, country-level and provincial-level organizations. Since then, it fought to create farmer-controlled food systems and promote farmer-to-farmer practices of knowledge sharing. The organization has grown in visibility due to its radical opposition to the liberalization of the rice market after South Korea, the third-largest Asian economy, joined the World Trade Organization (WTO) in 1995 and implemented a series of bilateral Free Trade Agreements (FTAs). With cheap food imports (especially rice) flowing into the country in increasing quantities due to continuous rounds of liberalization, agricultural prices have plummeted generating a four-fold increase in indebtedness and an exodus of smallholders from the countryside, decreasing from 6 million to 3.5 million (KPL, 2005).

In a context of corporate control of agriculture and food dumping, Korean farmers have been lobbying the government to include food sovereignty into law, guarantee fair prices for farmers (through public provisions) and compensation for their losses. Yet as the political and economic forces they confronted went beyond national borders, they simultaneously "globalized" their struggle by addressing their grievances against a series of WTO inter-ministerial meetings and negotiations. Meeting the challenges emerging from the international domain demanded forging new alliances, links and networks among peasant, worker and civil society organizations around the world. On September 10, 2003, a delegation of Korean peasants joined the protests at the Fifth Ministerial Conference of the WTO held in Cancun, Mexico, to discuss a new set of agreements about agriculture, access to non-agricultural markets, services and so on. In one of the most tragic and symbolic episodes of protests ever seen, Korean farmer Lee Kyung-hae stabbed a knife into his heart on the top of barricades and fences raised by police shouting, "WTO kills farmers". This extreme act of protest went to the heart of many farmers around the world, not only in Korea, and galvanized attention and support worldwide. His sacrifice highlighted the catastrophic social implications inscribed in the process of tout court liberalization of agricultural commodities, healthcare, education, culture, energy and other essential services. It called into cause not only the mechanics of the WTO's operation but also the conniving role of the Korean state and its ruling class.

KPL's struggle against trade liberalization and the resultant lowering of rural incomes and price-cost squeeze has continued unabated, despite ongoing FTAs being ratified, such as that between South Korea and the United States in 2011. In an interview at the margins of the mobilizations that ensued in 2012, Lee Gwangsuk reiterated KPL's adversity to industrial modes of farming: "Agriculture is perceived to be part of the industry. It is important for us to understand and raise awareness about the value of agriculture and food sovereignty to farming and non-farming people globally" (Gwangsuk, 2012). Neoliberal restructuring of agriculture, its integration within the circuits of industrial production and globalized trade, pushed peasants' organizations to continuously mobilize in order to reaffirm its centrality in the strategies of social reproduction of farmers. As a food-related activity, peasant agriculture has therefore to be re-imagined and re-framed as a pillar in the strategies of food sovereignty at national and global levels, reconnecting farmers and urban consumers, city and the countryside, through a series of horizontal interlinkages and short value chains (Van der Ploeg et al., 2012). And yet, the emergence of new global food empires, with their new norms and rules, has not gone uncontested. Social movements have in fact become key agents in shaping the emergence, formation and functioning, tensions and crises of various international food regimes (Friedmann, 2005).

BOX 9.1 TRANSNATIONAL AGRARIAN MOVEMENTS: LA VÍA CAMPESINA

The changing global political economy shaped by the power of corporate-driven industrialization of agriculture has posed peasants and rural workers around the world with a series of similar political and economic challenges.

Neoliberalism has enormously altered the dynamics of agrarian (re)production providing even higher power to transnational and domestic capital to dictate the terms of agricultural production and exchange (Borras et al., 2008b, p. 170). As the political and economic forces driving the capitalist transformation and restructuring of agriculture during the neoliberal era "globalized", peasant and farmer organizations around the world started to "internationalize" their struggles (Desmarais, 2007). The aim was to develop a political subjectivity and unified voice that would raise the visibility of peasant struggles around the world and help consolidate the power base of rural social movements within their countries. This scenario had profound implications on how the rural poor understand their conditions of social existence, assess the framework of political opportunities and respond to existing economic and political challenges (Martiniello & Nyamasenda, 2018, p. 147). In this sense neoliberal globalization produced both new challenges but also new opportunities for inter-exchange, communication and alliance-making (Edelman & Borras, 2016).

In such a context, in April 1993 a global peasant movement was created: La Vía Campesina (LVC). Its emergence coincided temporally with the Uruguay Round of the General Agreement on Tariffs and Trade (GATT), spurring representatives of rural organizations from North, South, East and West to coalesce into a single global peasant movement. At the moment, it includes more than 170 rural social movement organizations from Latin America, the Caribbean, North America, Eastern and Western Europe, Asia and Africa. LVC situated itself in the struggle against the corporate takeover of agriculture and food, denouncing the increasing rural poverty and growing hunger, and providing peasants in the South and farmers in the North with a common platform. Since its creation, LVC has been at the forefront of the global justice movement participating in anti-capitalist globalization marches held at various WTO ministerial conferences in Geneva (1998), Seattle (1999), Cancun (2003) and Hong Kong (2005). It was also involved in massive demonstrations against International Financial Institutions (IFIs) and G-8 countries in Prague (2000), Genoa (2001), Washington (2002) and Quito (2002), among others. In its effort to promote global solidarity, widen the inclusivity of the movement and support existing struggles for land, LVC moved its operative secretariat from Honduras to Indonesia in 2004, and more recently to Zimbabwe.

In world-historical terms, today's global peasant movement stands on the shoulders of previous movements for the right to self-determination (McMichael, 2008). From a world-systems perspective, we could define it as a genuinely anti-systemic movement (see

Arrighi et al., 1989) challenging the capitalist systems at its foundations. TAMs are thus movements, organizations, solidarity links and coalition networks of national peasant and farmer groups and their allies that cross national boundaries and seek to influence national and global policies. La Vía Campesina is the most well known of all the contemporary TAMs, networks and coalitions and has gained a considerable political reputation (Borras, 2004; Desmarais, 2007). According to Edelman and Borras (2016, p. 4), transnational alliances and actions often facilitate the mobilization of material, intellectual and symbolic resources and the identification of political opportunities. In a way, "it is a particular part of civil society that 'intervenes' in the development of agriculture, pulling it away from the route determined by the economy only" (Van der Ploeg, 2013, p. 10). TAMs represent an arena of action (Borras, 2008, p. 93), a space of interactions between an array of different organizations.

Yet TAMs are hardly new. Early transnational farmers' organizations sometimes manifested eclectic amalgams of agrarian populism, Communism, elite-led reformism and noblesse oblige, pacifism and feminism (Borras et al., 2008a, p. 173). Some movements and networks have been in existence for decades, for example, the Campesino a Campesino (Peasant to Peasant) movement, which generated a horizontal process of knowledge exchange in Central America and Mexico in the 1960s (Holt-Giménez, 2006; Boyer, 2010).

LVC claims to be fighting not only against transnational companies and agribusiness, capitalism and free trade but also against patriarchy (Vía Campesina, 2006). Its vision for a twenty-first-century agriculture is pivoted on notions of food sovereignty, land redistribution, agro-ecology and peasant's seeds, climate and environmental justice and dignity for migrant and waged workers while trying to galvanize international solidarity (Vía Campesina, 2019). In the last years, LVC has been more vigorously recognizing the central role played by women in food production and social reproduction, promoting gender diversity in the peasant movement. Its most significant international advocacy activities include the global campaign for agrarian reform (GCAR) (Rosset et al., 2006; Borras, 2006, 2008), the anti-GMOs campaign (Scoones, 2008), and the campaign for peasant agro-ecology, which is a set of place-specific practices, geared to recycling nutrients and energy on-farm, building healthy soils, promoting biodiversity and optimizing productivity of the farming system, rather than of individual species (Wittman et al., 2010; Rosset & Altieri, 2017). In doing so, LVC has defied the traditional forms of organizing and mobilizing the countryside, bringing in new innovative visions about work, nature, biodiversity and rural development.

Though LVC's main political motto has been the attempt to prioritize unity within diversity, it doesn't mean that internal differences do not exist as it pulls together a wide array of organizations. These differences range in terms of representation and agenda, political strategies and forms of actions, class basis and ideological and political differences. LVC's main effect has been to significantly contribute to reframing the terms of critical debates and practices in the field of international development with a thematic focus on issues such as environmental sustainability, climate change, food sovereignty, land rights and redistributive agrarian reforms, neoliberal trade policies, corporate control of genetic material and intellectual property rights. However, LVC is absent from Russia, Central Asia, the Middle East (with the exception of Palestine) and North Africa (MENA) region, and most notably China, which, together, host most of the world's rural poor (Borras et al., 2008a, p. 183). And yet, while according to some scholars, LVC provides an ontological detour that rejects the grand narrative of modernity (McMichael, 2008) and has the potential of challenging the dominance of capital in the Global South (Akram-Lodhi & Kay, 2009), others have adopted a more skeptical position. Bernstein (2009), for example, highlights their defensive, erratic, fragmentary and contradictory character. In a similar vein, Baletti et al. (2008) point to the internal contradictions and differences among various players within LVC.

Conclusion

The chapter explored the political economy and politics of rural social movements and their coalescence into transnational agrarian movements. It situated their emergence in the context of changing political economies and agrarian social relations at local, national and global levels. The study analyzed their origins, the social constituencies behind them, the ideologies inspiring their actions, and the visions driving their practices of contestation of often-authoritarian regimes. It identified the political dynamics that have led to the emergence of LVC, highlighting the dialectic between efforts toward localization and globalization of agrarian struggles. It pointed to elements of virtuosity exposed in their innovative political practices but also some of their internal differences, contradictions, failures and challenges.

It argued that studying rural social movements from an IPE perspective is fundamental to unpacking the emergence of various forms of contestation to state-led and capital-orchestrated agrarian restructuring (Martiniello, 2021). It allows connecting global processes and local practices paving the ways to new forms of understanding the dynamics of the making of international political economies. Despite these mobilizations do not exhaust the spectrum of the forms of resistance and the responses from below, they represent important entry points in the study of contentious politics in the Global South. It maintained that rural social movements (and their transnational articulations) represent important actors in shaping the trajectories of political and economic transformations at local, national and global scales. Their coalescence into transnational agrarian movements represents a historical tipping point in the making of truly anti-systemic social forces confronting global corporate and national capital, and the (transnational)state for equitable access to land, social justice and climate change.

Note

1 WSFs were essentially assemblies and platforms for the encounter, convergence and dialogue between different political organizations situated across the world around a set of common themes such as a critique of economic globalization, war, widening poverty, labor exploitation, environmental degradation, human and gender rights.

Bibliography

Akram-Lodhi, H., & Kay, C. (Eds.). (2009). *Peasants and globalization: Political economy, rural transformation and the agrarian question*. Routledge.

Alvarez, S. E., Dagnino, E., & Escobar, A. (Eds.). (1998). *Culture of politics: Politics of culture, re-visioning Latin American social movements*. Westview Press.

Arnold, D. (1984). Gramsci and peasant subalternity in India. *Journal of Peasant Studies*, *11*(4), 155–177.

Arrighi, G., Hopkins, T. K., & Wallerstein, I. (1989). *Anti-systemic movements*. Verso.
Baletti, B., Johnson, T. M., & Wolford, W. (2008). "Late mobilization": Transnational peasant networks and grassroots organizing in Brazil and South Africa. In S. M. Borras Jr., M. Edelman, & C. Kay (Eds.), *Transnational agrarian movements: Confronting globalization* (pp. 123–146). Blackwell Publishing Ltd.
Bernstein, H. (2009). Agrarian questions from transition to globalization. In A. H. Akram-Lodhi & C. Kay (Eds.), *Peasants and globalization: Political economy, rural transformation and the agrarian question* (pp. 239–261). Routledge.
Bernstein, H. (2010). *Class dynamics of agrarian change*. Fernwood Publishing.
Bezner-Kerr, R. (2017). Gender and agrarian inequities. In S. Sieglinde & B. Pound (Eds.), *Agricultural systems: Agro-ecology and rural innovation for development* (pp. 330–373). Academic Press.
Borras, S. M., Jr. (2004, October). *La Vía Campesina: An evolving transnational social movement* (Transnational Institute (TNI) Briefing Paper). Transnational Institute (TNI).
Borras, S. M., Jr. (2006). The underlying assumptions, theory and practice of neoliberal land policies. In P. Rosset, R. Patel, & M. Courville (Eds.), *Promised land: Competing visions of agrarian reform*. Food First Books.
Borras, S. M., Jr. (2008). La Vía Campesina and its global campaign for agrarian reform. In S. M. Borras Jr., & M. Edelman, & C. Kay (Eds.), *Transnational agrarian movements: Confronting globalization* (pp. 91–122). Blackwell Publishing Ltd.
Borras, S. M., Jr., Edelman, M., & Kay, C. (2008a). Transnational agrarian movements: Origins and politics, campaigns and impact. *Journal of Agrarian Change*, *8*, 169–204.
Borras, S. M., Jr., Edelman, M., & Kay, C. (2008b). *Transnational agrarian movements: Confronting globalization*. Blackwell Publishing Ltd.
Borras, S. M., Jr., & Franco, J. (2013). Global land grabbing and political responses "from below". *Third World Quarterly*, *34*(9), 1723–1747.
Boyer, J. (2010). Food security, food sovereignty, and local challenges for transnational agrarian movements: The Honduras case. *Journal of Peasant Studies*, *37*(2), 319–351.
Cabral, A. (1965). *Lutte nationale dans le colonies*. CONCP.
Davidson, B. (1974). African peasantries and revolution. *Journal of Peasant Studies*, *1*(3), 269–290.
De Janvry, A. (1981). *The agrarian question and reformism in Latin America*. Johns Hopkins University Press.
Della Porta, D., Andretta, M., Mosca, L., & Reiter, H. (2006). *Globalization from below: Transnational activism and protest networks*. University of Minnesota Press.
Della Porta, D., & Tarrow, S. (2005). Transnational processes and social activism. In D. Della Porta & S. Tarrow (Eds.), *Transnational protest and global activism*. Rowman and Littlefield.
Desmarais, A. (2007). *La Vía Campesina: Globalization and the power of peasants*. Pluto, Fernwood Publishing.
Dhawale, A. (2018). Remarkable farmers struggles in India: Some notes from Maharashtra and Rajasthan. *Agrarian South: A Journal of Political Economy*, *7*(2), 257–274.
Edelman, M. (2008). Transnational organizing in agrarian Central America: Histories, challenges, prospects. In S. M. Borras Jr., M. Edelman, & C. Kay (Eds.), *Transnational agrarian movements: Confronting globalization*. Blackwell Publishing Ltd.
Edelman, M., & Borras, S. M., Jr. (2016). *Political dynamics of transnational agrarian movements*. Fernwood Publishing.
Eschle, C. (2001). *Global democracy, social movements and feminism*. Westview Press.
Fanon, F. (1967). *The wretched of the earth*. Penguin Books.
Friedmann, H. (2005). From colonialism to green capitalism: Social movements and emergence of food regimes. In F. H. Buttel & P. McMichael (Eds.), *New directions in the sociology of global development*. Elsevier.
Guha, R. (1983). *Elementary aspects of peasant insurgency in colonial India*. Oxford University Press.
Guzman, S., & Martinez-Alier, J. (2006). Rural social movements and agro-ecology. In P. Cloke, T. Marsden, & P. Mooney (Eds.), *The handbook of rural studies*. Sage Publications Ltd., https://doi.org/10.4135/9781848608016
Gwangsuk, L. (2012). *Lee, Gwangsuk, president of the Korean peasant league*. Retrieved March 4, 2019, from https://www.youtube.com/watch?v=4MK8WXG4DbQ

Hetland, G., & Goodwin, J. (2013). The strange disappearance of capitalism from social movement studies. In C. Barker, L. Cox, J. Krinsky, & A. Gunvald Nilsen (Eds.), *Marxism and social movements*. E. J. Brill.

Hobsbawm, E. J. (1995). *The age of extremes: The short twentieth century (1914–1991)*. Abacus Books.

Holt-Ginénez, E. (2006). *Campesino a Campesino: Voices from Latin America's farmer to farmer movement for sustainable agriculture*. Food First Books.

Jung, C. (2022). Revisiting antisystemic movements in the global South: Struggles against exclusion and struggles against exploitation. *Third World Quarterly*, *44*(10), 2227–2245. https://doi.org/10.1080/01436597.2022.2106208

Korean Peasants League. (2005). *Launching resolution*. Retrieved March 4, 2019, from http://www.ijunnong.net/en/article/

Martiniello, G. (2015). Social struggles in Uganda's acholiland: Understanding responses and resistance to Amuru sugar works. *Journal of Peasant Studies*, *42*(3–4), 653–669. Special Issue on "Land grabs and politics from below".

Martiniello, G. (2021). Rural social movements/transnational agrarian movements. In H. Akram-Lodhi, B. McKay, B. Engels, & K. Dietz (Eds.), *Handbook of critical agrarian studies*. Edward Elgar Publishing.

Martiniello, G., & Nyamasenda, S. (2018). Agrarian movements in the neoliberal era: The case of MVIWATA in Tanzania. *Agrarian South: Journal of Political Economy*, *7*(2), 145–172.

Martins, M. D. (2006). Learning to participate: The MST experience in Brazil. In P. Rosset, R. Patel, & M. Courville (Eds.), *Promised land: Competing visions of agrarian reform*. Food First Books.

McMichael, P. (2006). *Development and social change: A global perspective*. Sage Publications Ltd.

McMichael, P. (2008). Peasants make their own history, but not just as they please. In S. M. Borras Jr., M. Edelman, & C. Kay (Eds.), *Transnational agrarian movements: Confronting globalization*. Blackwell Publishing Ltd.

Moyo, S., & Yeros, P. (2005). The resurgence of rural movements under neoliberalism. In S. Moyo & P. Yeros (Eds.), *Reclaiming the land: The resurgence of rural movements in Africa, Asia and Latin America*. Zed Books.

Nilsen, A., & Srila, R. (Eds.). (2016). *New subaltern politics: Reconceptualizing hegemony and resistance in contemporary India*. Oxford University Press.

Park, C. M. Y. (2019). "Our lands are our lives": Gendered experiences of resistance to land grabbing in rural Cambodia. *Feminist Economics*, *25*(4), 21–44.

Peluso, N. L., Afiff, S., & Rachman, N. F. (2008). Claiming the grounds for reform: Agrarian and environmental movements in Indonesia. In S. M. Borras Jr., M. Edelman, & C. Kay (Eds.), *Transnational agrarian movements: Confronting globalization*. Blackwell Publishing Ltd.

Peters, P. E. (2004). Inequality and social conflict over land in Africa. *Journal of Agrarian Change*, *4*(3), 269–314.

Razavi, S. (2009). Engendering the political economy of agrarian change. *Journal of Peasant Studies*, *36*(1), 197–226.

Rosset, P., & Altieri, M. (2017). *Agro-ecology: Science and politics*. Fernwood Publishers.

Rosset, P., Patel, R., & Courville, M. (2006). *Promised land: Competing visions of agrarian reform*. Food First Books.

Scoones, I. (2008). Mobilizing against GM crops in India, South Africa and Brazil. In S. M. Borras Jr., M. Edelman, & C. Kay (Eds.), *Transnational agrarian movements: Confronting globalization*. Blackwell Publishing Ltd.

Scott, J. C. (1975). *The moral economy of the peasant*. Yale University Press.

Scott, J. C. (1985). *Weapons of the weak: Everyday forms of peasant resistance*. Yale University Press.

Shanin, T. (1971). The peasantry as a political factor. In T. Shanin (Ed.), *Peasants and peasant societies: Selected readings*. Penguin Books.

Shanin, T. (1990). *Defining peasants: Essays concerning rural societies, expolary economies, and learning from them in the contemporary world*. Basil Blackwell.

Shin, G. (1994). The historical making of collective action: The Korean peasant uprisings of 1946. *American Journal of Sociology*, *99*(6), 1596–1624.

Stedile, J. P. (2002). Landless battalions: The Sem Terra movement of Brazil. *New Left Review*, *15*, 77–104.

Tarrow, S. (1988). National politics and collective action: Recent theory and research in Western Europe and the United States. *Annual Review of Sociology*, *14*, 421–440.

Thompson, E. P. (1978). Eighteenth-century English society: Class struggle without class? *Social History*, *3*(2), 133–165.

Tilly, C. (1978). *From mobilization to revolution.* Addison-Wesley.
Van der Ploeg, J. D. (2013). *Peasants and the art of farming: A Chayanovian manifesto.* Fernwood Publishing.
Van der Ploeg, J. D., Jingzhong, J., & Schneider, S. (2012). Rural development through the construction of new, nested, markets: Comparative perspectives from China, Brazil and the European Union. *The Journal of Peasant Studies*, *39*(1), 133–173.
Vía Campesina. (2006). *Gender diversity in the peasant movement.* Retrieved March 2, 2019, from https://viacampesina.org/en/gender-diversity-in-the-peasant-movement/
Vía Campesina. (2019). *What are we fighting for?* Retrieved March 2, 2019, from https://viacampesina.org/en/what-are-we-fighting-for/
White, J., & White, B. (2012). Gendered experiences of dispossession: Palm oil expansion in a Dayak Hibun community in West Kalimantan. *Journal of Peasant Studies*, *39*(3–4), 995–1016.
White, J. B. (2012). Gendered experiences of dispossession: Palm oil expansion in a Dayak Hibun community in West Kalimantan. *Journal of Peasant Studies*, *39*(3–4), 995–1016.
William, G. (1976). Taking the part of peasants. In P. W. Gutkind & I. Wallerstein (Eds.), *The political economy of contemporary Africa* (pp. 131–154). Sage Publications Ltd.
Wittman, H., Desmarais, A. A., & Wiebe, N. (Eds.). (2010). *Food sovereignty: Reconnecting food, nature & community.* Food First Books.
Wolf, E. R. (1969). *Peasant wars of the twentieth century.* Harper and Row.

10

CONCLUSION – CONTEXTUALIZING IPE AND FUTURES OF IPE

He who throws a stone in the market will hit his relative.

Yoruba Proverb

The Global South in IPE

In recent years advancements in the study of international political economy (IPE) have increasingly centered on the experiences of the Global South. This shift has allowed for a more comprehensive understanding of the complex dynamics that shape the economic and political landscape of these regions. Through the examination of various theoretical frameworks, empirical evidence and selected case studies, we have endeavored in this book to shed light on the challenges present, opportunities available and strategies adopted by the Global South to navigate the evolving global economic order.

One key advancement in the study of IPE concerning the Global South is the recognition of the importance of sociohistorical context. Understanding the historical legacies of colonialism, imperialism and exploitation is crucial to comprehend the current dynamics between the Global North and the Global South today, notably the schism between them. These key historical factors have shaped the economic structures, institutions and power dynamics within these regions. By incorporating historical analysis into the study of IPE topics, we have offered more nuanced explanations for the prevailing disparities between the Global North and South along a range of important topics.

Moreover, advancements in IPE studies have focused on the rise of South–South cooperation as a counterbalance to dominant yet unequal North–South relations. This has led to a renewed interest in studying the economic, political and social interactions among countries within the Global South. We are also witnessing the significance of regional integration efforts, such as the Association of Southeast Asian Nations (ASEAN), the African Union (AU) and the Caribbean Community (CARICOM) in promoting economic development, enhancing bargaining power and reducing dependence on the Global North. Furthermore, research has explored the role of

DOI: 10.4324/9781003264255-10

emerging powers such as Brazil, India and China in shaping the global economic landscape through their investment, trade and development policies.

Additionally, the advancements in IPE studies have emphasized the importance of incorporating a multidimensional analysis of power relations. Traditional notions of power solely derived from overwhelming military and economic prowess have been challenged. Concepts such as soft power, cultural hegemony, diplomatic solidarity and institutional power help us better understand the multiple ways in which power is exercised in the Global South. This has allowed for a more nuanced understanding of the strategies employed by the Global South to counter the dominance of the Global North and assert their own interests in international economic and political arenas.

Furthermore, the advancements in IPE studies have highlighted the complex role of multinational corporations (MNCs) in shaping the economic landscape of the Global South. Foreign direct investment (FDI), corporate social responsibility (CSR) and global value chains (GVCs) are certainly going to continue to exert much influence over development patterns in the Global South. These trends are also strongly connected to the growing presence of MNCs and how these actors influence economic policies, shape institutions and exploit the resources and labor of the Global South. We need a better understanding of the opportunities and challenges faced by the Global South in leveraging the presence of MNCs for their own developmental objectives.

Another significant advancement in the studies of IPE concerning the Global South is the exploration of the role of non-state actors. The agency and capacity of civil society organizations, social movements and grassroots activists to influence and shape the economic policies of the Global South is significant and has had major effects in some instances. This involvement of non-state actors as influential political and economic players reinforces the idea that the Global South is not just a passive recipient of global dynamics but an active participant in shaping its own economic and political destiny.

In conclusion, advancements in the study of IPE focusing on the experiences of the Global South have greatly contributed to providing a more nuanced portrait of the economic and political dynamics within these regions. The recognition of historical contexts, the rise of South-South cooperation, the multidimensional analysis of power relations, the role of MNCs and the agency of non-state actors have all shed light on the challenges, opportunities and strategies employed by the Global South in navigating the evolving global economic order. Moving forward, the continued exploration of these areas and the incorporation of further case studies will undoubtedly contribute to an even more comprehensive and insightful understanding of the complexities of life in the Global South.

Contextualizing IPE

There is a basic requirement of paradigm-shifting in IPE that necessitates changing the rules of the IPE game. As stated very early on in this book, the global political economy follows a set of rules set by space and time, social power and institutions such as states, MNCs and non-state actors. Changing the rules of the game can help us deal with issues of injustice resulting from the multiple inequalities in the global political economy. Not only do we need mechanisms of power parity and wealth distribution for the different players in the game but we also need to incentivize keeping the playing field the same way, for example, that we need to incentivize preserving our ecosystems, even if it is for a future we won't live in. To work for others is an act of love that serves the community.

When we look at the modern evolution of the global political economy, we find noticeable trends of growth in terms of population size, capital and appropriation of environmental resources (see Foster, 1999). Capital, which Piketty sees as the stock of all assets that can be traded in the market, has particularly expanded in the twenty-first century due to notable trends of policymaking such as rising social demands in the twenties, depression in the thirties and forties, and rising inequalities since the fifties (Piketty, 2014). Even if the creation of more wealth was accompanied by greater concentration of the ownership of capital since the fifties, social mobility also expanded greatly until the first crises of trade with the oil shocks of the seventies. These oil shocks were episodes of sudden high increases in oil and energy prices that had significant impacts on domestic economies around the world, by impacting employment and inflation. The main historical oil shock at that time, in 1973, was led by OPEC. OPEC countries, of which many are Arab states in solidarity with Palestine, limited the supply of oil, driving the prices up to pressure the United States to limit its arming of Israel.

Since then, we have seen a rolling back of numerous social programs around the world which led to a downfall of the relative increase in wages compared to capital, leading to a pauperization of the middle class (Piketty, 2014).

The problem of inequality can also be heightened with mechanisms such as transfer of capital ownership, such as inheritance or state acquisition, as opposed to trusting capital and other mechanisms of redistribution, and the consolidation of large real estate holdings by private corporations. The Islamic economic model is one model that can provide such mechanisms of redistribution through alimony, trusting and an ecological ethos (Warde, 2000; El Bernoussi, 2021).

In this book, contextualizing IPE was a key motif, and we tried to do it using different disciplines of social study. In our chapters on globalization and migration, we saw emphasis on social relations and social formations, given Garriga Lopez's anthropological lens. In our chapters on value and security, we saw emphasis on genealogies and how concepts mean different things at different times, given Saade's political theory lens. In our chapters on food and social movements, we saw emphasis on the political and economic making of a world food regime and the ensuing social struggles for survival, given Martiniello's political ecology lens. And lastly, in our chapters on labor and finance, we saw the importance of the power bargain and struggle for interest locally and internationally, given El Bernoussi's political science lens.

Futures of IPE

The list of topics we discuss in this collection is not meant to be exhaustive – it represents a grid of themes that in some way help us depart from traditional IPE core interests, those being the big actors (rich countries) and the big topics (international trade). The topics reflect our own individual epistemes, collective aesthetics, disciplinary specializations and political sensibilities. And yet a set of emergent issues that are shaping the face of the polity and economy of the global capitalist system would have deserved being accurately dealt with. We offer here a series of bullet points opening to new areas of research in the field of IPE.

- The first question has to do with the emergence of a new block of power and affluence known as the BRICS (Brazil, Russia, India, China, South Africa), which is contributing to the current multi-polarity of the global economy. Driven by the spectacular economic growth of China, and to a lesser extent India, this new alliance is paving the way for the emergence of new financial institutions, such as the BRICS Development Bank, which are shaping a new global financial and currency architecture reflecting a decline in the global hegemony of the US dollar (see Wade, 2013). While the question of the relations between systemic cycles of accumulation and hegemonic transitions has been posed in the most critical IPE literature (Arrighi & Silver, 2005; Arrighi, 2001), what seems less explored are the global implications of spreading capitalism to high-population countries such as India and China and the consequences in terms of pressures over natural resources (see Singh, 2023).

- Within an energy paradigm still based on fossil fuels and in a context of growing demand for raw materials, nature has been working as a material basis for the extraction/subtraction of natural resources – faster than its regeneration rate – and as a "sink" – receiving all that is expelled from the productive process in the form of high levels of chemicals and waste. Widespread deforestation, greenhouse gas emissions, biodiversity reduction, desertification, species extinction and atmospheric oceanic pollution are some of the most destructive manifestations of the intersection between politics, economics and ecology. Nature and ecologies do not seem to find a place within IPE unless when they are seen as triggers of migration and security issues (Peluso & Watts, 2001) or when they are considered externalities to the production process. And yet debates over market-driven solutions to the environmental question, such as paying for pollution or green incentives, have been permeating the discipline of IPE especially because of their achievability "within" the frame of green capitalism. On the other hand, we see the emergence of new epistemologies such as eco-socialist, eco-anarchist and eco-feminist perspectives questioning this eco-modernist perspective which frames market and technologies as the core to resolve the environmental challenges of our times. Greening IPE would therefore require a re-conceptualization of capitalism as not only embedded in social relations, as in Western socialist traditions, but embedded in the biosphere (see Moore, 2015) and even in the regulatory frameworks of environmentalism and so-called green capitalism (Bond, 2022).
- Third, the development of mega-infrastructural projects in Africa and globally in the last decade has massively contributed to expanding the integration of the continent and other regions within the global political economy. The idea is to develop these new infrastructural nodes in order to exploit the large potential of "empty", "unused" or "under-utilized" land allegedly available in Africa. Mega infrastructural projects such as the Southern Agricultural Growth Corridor of Tanzania (SAGCOT), the Lamu Port and Southern Sudan Ethiopia Transport Corridor (LAPSSET), the Beira and Nacala corridors in Mozambique, just to cite a few, aim to trigger the growth of agricultural and mining corridors by connecting remote geographic areas with high farmland and natural resources potential to international markets. Yet, given the high costs of gigantic transport infrastructural development, which African governments alone cannot afford, new emerging political complexes (bilateral donors, International Financial Institutions, development agencies and African governments) and economic interests (agro-chemical and seed companies, mining and energy capital) are aligning behind the making of these corridors. One example is the East African Crude Oil Pipeline (EACOP), possibly the longest pipeline (1443 km) on the African continent, which is funded by French multinational oil corporation Total alongside the state-owned China National Offshore Oil Corporation (CNOOC) and a mix of finance institutions such as South Africa's Standard Bank and the Industrial and Commercial Bank of China. The pipeline costs four billion USD and will transport crude oil from the city of Kabale in Hoima district in Uganda to the Chongoleani Peninsula near the port of Tanga in Tanzania. This example shows the very large

magnitude of investments involved. This convergence of power and expertise which imposes its vision upon existing modes of control, access and use of land, and existing livelihood activities, threatens to displace communities, endanger wildlife and tip the world closer to catastrophic climate change. In a similar vein, the Belt and Road Initiative (BRI) represents one manifestation of the relation between transport and logistic infrastructural changes and expanding frontiers of capitalist development.

- We write in a period of escalating military and territorial conflicts with a growing militarization of international relations. Seen from the MENA, the region has been ravaged by five imperialist, sub-imperialist and settler-colonialist wars in Iraq, Libya, Syria, Yemen, Palestine and Lebanon. The role of war, especially when associated with the raison d'état has found a place in realist accounts of IPE. Indeed, we see a recurrence and a persistence of imperialism as key dynamics governing international relations, notably in relation to the regions of Africa and the Middle East where war and conflict are rampant (see Capasso, 2023). As a counterpunch, we also see the emergence of revolutionary anti-imperialist movements as seen with the recent anti-French coups in Niger and Gabon and previously in Mali and Burkina Faso.
- The war in Syria generated the largest mass exodus since WWII, while labor migrants have become increasingly indispensable to the operation of the world economy. Understanding the role of mobilities, national and international, seems necessary to grapple with the unfolding of both international markets and state policies. IPE has the opportunity to contribute to a deeper understanding of the nexus between migrations, the logic of capital accumulation and the mechanics of state regulation.

Moving Forward

Studying the international political economy is increasingly crucial for anyone interested in the political economic foundations of our contemporary world as consumption and production connects us to one another through circulation and to an ecosystem of resources, stretching over space and time.

A key takeaway from this book is to start to study IPE by contextualizing our topics in space and in time to reveal the processes of structuring the international capitalist economy and to evaluate actual policies dealing with all sorts of resources (human, natural, financial, military, etc.). The context of the Global South is essential for a more profound understanding and reading of IPE, despite its economic marginality and political subordination because it is a site of heightened problems that jeopardize the wellbeing and livelihood of everyone. Think about issues of climate change. The Global South represents the majority of the world's population and covers most of the world's territory, and as such disasters and ecological problems anywhere in the Global South impact every one of us.

Political economist Ha-Joon Chang argues that the view that development happens through "good policies" of opening and liberalizing the economy is factually wrong. In actuality history shows that when countries follow supposedly "bad" policies of subsidies and infant industry protection that is what helps their economy. Infant industry is a concept in economics that refers to an industrial sector in an economy that receives aid from the government in an effort to grow the industry and make it competitive in the international market. In fact, Western economies became rich exactly by following those "bad policies", and then, they have been instructing new independent economies of the Global South not to follow their model and follow instead the so-called good policies that harm their weak economies even further. As such, rich countries have been "kicking away the ladder" of economic development from countries of the Global South for decades. This reveals a central problem in IPE; rich countries have influence, control and power over poor countries, and they push them into economic and political actions that go against their local interests and in favor of foreign corporate and state interests. As discussed in the introduction of this book, this leads to a form of cognitive dissonance in the policymaking of the Global South because policymaking is captured by the Global North through precisely the dynamics here described (El Bernoussi, 2024). Rising political economist Joma Geneciran of the Philippines tells us another important story: the need for radical thinking within the politics of decoloniality (2024). Decoloniality was for us a key concern given our struggle with Western-centric theorizations in IPE and in understanding the Global South. Geneciran argues for the need to rely on historical materialism, not just linguistics and semantics in the project of decolonization (2024). As such, we need to be specific about engaging with the hegemony of capitalist modes of production and reveal their connection to the social formation of the power layout. And we must demand change.

Arguing against the notable critic of modernity theory Walter Mignolo, Geneciran cautioned about the risk and danger of detaching decoloniality from politics, because we run the risk of accepting the economic order (i.e., save and grow the economy) and defeating the decolonial project, as has happened repeatedly in the history of the postcolonial world (Geneciran, 2024). This call for bringing back historical materialism into the project of decoloniality finds echo with another radical call, that of ontic capaciousness. The argument here is that efforts to suggest radical thinking in social study, for problems such as discrimination, hierarchy and exploitation, have often relied on ontological pluralism (see anthropology as a discipline). This ontological turn prescribes the need to accept the diversity of our communities as a way to solve our problems. This ontological pluralism, however, remains ideational and makes concrete, material actions of resistance and change ineffective (Vasantkumar, 2022). What is needed instead is ontic, as in the imagination of the real and unreal, capaciousness; a more radical and material outlook to thinking and changing our communities, including a project of decoloniality.

Most importantly, like the epigraph in this concluding chapter, harming another is harming oneself, as we share a planet and a universe. History has shown how much destruction we have inflicted on one another and for that to stop we need radical thinking in IPE.

Bibliography

Arrighi, G. (2001). Capitalism and world (dis)order. *Review of International Studies*, *27*, 257–279.

Arrighi, G., & Silver, B. J. (2005). Hegemony unravelling. *New Left Review*, 83–116.

Bond, D. (2022). *Negative ecologies: Fossil fuels and the discovery of the environment.* University of California Press.

Capasso, M. (2023). IR, imperialism, and the global South: From Libya to Venezuela. *Politics*, *43*(4), 553–568. https://doi.org/10.1177/02633957211061232

El Bernoussi, Z. (2021). Developing the halal market: China's opportunity to strengthen MENA ties and address Uighur/Hui issues. In A. U. Yakin & L.-L. Christians (Eds.), *Rethinking halal: Genealogy, current trends, and new interpretation*. Muslim Minorities Series (37). E. J. Brill.

El Bernoussi, Z. (2024). The high stakes of differentials. *International Studies Review*, *26*(3), 1–3.

Foster, J. B. (1999). *The vulnerable planet: An economic history of the environment*. Monthly Review Press.

Geneciran, J. (2024). Global historical materialism and decoloniality. *Review of African Political Economy*, 1–9. https://doi.org/10.62191/ROAPE-2024-0035

Moore, J. W. (2015). *Capitalism in the web of life: Ecology and the accumulation*. Verso.

Peluso, N., & Watts, M. (Eds.). (2001). *Violent environment*. Cornell University Press.
Piketty, T. (2014). *Capital in the twenty-first century*. Harvard University Press.
Singh, P. (2023). Celebrating the 50th anniversary of Schumacher's small is beautiful: An eco-socialist perspective. *Capitalism Nature Socialism*, *34*(4), 1–19. https://doi.org/10.1080/10455752.2023.2282135
Vasantkumar, C. (2022). Not "multiple ontologies" but ontic capaciousness: Radical alterity after the ontological turn. *Journal of Ethnographic Theory*, *12*(3), 819–835.
Wade, R. (2013). How Western states keep the lead in global organizations. *Challenge*, *56*(1), 5–39.
Warde, I. (2000). *Islamic finance in the global economy*. Edinburgh University Press.

INDEX

For Product Safety Concerns and Information please contact our EU
representative GPSR@taylorandfrancis.com
Taylor & Francis Verlag GmbH, Kaufingerstraße 24, 80331 München, Germany

www.ingramcontent.com/pod-product-compliance
Ingram Content Group UK Ltd.
Pitfield, Milton Keynes, MK11 3LW, UK
UKHW050233200926
475702UK00020B/3004
* 9 7 8 1 0 3 2 2 0 5 7 4 8 *